Reframing Reality
The Aesthetics of the Surrealist Object in French and Czech Cinema

Alison Frank

intellect Bristol, UK / Chicago, USA

First published in the UK in 2013 by
Intellect, The Mill, Parnall Road, Fishponds, Bristol, BS16 3JG, UK

First published in the USA in 2013 by
Intellect, The University of Chicago Press, 1427 E. 60th Street,
Chicago, IL 60637, USA

Cover designer: Ellen Thomas
Cover image: *A Blonde in Love* (1965)
   © CBK/Filmové studio Barrandov/The Kobal Collection
Copy-editor: MPS Technologies
Index: Lyn Greenwood
Production manager: Jelena Stanovnik
Typesetting: Contentra Technologies

Print ISBN: 978-1-84150-712-5
ePDF ISBN: 978-1-78320-169-3
ePub ISBN: 978-1-78320-168-6

Printed and bound by Hobbs, UK

Reframing Reality

Contents

Acknowledgements

I would like to thank Reidar Due, my thesis supervisor at the University of Oxford, for his guidance and valuable advice. Michael Sheringham provided helpful insights in the early stages. My college adviser, Michael Hawcroft, was a source of friendly support throughout my studies. I specially wish to thank Xon de Ros and Dorota Ostrowska for their encouragement.

I am grateful to the Keble Association for their contribution towards my year abroad at the École Normale Supérieure, and for supporting trips to Karlovy Vary (2008) and Łodz (2006), where I presented my research at the 'Rediscovering Polish Cinema' conference. I would also like to thank Oxford University's Department of Medieval and Modern Languages for their support of the Łodz trip.

Vanya Murray, former film librarian at the Modern Languages Faculty Library, was of great help in obtaining the necessary books and films. Thank you also to Jelena Stanovnik at Intellect for her enthusiasm and dedication.

I wish to express my gratitude to Diane Watson for including films as part of her English class at Branksome Hall, and to Bart Testa for his comprehensive and inspiring 'Introduction to Film' course at the University of Toronto.

Thank you to Mićo Tatalović for unwavering encouragement throughout my postgraduate career. Finally, I would like to thank my parents, Barbara and Richard Frank, to whom this book is dedicated, for supporting my studies wholeheartedly from the very beginning.

Parts of Chapter 3 have been published previously in modified form. The section on Věra Chytilová was reworked into an article, 'Formal Innovation and Feminist Freedom: Věra Chytilová's *Daisies*', first published in *CineAction* no. 81 (2010), 46–49. The sections on Miloš Forman, Ivan Passer and Jiří Menzel formed the basis of the peer-reviewed article, 'Czech Surrealism and Czech New Wave Realism: The Importance of Objects' in *Kinema: A Journal for Film and Audiovisual Media* no. 36 (Fall 2011), 39–58.

Introduction

cademic accounts of surrealism and cinema have tended to define the relationship between them either very narrowly or quite broadly. Accounts from the 1970s and 80s by authors such as J. H. Matthews, Linda Williams, Steven Kovács and Alain and Odette Virmaux have focused primarily on the early work of Luis Buñuel (*Un Chien andalou*, 1929 and *L'Âge d'or*, 1930), and may include consideration of *La Coquille et le Clergyman/The Seashell and the Clergyman* (1928), the film made by cinematic impressionist Germaine Dulac for surrealist Antonin Artaud. They may also discuss Buñuel's later work, based on the argument that the director remained a surrealist all his life, and only needed the artistic freedom to express it. However, films influenced by surrealism but not directly related to the movement receive far less attention, if any.

By the 1990s, the focus was beginning to broaden: Ramona Fotiade, for example, made a convincing case for the cultural influence of surrealism in postmodern French cinema, specifically Jean-Jacques Beineix's *37°2 le matin/Betty Blue* (1986).[1] In the 2000s, *The Unsilvered Screen* (edited by Graeme Harper and Rob Stone) and Michael Richardson's *Surrealism and Cinema* included chapters on Buñuel but also argued for expanding the definition of surrealism in film to include examples taken from Hollywood, American classical animation, British cinema, documentary and works by directors such as David Lynch, Raúl Ruiz, Walerian Borowczyk, Andrei Tarkovsky and Alejandro Jodorowsky.

Both narrow and broad approaches to defining surrealism in cinema correspond in different ways to the surrealists' own approach. In terms of granting its official approval (and the accompanying label 'surrealist') to any film, the group was extremely selective, choosing only Buñuel's first two films: they rejected *La Coquille et le Clergyman* essentially because it defined itself as dream-based and distanced itself too radically from reality through the use of special effects. However, Ado Kyrou's volume *Le Surréalisme au cinéma* (1963) was liberal in identifying what he called surrealist moments in a wide variety of examples of past and contemporary European and American films, from *Fantômas* (1913) to Russ Meyer.

Between the surrealist selectiveness of the 1920s and 30s and Kyrou's efforts as a post-war spectator to discover surrealist moments in film lies the story of surrealism's troubled relationship with the medium. It was a story narrated by André Breton himself in his 1951 essay 'Comme dans un bois'/'As in a Wood': as a young man, he would spend his Sundays with his friend Jacques Vaché, immersing himself in the pure pleasure of film's *'pouvoir de dépaysement'/'power of defamiliarisation'*[2] by wandering from cinema to cinema at will, not bothering about conventional concerns such as the name of the film or watching it from beginning to end.[3] The surrealists were united by their admiration for Chaplin's film comedy; for Henry Hathaway's vision of the power of love in his 1935 film *Peter Ibbetson*; for Feuillade's portrayal of the marvellous infiltrating the fabric of everyday reality; for, above all, cinema's general conduciveness to transgression of restrictive social and moral codes of behaviour and the limitations that they impose on the imagination.

As the surrealists formulated the principles of their own movement, they naturally looked to cinema as a powerful and popular modern medium through which they could communicate their ideas in a manner that would convince a wide audience of their relevance. Fundamental to this power was the fact that cinema was an art form which seemed most faithfully to reproduce life as it is experienced. The surrealists wanted to demonstrate that their revolution was not limited to the mind, and to do so they needed to prove that a revolution of the mind would have a real impact on everyday life. The source of the difficulties that the surrealists encountered with cinema, however, was the fact that their primary concern was the unconscious. They soon realised that it was impracticable to use cinema as a more vivid and immediate form than language for the expression of the director's unconscious; however, it would take longer for them to realise that it was almost equally difficult to use cinema as a means of influencing the audience's unconscious.

Breton as a young man had taken an unusually active role in creating his film experience, putting together a mental collage of the film fragments he had seen on his Sunday afternoon at the cinema. Kyrou, too, in *Le Surréalisme au cinéma* described a subjective approach to watching movies, citing Man Ray's practice of obscuring his vision as a means of altering his experience of a film, or his own tendency to deliberately confuse his understanding of a film by recalling plots and characters from other films as he watched it.[4] Rudolf Kuenzli argues, however, that while the surrealists advocated 'active' viewing of popular films, a 'passive' viewer was required for their own.[5] While the surrealists were arguably within their rights to believe that their own films did not require imaginative transformation in order to stimulate the viewer, they were perhaps over-ambitious in the specific effect that they hoped their films would have. They aspired to a cinema that would have a transformative effect on the viewer. Most mainstream cinema is primarily designed to entertain its audience, however, not transform them. Although cinema can present a new point of view, it is unlikely to bring about any radical revolution in the audience's perspective on the world. However quixotic it appears in retrospect, such a radical revolution was precisely the surrealists' goal.

Initially, the surrealists had been excited by the fact that cinema used images as its basis of communication. Even before any actual surrealist film production took place, surrealist writing reveals the way in which cinema had captured the group's collective imagination. Like their avant-garde predecessors including Guillaume Apollinaire and Blaise Cendrars, the surrealists were inspired by cinema's promise to broaden expressive possibilities: writing modelled on cinema, it was hoped, would offer liberation from the weight of literary precedent.[6] This new approach to writing also aimed to make use of cinema's ability to 'accentuate the external, visual side of an object, stripping it of the semantic content that literature imposes'.[7] Between 1925 and 1933, surrealists including Artaud, Philippe Soupault,

Robert Desnos and Benjamin Fondane published numerous 'unfilmable scenarios'.[8] Paul Hammond's *The Shadow and Its Shadow*[9] and the anthology section of Virmaux also reveal the considerable number of cinema-inspired poems, film reviews and essays written by surrealists. The group's relatively modest involvement in actual film-making, then, takes place against a background of active engagement in cinema-inspired writing.

For the surrealists, the cinema was also a promising medium because, being image-based, it seemed to provide an expressive analogy to dreams, the means by which the unconscious communicates most directly with us. They soon perceived a contradiction between the demands of the unconscious and the demands of realism, however. Dream images, after all, may not correspond to photographic realism: for example, people and objects in dreams often take on dual identities, and this cannot be captured on film without camera tricks; if camera tricks are used, then film's persuasively realistic quality will disappear, and the audience may then cease to take the dream-like film and its message seriously.

As writers, the surrealists were accustomed to a medium of expression that would allow for remarkably precise expression of subjectivity and psychology. Cinema, for all its photographic realism, cannot reproduce the psychological dimension of our experience of reality, unless it is through subjective images or an interior monologue; the latter was not available during the silent era, and both techniques again take away from cinema's illusion of reproducing an objective vision of reality. In general, it was difficult for film to represent interiority in a manner that was not intrusive; this meant that expressing the unconscious was equally challenging. The challenge would only become more pronounced when the dominance of image, which the surrealists saw as intimately connected with the unconscious, was undermined by the arrival of sound: the logical demands of dialogue and narrative grew as feature film-making became the established norm. The surrealists had to accept that short silent films were no longer the means by which to reach a popular audience. Unfortunately, the surrealists chose not to take up the challenge of making feature-length films with dialogue. Indeed, in 'Comme dans un bois', Breton locates the demise of surrealism's hopes for cinema in 'une action de type théâtral'/'a theatrical type of action': in narrative, then, or at least a certain type of convoluted narrative.[10] Although Kuenzli pinpoints the principal difference between dada and surrealist cinema as the way in which the latter draws its audience in through the use of narrative and avoidance of tricks of the medium,[11] the logical cause-effect relationships of conventional narrative would not be surrealism's natural milieu; as Harper and Stone observe, 'it was in the gaps between words and images that surrealism could flourish',[12] or in other words, the very places where conventional narrative breaks down.

While the surrealists themselves may have withdrawn from practical film-making to their previous position as spectators, it does not mean that their influence on cinema is limited to the three films issued directly from the movement. The corpus of films that I will examine here is similar in some ways to the conventional scope of surrealist film as defined by scholars of the 1970s and 80s in that it includes a brief discussion of *Un Chien andalou*; it also features a detailed discussion of three of Buñuel's late films and, with respect to two of them, builds on Linda Williams' observations in her 1981 book *Figures of Desire*.

The inclusion of Jan Švankmajer in Chapter 3 is also not a radical expansion of the definition of surrealism in film: although the films that will be examined in fact predate the Czech animator's membership in the Czech surrealist group, even scholars who applied a conservative definition of surrealism in film would most likely have included this film-maker, albeit one from a different surrealist tradition, had his work been available in the West at the time they were writing.

Where my study moves beyond conventional definitions of surrealist film is in its inclusion of René Clair's *À Nous la liberté* (1931), a selection of Czech New Wave films[13] and Jean-Pierre Jeunet's *Le Fabuleux destin d'Amélie Poulain* (2001) (henceforward abbreviated to its English title, *Amélie*). Unlike some films covered in Richardson's book and *The Unsilvered Screen*, however, all of these (with the exception of Jeunet's) have a more or less direct relationship with surrealism. René Clair was a contemporary of the Paris group and directed the dada film *Entr'acte* (1924) early in his career. In the case of Jeunet, by the postmodern period surrealism had become a part of the cultural landscape in France (however distanced from its original ambitions): as this book's final chapter will explain, Jeunet's work may be classed as part of the *cinéma du look* tendency and thus it is worth comparing its adoption of surrealism with the way in which Beineix incorporated surrealist ideas, as discerned by Fotiade.

The Czech New Wave directors hail from a country with its own distinct surrealist tradition which, unlike the French movement, did not decline after the end of World War II, and in fact has continued to exist up to the present day. Certainly, many countries aside from France had their own surrealist movements: Belgium, Denmark, Poland and the former Yugoslavia are well-known examples, and Effie Rentzou's recent monograph, *Littérature malgré elle: Le Surréalisme et la transformation du littéraire*,[14] explores surrealism in Greece. As Elza Adamowicz points out, from the mid-1930s French surrealism felt the need to internationalise as it was becoming accepted (and hence domesticated) by the middle classes and commercial interests, while failing to convince the Communist party that surrealist artistic goals were compatible with leftist politics.[15] There are several reasons for devoting a substantial chapter, accounting for a full third of the present book, to surrealism in Czech cinema in particular. First, there is Jan Švankmajer, already mentioned, whose work, past and present, exemplifies the strong surrealist movement in the former Czechoslovakia. Secondly, in one of his early articles on Czech New Wave cinema, Peter Hames gave special prominence to the Czechoslovak capital in the history of surrealism, noting that 'Paris and Prague have sometimes been described as the "twin poles of surrealism"'.[16] Hames's later comprehensive monographs on Czechoslovak cinema[17] continued to highlight traces of surrealism; most recently, Jonathan L. Owen's *Avant-Garde to New Wave: Czechoslovak Cinema, Surrealism and the Sixties* (2011) has explored surrealist influence on the Czech New Wave in greater detail. Finally, over the past ten years, Czech New Wave cinema has become more widely available on DVD, so readers are increasingly able to assess for themselves the examples of surrealism highlighted in scholarly writing on the subject.

In addition to the directors' links to surrealism, the corpus is justified by the hybrid nature of the films themselves. Although the surrealists did not venture into mainstream narrative feature film-making, their sympathies had always lain squarely with popular cinema rather than self-consciously aesthetic or avant-garde films aimed at intellectual audiences. Unfortunately, the surrealists' own experience had shown them that popular cinema was often dull and disappointing unless one took a wilfully subjective approach to watching it. An academic analysis, too, will have difficulty locating the kind of ruptures in mainstream cinema's reality that may allow surrealism to exist. It is for this reason that I have chosen films that, while they can be considered *auteur* insofar as they represent the personal artistic vision of their directors, also maintain their popular appeal, principally through their use of comedy. The films made in the 1960s (Buñuel and Czech New Wave cinema) tend to engage in a modernist experimentation with form; as a result, these films offer many examples of narrative ruptures that leave space for surrealism. It has been suggested that Jeunet is part of a trend of French directors who achieve popular appeal through a return to a classical approach to film-making, characterised by conventional narrative form and an emphasis on technical perfection.[18] This apparent return to French cinema's tradition of quality brings Jeunet closer to Clair in terms of both approach and success: *Amélie's* international audiences totalled approximately 30 million,[19] and Clair was, during his time, 'arguably the most celebrated film artist in the world'.[20] Although Jeunet's and Clair's films conform to conventional narrative much more closely than the films of the 1960s, my study will nonetheless attempt to identify those moments where their rational organisation leaves room for a kind of liberation.

The principal way in which my study departs from past accounts of surrealism in cinema is in its definition of the means by which a form of surrealism may exist within more or less conventional narrative cinema. Other studies of surrealism in cinema have tended to define surrealism based on films' having themes sympathetic to the movement (such as explicit reference to the power of dreams and the unconscious) or through visual characteristics linking the film image to surrealism in painting: this seems to reiterate Kyrou's approach to discovering surrealist moments in cinema, however. Of all surrealist methods of increasing contact with the unconscious, the surrealist object is most suited to film: this is the case because even if the effect of the surrealist object relies on the intervention of the unconscious, the object component invariably maintains a grounding in the material world. The first chapter of this book will explain the concept of the surrealist object in greater detail, but a simple account will be of use here. Although the first surrealist object was based on the meeting of two objects in a place common to neither one, the term came to include any object that shed light on the functioning of the unconscious: this could occur symptomatically (an object that draws one's attention was thought to be indicative of one's unconscious preoccupations) or productively (an object or combination of objects was supposed to lead the unconscious to engage creatively with them, perceiving an unexpected similarity between the objects, for example).

In spite of the fact that objects are easily inscribed in a photographically realistic context, the surrealists never explicitly formulated a theory of how surrealist objects could be incorporated in cinema. The first chapter of this book will examine whether any of the objects in *Un Chien andalou* may be considered surrealist objects, even if they were not labelled as such by the surrealists themselves. However, the rest of the book will not be concerned with examining films for the presence of surrealist objects, at least not according to their conventional surrealist definition. In the context of the corpus of films proposed, I will refer to 'hybrid objects' rather than surrealist objects. They will be defined as physical objects that have more than just a narrative function or a single symbolic meaning. Hybrid objects serve a multiplicity of narrative, aesthetic and semiotic roles. They will often take on a comic function that will endow them with additional layers of resonance. Whether or not they contribute to comedy, the objects' multiple meanings will act as a source of instability in the film, altering the audience's habitual perception of the film and its definition of reality, and destabilising its established moral assumptions and rules. The hybrid object may thus be said to fulfil surrealist goals through its multiple meanings and its associated subversive effect. The surrealists were keen to see society's repressive rules replaced by the liberating rule of desire; for them, multiple meaning not only highlighted the complexity of reality but specifically favoured the unconscious and its tendency to connect objects by perceiving similarity rather than difference.

While it fulfils surrealist goals, the hybrid object in cinema is quite different from the surrealist object in real life: its effect is not based on the psychological impression it may make on the viewer, nor are the associations it develops based in the unconscious. It is for this reason that I will refer to the 'audience' rather than the 'spectator', as the latter supposes a particular role for the viewer (which the surrealists wanted to define for viewers of their films), whereas my concept of the hybrid object leaves the viewer a more open-ended role with respect to discerning meaning. The object as a psychological symptom in film is in fact a conventional option: in popular cinema, objects regularly function as a simplistic key to a character's psyche, and the audience is invited to psychoanalyse the character by interpreting the object. In the films studied here, by contrast, the multiple meanings that objects take on will tend to be transparent; those objects associated with a more mysterious meaning will be resistant to interpretation. The hybrid object is also different from the surrealist object because the associations that it develops will not stem from the play of the unconscious, but from the circulation of the object through the film. This constitutes a cinematic and thereby less intrusive means of creating multiple meanings in an object: the object will accumulate meaning naturally, as it were, through the way in which it is used in the narrative, the contexts in which it appears, the objects with which it is juxtaposed and any comic situations in which it participates. Although it arrives at its effect in a different way than the conventional surrealist object, the hybrid object through its functioning in narrative cinema highlights for the audience the notion that hybridity does in fact arise in everyday life, outside the cinema, as a form of rupture in the fabric of appearances.

In Chapter 1 I will discuss the notion of the surrealist object in greater detail, as well as the surrealists' relationship with cinema. The chapter will include a brief analysis of Buñuel's *Un Chien andalou* to examine the way in which objects work in a film directly associated with the surrealist movement. In Chapter 2, on René Clair's *À Nous la liberté*, I will begin a demonstration of my theory of hybrid objects: they participate in comic situations and, through their circulation through different situations in the film, accumulate sometimes contradictory meanings that create an instability even in this solid example of mainstream popular cinema. Chapter 3 is chiefly devoted to seven examples of Czech New Wave cinema, with a smaller section on contemporaneous short films by Jan Švankmajer. The chapter will begin with an explanation of the historical, cultural and political background of the Czech New Wave, including an account of the development and specificity of Czech surrealism. Then, I will trace the way in which physical reality and humour multiply the meaning of objects in these films. Chapter 4 will analyse the way in which generic hybridity modulates object meaning in three films from Buñuel's later career. In this chapter I will argue that by shifting from one genre to another Buñuel changes the criteria by which the audience judges objects as plausible within their context, and thereby also alters the type of meaning that is assigned to objects. Finally, Chapter 5 will highlight in *Amélie* a peculiar prevalence of objects related to communication, which I will refer to as 'media objects': despite Jeunet's whimsical adoption of certain surrealist notions (such as desire making chance appear as destiny or the influence of the unconscious on conscious perception), hybrid objects in this film are less disruptive to a totalising concept of reality than in a film that is superficially more conventional such as *À Nous la liberté*. The conclusion will move from this observation to define possible areas for future research on hybrid objects as a means for the presence of surrealism in cinema.

Notes

1 'The slit eye, the scorpion and the sign of the cross: surrealist film theory and practice revisited', *Screen* 39 (1998): 122–23.
2 Here and throughout, translations from French sources are the author's own.
3 In *Les surréalistes et le cinéma*, eds. Alain and Odette Virmaux (Paris: Seghers, 1976) 278–79.
4 In *The Shadow and Its Shadow: Surrealist Writings on the Cinema*, 3rd edn, ed. and trans. Paul Hammond (San Francisco: City Lights, 2000) 131.
5 'Introduction', *Dada and Surrealist Film*, ed. Rudolf E. Kuenzli (Cambridge, MA: MIT Press, 1996) 8–9.
6 Mikhail Iampolski, *The Memory of Tiresias: Intertextuality and Film*, trans. Harsha Ram (Berkeley: University of California Press, 1998) 128, 162–63; Richard Abel, 'Exploring the Discursive Field of the Surrealist Film Scenario Text', *Dada and Surrealist Film*, ed. Rudolf E. Kuenzli (Cambridge, MA: MIT Press, 1996) 59.
7 Iampolski 167.
8 Abel 58; Iampolski 162.
9 *Surrealist Writings on the Cinema*, 3rd edn (San Francisco: City Lights, 2000).
10 In *Les surréalistes et le cinéma* 282.
11 10.

12 'Introduction: The Unsilvered Screen', *The Unsilvered Screen: Surrealism on Film*, eds. Graeme Harper and Rob Stone (London: Wallflower, 2007) 4.

13 I use the term 'Czech New Wave' in part as shorthand for 'Czechoslovak New Wave', in part because the New Wave films that will be considered here are all in the Czech language, and primarily made by Czech-born directors (with the exception of Jaromil Jireš). For a consideration of the specificity of Slovak cinema of the 1960s, see (for example) the chapter on Juraj Jakubisko in Jonathan L. Owen's *Czechoslovak Cinema, Surrealism and the Sixties* (Oxford: Berghahn, 2011) as well as Peter Hames's two monographs, *The Czechoslovak New Wave*, 2nd edn (London: Wallflower, 2005) and *Czech and Slovak Cinema: Theme and Tradition* (Edinburgh: Edinburgh University Press, 2009).

14 Paris: Editions Pleine Marge, 2010.

15 'Introduction', *Surrealism: Crossings/Frontiers*, ed. Elza Adamowicz (Bern: Peter Lang, 2006) 11–12.

16 'Czechoslovakia: After the Spring', *Post New Wave Cinema in the Soviet Union and Eastern Europe*, ed. Daniel J. Goulding (Bloomington: Indiana University Press, 1989) 131.

17 *The Czechoslovak New Wave* (2005) and *Czech and Slovak Cinema: Theme and Tradition* (2009).

18 Jean Cluzel, *Propos impertinents sur le cinéma français* (Paris: PUF, 2003) 100.

19 Isabelle Vanderschelden, *Amélie*, French Film Guides (Urbana and Chicago: University of Illinois Press, 2007) 1.

20 Dudley Andrew, *Mists of Regret: Culture and Sensibility in Classic French Film* (Princeton: Princeton University Press, 1995) 55.

Chapter 1

Surrealist Objects and Cinema

Introduction

In order to provide a clear picture of the inspiration behind my theory of the hybrid object, this chapter will explain the notion of the surrealist object in greater detail, describing it in its various manifestations and explaining how it fits into a larger scheme of surrealist thought. I will then go on to highlight, in a shorter section, the ways in which the hybrid object differs from the surrealist object and why, in the context of film, this must be so. The chapter will conclude with a brief analysis of Luis Buñuel's *Un Chien andalou* (1929) in order to examine the way in which objects were used in a surrealist film. I will argue that although these may be considered a form of surrealist objects in cinema, they would have to be developed further and ultimately transformed if they were to make the transition from the context of short experimental films to that of the relatively popular narrative feature film after the advent of sound.

The notion of the surrealist object

Crise de conscience: crise de l'objet

In the *Second Surrealist Manifesto*, André Breton said that the movement's success or failure could be judged based on whether or not it succeeded to 'provoquer, au point de vue intellectuel et moral, une *crise de conscience* de l'espèce la plus générale et la plus grave'/'provoke, intellectually and morally, the most widespread and serious *crisis of consciousness*'.[1] The surrealists sought to achieve this 'crisis of consciousness' through diverse means, all of which shared the basic characteristic of demonstrating and investigating the power of the unconscious: early surrealist experiments in automatic writing highlighted the creativity of the unconscious, and dreams, when interpreted, showed that the unconscious held valuable information about individual desire. From 1928, Breton began to speak of a 'crise de l'objet'/'crisis of the object' in *Le Surréalisme et la peinture/Surrealism and Painting* (1928), *Qu'est-ce que le surréalisme?/What is Surrealism?* (1934) and 'Situation surréaliste de l'objet: situation de l'objet surréaliste'/'Surrealist Situation of the Object: Situation of the Surrealist Object', a lecture which he gave in Prague in 1935. Like surrealism's more general 'crisis of consciousness', a crisis of objects would take place by demonstrating and attempting to increase the intervention of the unconscious in relation to objects.

The inspiration behind the surrealist object

The sixth canto of Lautréamont's *Les Chants de Maldoror* found beauty in 'la rencontre fortuite sur une table de dissection d'un parapluie et d'une machine à coudre'/'the chance meeting of an umbrella and a sewing machine on a dissecting table' and inspired the surrealists to define a surrealist object as one which brings together two objects in a place common to neither one.[2] Lautréamont's image was considered to describe a surrealist object because objects were defamiliarised by taking them out of their usual environment: this would lead the viewer to stop ignoring these objects as a familiar part of everyday life, and to imagine a new relationship that these objects might have with their new environment. The juxtaposition of an object with another object with which it is not usually seen will lead the viewer to consider how they might be related: hence the significance of the word 'dissection', which suggests more than looking for a common bond between the two objects and instead considering how they might be used in combination, as one object.

Basic characteristics of surrealist objects and their relation to the unconscious

The surrealist object based on Lautréamont highlights three fundamental features common to all surrealist objects that the surrealists would go on to define: defamiliarisation, association and mysterious power. It was through these fundamental features that all surrealist objects demonstrated the intervention of the unconscious in relation to physical objects in waking life. In order to understand the way in which defamiliarisation, association and mysterious power are related to the unconscious, it is necessary to look to *The Interpretation of Dreams*, a text with which the surrealists were very familiar.[3] In this text, Freud explained that dreams are formed based on two key processes: condensation and displacement. Objects that appear in dreams may be there because they connect a number of different thoughts: the unconscious has selected these objects not because they are necessarily important per se, but simply by virtue of their chance frequency in thoughts that are significant to the dreamer.[4] The process by which the unconscious selects an object to represent more than one thought is called 'condensation'.[5] Displacement refers to the way in which that object, when it appears in the dream, takes on the importance of the thoughts connected to it.[6] The reason why dreams have a power to impress and disturb the dreamer is that, as Freud explained, while the 'manifest content' (that which actually appears in the dream) may appear ridiculous, the 'latent content' (the original thoughts) offers us important insights into ourselves.[7] There is a mystery to dreams and their power to move us, however, because condensation and displacement make it very difficult to discover the dream's latent content, otherwise known as 'interpreting the dream'.[8] Freud said that dreams are 'scant, paltry, laconic in comparison to the range and abundance of the dream-thoughts' and that, as a result, 'one is never certain of having interpreted a dream in its entirety'.[9]

In the context of surrealist objects in waking life, processes of association and defamiliarisation are characteristic of the unconscious and thus point to or elicit its intervention: just as the unconscious is skilled in discovering a common element linking two important thoughts in a dream (condensation), so it will easily intervene to find similarity between objects in waking life (association). The shock of seeing an object in a new environment, or otherwise defamiliarised, also evokes the way in which the object of condensation circulates bizarrely through a dream, acting as visual representative of the original thoughts while remaining semiotically dissociated from them. The bizarre and sometimes inexplicably powerful effect of the surrealist object is comparable to the way in which unimportant objects in dreams seem inordinately important because they have taken on the significance of the thought that they represent (condensation and displacement). Breton said, in relation to a surrealist object's associations, 'malgré mon effort d'objectivité, je n'oserais prétendre avoir extrait le meilleur, ni le plus significatif'/'in spite of my attempt at objectivity, I would not dare claim that I have extracted the best or the most significant'.[10] A surrealist object could thus take on as much mystery as a dream object: its significance and the associations it provoked would always be to some degree mysterious because they were elaborated by the unconscious.

Johanna Malt offers an alternative reading of surrealist objects in *Obscure Objects of Desire: Surrealism, Fetishism and Politics*.[11] She sees the surrealist fixation on objects as symptomatic of their 'fetish' function, both in the original sense of 'personal talismans or totems' and in the Freudian sense as sexually charged objects, which the surrealists used to provoke scandal and to work through 'private obsessions'.[12] Although Malt is not the first to have discerned fetishism in the surrealist relationship to objects, her theory differs in that it does not see the fetish as inward-looking or an unhealthy product of neurosis: rather, it adopts Christian Metz's and Laura Mulvey's view of fetishes as having 'to some extent, an enabling function', which 'permits a paradoxical fluidity in ways of thinking the world, even while tending towards fixity and repetition in its detail'.[13] Moving beyond the object's significance to the individual, Malt highlights the socio-historical resonance of surrealist objects, which results from the surrealists' awareness of 'the erotic allure of the object as commodity'.[14] Casting commodities as fetishes, the surrealists point to the historical and ephemeral quality of products presented as timeless, and to the absence lurking behind these products' promises to satisfy our desires.[15]

Types of surrealist object

A survey of the different types of surrealist object named by Breton in the essays mentioned earlier will reveal the way in which all point to the intervention of the unconscious. One of the most familiar, which Breton names as part of the history of the 'symbolic object', is Duchamp's readymade art, which transposes an everyday object to the museum, adding an unexpected title such as 'fountain' to a urinal.[16] This constituted more than an arbitrary method of defamiliarisation, as the artist had to engage in a detailed consideration of the object's normal use in order to select a combination of object and title that would most effectively subvert the habitual associations that one would make with the object. Breton explained the effect as follows: 'une lumière intense se répand [...] non plus sur l'objet étroit, [...] mais sur toute une opération de la vie mentale'/'not just the object itself, [...] but a whole operation of mental life [...] is illuminated'.[17] As it provokes the unconscious to seek unexpected similarities between different objects, the readymade as a surrealist object sheds light on the workings of the mind.

Some surrealist objects recall the example from Lautréamont: collage, which Breton considered a type of surrealist object, was based on the same principle of juxtaposition of diverse objects in a new location.[18] The 'image double'/'double image' brought together two diverse objects, but allowed them to exist within a single object in which the objects could be seen alternately but not simultaneously: one common example is an image which can be perceived as a duck or a rabbit, depending on how one interprets its different parts.[19]

Objects like Duchamp's readymade were able to become surrealist without involving physical juxtaposition with another object: the object put to an unconventional use, for example, or the renamed object, used strategies of defamiliarisation similar to that of the readymade.[20] Frottage was a more radical means of defamiliarisation, where a rubbing was taken of an object in order to disguise its usual appearance and draw out characteristics that one might not normally notice.[21] An object that had been damaged or worn could be surrealist because it was not only defamiliarised but also reflected, through its physical metamorphosis, the semiotic instability of any object.[22] The more general 'symbolic object' was surrealist precisely because it destabilised the object's everyday meaning: it could simultaneously be a familiar physical object and represent any number of different ideas.[23]

Last, but certainly not least, found objects were a type of surrealist object that held special interest for the surrealists. In one of his novels, Breton speaks fondly of the objects he finds at the Paris flea markets: objects that are 'démodés, fragmentés, inutilisables, presque incompréhensibles, pervers enfin au sens où je l'entends et où je l'aime'/'outmoded, fragmented, unusable, almost incomprehensible, ultimately perverse, in the way I understand and love this term'.[24] His description here implies that the found object is simply a combination of several types of surrealist object mentioned earlier (one that has been damaged, worn, renamed, or had a new use invented for it). However, in *L'Amour fou/Mad Love*, Breton attributed a more clearly personal interest to the found object: again at the Paris flea market, Alberto Giacometti happened to find a mask which gave him the inspiration he needed to complete one of his sculptures.[25] Breton described such apparent coincidences as 'le hasard objectif'/'objective chance', a case of the unconscious influencing perception so that chance occurrences (such as finding an object) take on immense relevance to the individual.[26]

The surrealist object as symptom of the unconscious

All surrealist objects may be considered personal because the associations that the unconscious suggests in relation to the object will be symptomatic of the individual's preoccupations; the found object foregrounds the influence of the unconscious in a more insistent manner, however. Whereas other types of surrealist objects are calculated to provoke the unconscious, in the case of the found object it is the unconscious that provokes the conscious mind. Breton remarked on the power of the unconscious over perception in *Les Vases communicants/Communicating Vessels*, noting that 'l'exigence du désir à la recherche de *l'objet* de sa réalisation dispose étrangement des données extérieurs, en tendant égoïstement à ne retenir d'elles que ce qui peut servir à sa cause'/'the demand of desire, when looking for the *object* that will fulfil it, arranges outside appearances strangely, tending egotistically to only register that which is of use to it'.[27] Giving a chance discovery the impression of destiny, found objects demonstrate most strikingly the way in which the unconscious directs one's conscious attention to objects that are relevant to one's desires. Breton explained Giacometti's found object as follows: 'la trouvaille remplit ici rigoureusement la même office que le rêve, en ce sens qu'elle libère l'individu de scrupules affectifs paralysants, le réconforte et lui fait comprendre que l'obstacle qu'il pouvait croire insurmontable est franchi'/'the found object serves the same purpose as dreams, in the sense that it liberates the individual from paralysing emotional doubts, comforts him/her and makes it clear that the obstacle which seemed insurmountable has been overcome'.[28] Having understood that it was not destiny that led one to find an object but the unconscious, the surrealists were excited by the idea that objects which hold an inexplicable fascination for us in everyday life might hold as much information as dreams do about our deepest motivations.

The unconscious and the everyday object

Breton believed that everyday encounters with objects would make one intimately aware, consciously or unconsciously, of their details. He declared that he was only able to gain a *'conscience poétique des objets'*/*'poetic awareness of objects'* through 'leur contact spirituel mille fois répété'/'spiritual contact with them, repeated a thousand times'.[29] The surrealists' experience with automatic writing led them to identify the unconscious as the source of creativity: they saw the mark of unconscious methods of association in poetic imagery, which links two realities based on a small detail. Like Breton, Louis Aragon sensed that the everyday could be a source of rich unconscious associations. He emphasised that 'on n'approchera jamais assez du quotidien'/'one can never get too close to the everyday', and felt that 'il y a de quoi frémir à voir une famille bourgeoise qui prend son café au lait du matin, sans remarquer l'inconnaissable qui transparaît dans les carreaux rouges et blancs de la nappe'/'there is something to make one tremble when one watches a middle-class family drink their morning coffee with milk, not noticing the unknowable which appears in the red and white check of the tablecloth'.[30] Aragon was excited by the contrast between familiar everyday items and the power of unconscious association that they held: 'les simulacres des temps modernes empruntent à l'anodin même de cet accoutrement une force magique inconnue à Éphèse ou à Angkor'/'the simulacra of modern times take from their very harmless appearance a magical force that was unknown even in Ephesus and Angkor'.[31] He was enchanted by the idea that the marvellous was located precisely in the familiar objects with which people interact comfortably all the time: the surrealists felt that mysterious power was enhanced by its proximity to everyday life.

Everyday reality as a privileged space for surrealism

The surrealists were interested in the everyday as a locus for unconscious associations. Moreover, it was surrealism's goal to show that the unconscious was a valuable dimension of waking life. In surrealism's first manifesto, Breton summarised the movement as aiming towards a reconciliation of conscious and unconscious minds, of dreams and waking reality: 'Je crois à la résolution future de ces deux états, en apparence si contradictoires, que sont le rêve et la réalité, en une sorte de réalité absolue, de surréalité'/'I believe that in future these two seemingly contradictory states of dream and reality will be resolved into a sort of absolute reality: a surreality'.[32] Having engaged in automatic writing during the early years of the movement and having analysed their own dreams, the surrealists needed a new area of research that would make the public understand that the unconscious is already a part of waking life, and encourage people to embrace unconscious interventions. Aragon noted the extraordinary degree of persuasive power held by physical proof: 'ce caractère de matérialisation [...] a sur l'homme un grand pouvoir [...] il lui ferait croire à une impossibilité logique au nom de sa logique'/'that which exists in material form [...] has great power over people [...] making them believe, for the sake of their logic, in a logical impossibility'.[33] In terms of surrealism's relationship and relevance to the general public, surrealist objects as a point of contact with the unconscious would be more visual and familiar than automatic writing and could seem more real and relevant than dreams.

The surrealist emphasis on thought over physical reality

The surrealist object thus seemed to represent a move towards surrealism's professed interest in discovering a balance between physical reality and the unconscious. Aragon called for a movement away from the modern habit of thinking abstractly and a return to thinking 'simplement, comme il semble naturel, suivant ce que je vois et ce que je touche'/'simply, naturally, following the senses of sight and touch'.[34] However, even in relation to surrealist objects, the group took care to stress that it was thought that was important: through their privileging of the activity of the mind, at the expense of the object that inspired that activity, the surrealists themselves emphasised the abstract over the physical. Breton, for example, considered it an advantage that the juxtaposition of objects enabled the viewer to 's'élever au-dessus de la considération de la vie manifeste de l'objet, qui constitue généralement une borne'/'rise above the consideration of the manifest life of the object, which has a restrictive tendency'.[35] His statement epitomises the surrealist sense of the object as a mere springboard for a more important psychological process. 'On finira bien par admettre'/'We will ultimately concede', said Breton elsewhere, 'que tout *fait image* et que le moindre objet, auquel n'est pas assigné un rôle symbolique particulier, est susceptible de figurer n'importe quoi'/'that everything *creates an image* and that the most lowly object, which doesn't have a particular symbolic role assigned to it, is in a position to represent anything at all'.[36] Here Breton takes the primacy of the unconscious one step further: he asserts that the unconscious can assign any meaning at all to an object, being limited in this activity not by the physical characteristics of that object, but only by other psychological associations that the object may already hold.

This neglect of the object in favour of thought was partially due to the fact that the group interpreted surrealist objects in the same way as dream objects: in dreams, the object is irrelevant, no more than a device connecting important thoughts. However, to think of the surrealist object in this way is to overlook an important difference. Even if the unconscious adopts dream-like processes of association in relation to objects in everyday life, it is not typically an important thought but rather a physical object that is the starting point of these associations. In the case of the found object, which does have an unconscious desire at its origin, physical characteristics nevertheless have more importance than they would in a dream object: it was, after all, the design of the mask that he found that inspired Giacometti to complete his sculpture.

The ethereal unconscious

It was perhaps natural that the surrealists should have moved away from the physical aspects of the object, however: the importance of the found object, and the associations inspired by all surrealist objects, came from the unconscious, and this meant that such objects maintained a mysterious and ethereal quality that distanced them from physical reality. Being unique to the individual, the unconscious will create associations that are very personal and thus inaccessible to other people unless they are explained. It is impossible to know, or understand, even one's own unconscious completely: as a result the associations that it creates will, like dreams, retain a degree of mystery. The surrealists described many instances in which an object took on great personal significance, offering renewed hope, and yet they were often unable to explain exactly where this power came from. Breton, for example, in *Les Vases communicants*, describes a girl buying gherkins, and the importance he assigns to them seems too great for their symbolism to be merely sexual: 'ces cornichons m'ont tenu lieu de providence, un certain jour'/'these gherkins acted as providence for me, one day', he declares, but does not specify the reason for their importance, which was perhaps unknowable even to him.[37]

The question of objectivity

The surrealists' sense of the influence of the unconscious over conscious perception was so extreme that it cast doubt on the very idea of objectivity. Dalí, for example, invented 'paranoiac-critical activity', in which the practitioner selects an 'idée obsédante'/'obsessive idea' and relies on the unconscious to find physical proof of its omnipresence in the outside world.[38] The surrealists called this practice 'une force organisatrice et productrice du hasard objectif'/'a force that organises and produces objective chance':[39] in other words, it is characterised by the unconscious directing one's conscious attention, just as it does in the case of the found object, resulting in the impression that chance events have personal significance. The difference is that the practitioner of paranoiac-critical activity deliberately provokes the unconscious to influence perception in a more sustained way and in relation to an idea that has been consciously chosen.

Although Breton said that it was important for the practitioner to check with other people to determine whether his impressions had an objective basis,[40] paranoiac-critical activity nonetheless offered an even more extreme example than the found object in terms of demonstrating the degree to which the unconscious can interpret objective reality, creating meaning where none was intended, and making perception intensely personal. The surrealists believed that this was in fact the natural state of all perception, which paranoiac-critical activity, like found objects, merely served to magnify: 'je suis intimement persuadé'/'I am firmly convinced' declared Breton, 'que toute perception enregistrée de la manière la plus involontaire [...] porte en elle la solution, symbolique ou autre, d'une difficulté où l'on est avec soi-même'/'that all perception, registered in the most involuntary way [...] holds within it the solution, symbolic or otherwise, to a personal difficulty that one is dealing with'.[41] In other words, according to the surrealists, that which one perceives in everyday life is not perceived objectively but is subjectively interpreted by the unconscious.

Surrealist objects as reconciling subjectivity and objectivity

Breton considered it surrealism's collective mission to 'travailler à ce que la distinction du subjectif et de l'objectif perde de sa nécessité et de sa valeur'/'work towards making the distinction between subjective and objective unnecessary and worthless':[42] the separation that is conventionally made between subjectivity and objectivity was thus one of the many boundaries that surrealism sought to break down. In spite of their tendency to take on intensely subjective and even mysterious meaning, surrealist objects were nonetheless typically able to function on both subjective and objective levels. As art objects, that is to say surrealist objects created for a general audience, they had objective value insofar as they successfully provoked the unconscious to engage creatively with the object, whatever subjective direction that engagement might then take. More personal types of surrealist object would become objective by means of an explanation of their relevance to the individual: the example of Giacometti's mask, for instance, has a clear objective value because it demonstrates that his unconscious led him to find an object that enabled him to complete an artistic project. In the case of symbolic objects that have a mysterious personal power that cannot be explained (Breton and the gherkins, for example), their objective value lies not in their detail but in the familiarity of the general impression of ineffable significance, something which most people will have experienced in relation to an object. As to the ability of surrealist cinema, which is based on very personal ideas, to appeal to a broad audience, Jean Goudal argued that it would have 'un caractère suffisamment pénétrant et humain du seul fait qu'il sera sorti du cerveau d'un de mes semblables'/'a sufficiently insightful and human quality simply because it has emerged from the mind of a fellow human being'.[43] For Malt, surrealist objects transcend their status as personal fetishes and gain a broader and lasting value through their status as commodity fetishes, exposing the lack that exists behind objects of consumer desire.[44]

The hybrid object versus the surrealist object; cinema versus surrealism

The hybrid object in film is a physical object that cannot be explained simply by its narrative function, aesthetic qualities, its comic function or its symbolism alone. It takes on a multitude of roles and thus becomes hybrid, its ambiguous meaning creating a source of disruption in the film. This multiple meaning and associated instability make the hybrid object similar to a surrealist object; unlike the surrealist object, however, the multiplicity of meanings and subversive force of the hybrid object do not typically find their source in the unconscious. Rather than developing multiple meanings by triggering a series of mental associations in the unconscious, as the surrealist object does, the hybrid object accumulates meanings as it circulates through the film; it may enter into juxtapositions with other objects, its details may be brought to the audience's attention via close-ups, it may be put to an unusual use or be found in an unusual environment. The film may draw hybrid objects to the audience's attention through methods similar to those used in surrealist objects; however, hybrid objects take on a different type of meaning because their meaning is produced by the film, not by the unconscious. Whereas the surrealist object's meaning is often mysterious and very personal, the hybrid object's meaning is almost always transparent and, from the audience's point of view, objective: meaning may be shown to be dependent on a particular character's state of mind, but the audience will be in no doubt as to what that meaning is. In those cases where the meaning of a hybrid object is not entirely clear, there will be no invitation to the audience to interpret the object from a Freudian perspective: instead, the object will tend to be resistant to interpretation and simply exist in the film as a locus for a collection of diverse and sometimes contradictory meanings.

The differences between the hybrid object in film and the surrealist object are necessary, given cinema's specificity and the dominant mode that it gradually came to adopt following the arrival of sound. Cinema's basis in photographic realism predisposes it to portraying physical reality more or less objectively; this impression of objectivity persists for the audience, as they are typically able to forget about the director whose role it is to shape that reality. The surrealist object has both objective and subjective dimensions, as discussed earlier, and its objective dimension could be easily portrayed on film: indeed the hybrid object often makes use of the surrealist object's physical form. It would be more challenging, however, to portray the surrealist object's subjective, unconscious dimension on film, as the world of the mind is often quite different from physical reality: in fact, to attempt to simulate a subjective vision of reality on film would detract from the medium's power of objective realism. That realism is crucial in order for the diegesis to support a narrative which, however many surprises it may contain, in its mainstream form remains grounded in the realm of logical causes and effects. Although the advent of sound allowed cinema to make use of voice-over and dialogue to communicate characters' thoughts and feelings in greater detail, the cinema has remained primarily a visual medium that favours action over interiority. Moreover, since the arrival of sound, cinema's dominant mode has been narrative, the goal of which is to entertain the audience with a story based on events, not, as the surrealists would have preferred, transforming the audience through an exploration of the unconscious.

The cinema was thus its own medium with its own goals, but the surrealists ignored this, just as they ignored the physical nature of the surrealist object: their interest in any given form of expression was in direct proportion to its ability to portray and explore the workings of the unconscious. René Clair pointed out the potential conflict between film form and surrealist practice in his response to Jean Goudal's article that had cast cinema as an ideal medium for surrealism: 'si le surréalisme a sa technique propre, le cinéma a la sienne aussi'/'surrealism may have its own particular techniques, but so does cinema', Clair warned.[45] The surrealists would discover this conflict when they attempted to put their theories of automatic cinema and filmed dreams into practice. Although the surrealists were also excited by cinema's ability, through montage, to bring together different realities, their attention to film form was again shaped by its usefulness to their own movement. As a result, the surrealists continued to believe that cinema would be a useful tool for exploring the unconscious, even when their practical experiments with film form suggested that this was not the case. When cinema's evolution as a medium turned decisively towards feature films with a logical narrative progression, and thus away from surrealistic psychological digressions, the group's experiments with film-making came to an end.

Objects in surrealist cinema: *Un Chien andalou*

Buñuel and Dalí were novice film-makers and not yet surrealists when they collaborated to make *Un Chien andalou*. The film nonetheless became the most famous example of surrealist film-making, and the one most consistently praised by the surrealists themselves: in fact, when he saw the film, Breton personally invited Buñuel and Dalí to become members of the group.

Buñuel said that he and Dalí made the film based on images taken from their dreams, selecting them for their irrationality; however, Buñuel biographer John Baxter points out that many of *Un Chien andalou*'s configurations are in fact lifted from Freud and from other films, advertisements, art and cultural detritus of the time.[46] Linda Williams' analysis of the film suggests that, in spite of Buñuel and Dalí's lack of experience as directors and as surrealists, the film is more than a random collage of influences: she believes that it testifies to a careful consideration of the way in which the medium could be used to represent the unconscious.[47] The following summary of her argument will show Williams to be correct in her assessment of *Un Chien andalou* as demonstrating an effective strategy for the filmic portrayal of the unconscious in general. However, when it comes to objects, Williams fails to recognise that Buñuel and Dalí's approach was far less convincing: although the directors successfully reproduced the forms of unconscious association, these forms were effectively dissociated from their complexity of meaning. This left the audience unsure of how to engage with objects in *Un Chien andalou*.

Portraying the unconscious on film
Williams says that rather than simply reproducing dreams on film, as the surrealists had thought of doing, Buñuel and Dalí made a subtler use of the medium and portrayed the workings of the unconscious in a more organic way.[48] If the unconscious was to be accurately

represented, its contents could not be given explicitly.[49] Instead, in *Un Chien andalou* Buñuel set the precedent for a practice that would become familiar throughout his late work: that of expressing the unconscious filmically through 'the disruption of one level of discourse by another', in imitation of the way in which the unconscious intervenes in an unexpected and destabilising manner in waking life.[50] In this way, the portrayal of the unconscious becomes more universal: it appeals to the experience of all audience members in a way that a film of one individual's dream cannot.[51]

The specific way in which this disruption occurs in *Un Chien andalou* reflects the surrealists' developing understanding of the exigencies of the medium in relation to reception; they saw that the major difference between dream and film was that in dream the signifier is more believable than the signified, whereas in film the opposite is true.[52] The surrealists realised that in order to make films that imitated the workings of dream more closely, they needed to make the signified less believable: the audience would then be made to believe more in the signifiers that appeared before them, and the experience of the film would be much more similar to a dream.[53] However, if this technique was taken too far, and there was too radical a disruption of the level of discourse with which the audience normally engages, there was the danger that the audience would fail to engage with the film at all.[54] This was in fact the case with *Un Chien andalou*, at least to a degree, as the apparent inability of its signified to be properly grasped was taken to mean that it was an 'avant-garde' film: the audience believed that that film was not meant to be understood, and thus failed to engage with it in the way that the surrealists hoped.[55] Arguably, whatever their true intentions, the surrealists' approach to film compelled the audience to be as passive when watching a surrealist film as they would be if they were dreaming.[56] Rather than provoking active audience engagement, the surrealist portrayal of the unconscious was ultimately demonstrative: this is a concept which will be important later, as it will help to explain why the objects in *Un Chien andalou* function fully neither as surrealist objects nor as dream objects.

Un Chien andalou may be considered narrative insofar as there is a general semblance of story, centred on a largely antagonistic relationship between a man and a woman; however, just as in a dream, and unlike in a film, it is impossible to predict the direction that the narrative will take. As the film is visually engaging, however, it is possible simply to abandon oneself to the flow of events, precisely as one would in a dream. The film resembles dream in that people and objects succeed in being one thing and another at the same time (as in the dream process of condensation). In terms of characters, the simplest manifestation of this duality is the androgyne, who appears with both masculine and feminine aspects.[57] The central male character (played by Pierre Batcheff) also has feminine elements to his dress when he is first seen riding a bicycle; his dual nature is more radical, however, as he literally becomes two people at one point in the film, when a sterner version of himself confronts the weaker version.[58] The central female character's body serves as a liminal location when Batcheff's character caresses her breasts, which briefly turn into buttocks as the result of a camera trick.[59] Such tricks were theoretically discouraged by the surrealists as they believed that they would destroy the film's impression of reality, which they considered a powerful persuasive tool for convincing people that the surrealism portrayed in the film could exist in everyday life; fantastic occurrences, on the other hand, could allow the film to be classified as a dream and therefore, in the public's eyes, become irrelevant. *Un Chien andalou*, however, clearly gives an impression of dream, and accordingly features several examples of such special effects.

The role of objects

While the experience of the narrative, with its disruption of discourses, reflects a careful consideration of film form in order to alter the spectator's relationship to it, the way in which objects are portrayed is less subtle. The subjective point of view is suggested in this film through shots of characters staring intently at objects. For example, the female character fixes her gaze on the male character's accessories which she has arranged on the bed, or a death's head moth on the wall. The stare and its object are divided, as the stare is shown in one shot, and the object of the stare in a subsequent shot. This forces the spectator to watch another character staring at something that may or may not be of obvious interest. In the case of the clothes on the bed, the woman's stare is contemplative. In the case of the moth, the woman shows more emotion, but the way in which Buñuel and Dalí magnify the subjective power of what she sees is through literal magnification of the image (a more distant shot fades in stages to an extreme close-up); at one point the directors even use an iris to zero in on the death's head on the moth's abdomen. In the case of the clothes on the bed, the woman's contemplative stare is uncinematic: it is a shot without movement, has no event associated with it, and does not give the spectator the means to consider what the character might be thinking because the film does not explore her psychology. The audience's own inactivity is brought to their attention as they are reminded that they are passively watching a character who is watching something else. It is easier to understand the power of the death's head moth to motivate the character's stare, but even here, the way in which the series of closer shots and the iris are used to evoke that interest is intrusive and points to the power of the director to control what the audience sees.

A more interesting conjunction of a stare and its object occurs when Batcheff's character discovers a hole in his hand from which ants are emerging. It begins with a kind of establishing shot that was missing in the previous examples: a medium shot of Batcheff in profile staring at his hand, which is included in the frame. The next shot is a close-up view of the palm of his hand (figure 1.1), revealing the hole and the ants emerging from it, which were not visible in the previous shot. This image will become the basis for a series of transformations effected by means of dissolves. The transformations are interesting in themselves: the ants emerging from the palm of Batcheff's hand are transformed into underarm hair (of a man on the beach) (figure 1.2), which turns into a sea urchin (figure 1.3), which then becomes the head of the androgynous woman in the street, seen from above (figure 1.4). The objects are linked through the general round shape that they share, certainly, as Linda Williams points out.[60] More evocative, though, is the series' theme and variation based on natural textures: the creepiness of insects' hair-like legs tickling a palm, the fluffy hairs in the armpit, the sharper hair-like protrusions of the urchin's needles and finally the smooth hair of the androgynous woman's head. These textures and their locations not only have sexual resonance, but involve more instinctive methods of association (touch, for example), all characteristic of the unconscious.

The juxtaposition of ants in a palm, hairs in an armpit, the spines of an urchin, and hair on a head may be considered an example of a surrealist object transposed to film. However, in spite of Buñuel's use of dissolves, a technique specific to cinema, the series of images is not cinematic: after the initial image, which features the movement of the ants, the objects are static and isolated from their environment, creating a comparison that could have taken place as easily through a series of photographs. Moreover, this series creates an intrusive pause in the film's narrative. There is a sense that the director is putting the cinematic apparatus at the service of surrealism, and the effect is as stilted as the previous shots of the female character's stares.

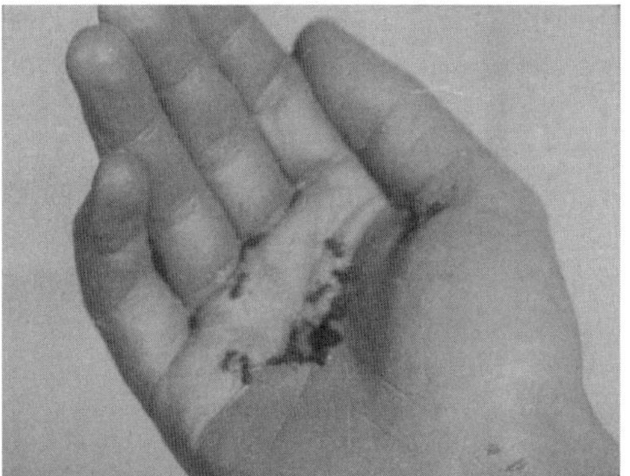

Figure 1.1: Ants emerging from the male character's palm in *Un Chien andalou*.

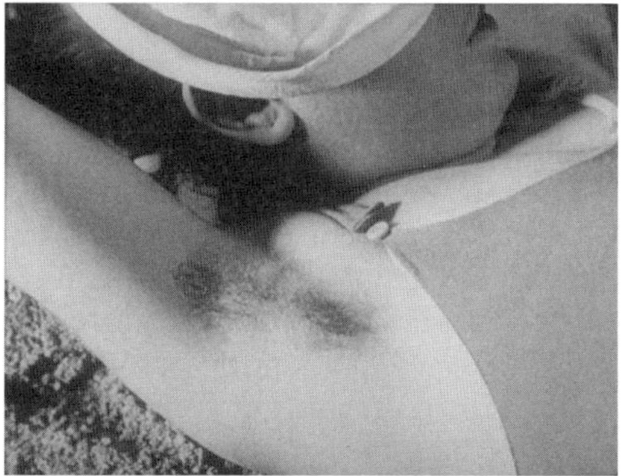

Figure 1.2: The underarm hair of a man on the beach in *Un Chien andalou*.

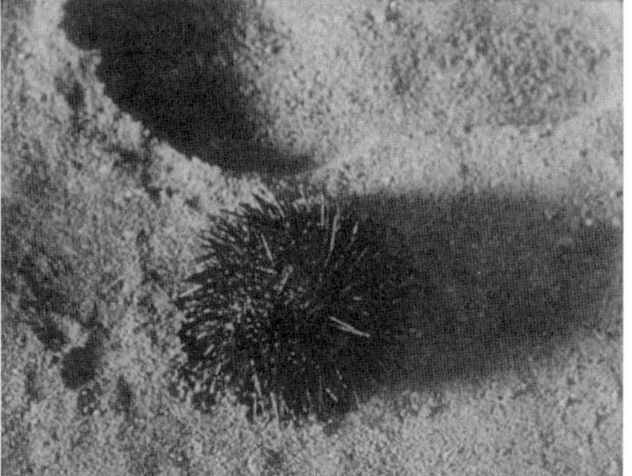

Figure 1.3: A sea urchin in *Un Chien andalou*.

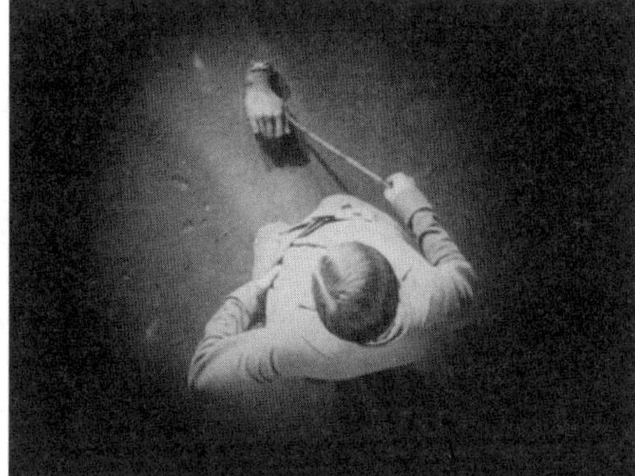

Figure 1.4: The androgynous woman in the street in *Un Chien andalou*.

The isolation of the images in the series of comparisons also reflects their separation from the narrative. The transformations were most likely intended to portray the subjective associations that Batcheff's character is making based on what he sees in his palm (the ants themselves perhaps being the symbolic representation of a sexual urge). Whether or not these associations are the product of the Batcheff character's unconscious is irrelevant to the audience, however, as they can have no more than the most basic Freudian understanding of his psychology. Indeed, although Williams points out that there are many shape-based comparisons in the film, which are characteristic of unconscious methods of association, she herself cannot locate a meaning for them except as Freudian symbols.[61] She argues that Buñuel makes use of the specificity of the filmic medium by portraying the way in which desire, or the unconscious, influences perception by means of figures such as metaphor and metonymy, and that the director thus shows the form of unconscious desire, not just its content.[62] However, she does not question whether Buñuel's use of the specific techniques that cinema makes available is in fact a cinematic use.

Williams' assessment of Buñuel's portrayal of unconscious desire begs the question of whether the form of that desire can be effectively portrayed without its content (or, rather, with an oversimplified Freudian content). While I agree that the disruption of one level of discourse by another may be an effective way of evoking the experience of the intervention of the unconscious in general, I disagree that the influence of the unconscious over our perception of objects can be portrayed without indicating the reason why this is of interest. Certainly, *Un Chien andalou*'s first famous example of an unusual juxtaposition of objects (eyeball-razor) and their shape-based association with a distant reality (the moon and a cloud) is so shocking that it communicates a psychological effect without the need for meaning. In most cases, however, the film presents the spectator with the form of surrealist objects accompanied by a basic Freudian resonance that creates insufficient impact.

In '*Un Chien andalou*: The Talking Cure', Stuart Liebman offers a daring interpretation of objects, one that avowedly sounds 'far-fetched' but is thereby all the more intriguing: faced with 'striking visual incongruities', Liebman looks to wordplay as a way of explaining how objects, bodies and movements interrelate.[63] His interpretation of the (eye) opening scene links the diverse visual elements of this sequence by associating them with a punning range of *gros mots* and expressions characteristic of the 'transgressive impulses of the unconscious'.[64] His analysis of the connections between the ants in the palm and sequence of images that follow seems rather thin by comparison. Starting with the French word for ant, '*fourmi*', he uses this word to trace a relationship with ensuing object images based on the '*our*' sound: the sea urchin is an '*oursin*' and the crowd of people (around the androgynous woman) seen from above, swarming like ants, '*fourmillent*' (the inconvenient exception formed by the *poils de l'aisselle*/underarm hair is ignored).[65] Liebman believes that Buñuel and Dalí used film form to represent the way in which dreamwork 'transform[s] [...] a latent verbal thought into manifest verbal images'; as a result, images in the film can be compared to the Freudian rebus and in order to understand them 'the film analyst, like the psychoanalyst, must break apart each image into the words or syllables that compose it'.[66]

Liebman's is a stimulating approach to understanding objects in *Un Chien andalou* because it does not only describe how the directors used film form to represent unconscious processes in general; it also attempts to discover, in detail, the original, specific content encoded in this form. A significant problem remains, however: while the possible meaning discovered by this approach is (in some cases) rich, will the average audience member really be 'induce[d] to "hear" the murmuring speech beneath the evolving spectacle'?[67] Liebman's 'we' clearly refers to film critics and scholars: those who have the patience to watch one film many times over, scrutinising the images and thinking about them in depth. Indeed, he concludes by declaring that, specifically, '*critics* must listen as well as look at the film text' [my emphasis].[68] Thus, even in light of an approach that assesses the form and content of the film equally, its surrealist objects cannot be said to fulfil the surrealists' goal to revolutionise the general public's way of thinking.

While a viewer of a surrealist sculpture or painting in an art museum would be prepared to think creatively in order to discover the link between juxtaposed objects, cinema audiences are unused to engaging subjectively with a film; the normal point of engagement with an object is mediated by the narrative, and therefore we typically relate to objects based on their physical place in the diegesis, their significance to the characters, and their role in advancing the story. *Un Chien andalou* does not give sufficient provision of any of these cues: as explained earlier, its dream-like narrative encourages passivity in the viewer. As a result, what Buñuel intended as a 'call to murder' washed over the audience, who had been deprived of the orientation points they needed to engage actively with the film.

Conclusion

The fatal flaw in surrealist cinema and its portrayal of objects was to expect active engagement from an average audience when the film equipped them for a passive role. My theory of the hybrid object will not, in general, base itself on the idea that the audience must engage actively in order to discover the multiple meanings of the hybrid object. The hybrid object will be unusual in the context of film by virtue of the fact that its meaning exists on many levels; the audience will be able to assimilate this meaning, however, because it will typically be transparent and, most importantly of all, will be produced by the film itself, through the means that are specific to it, and for the sake of narrative, not for the sake of surrealism.

Notes

1 *Les Manifestes du surréalisme* (Paris: Le Sagittaire, 1946) 51. In this and other quotations from Breton, the italics are his.

2 André Breton, 'Situation surréaliste de l'objet: Situation de l'objet surréaliste', *Position politique du surréalisme, André Breton: Oeuvres complètes*, ed. Marguerite Bonnet, 3 vols (Paris: Gallimard, 1992) 2: 492.

3   *The Interpretation of Dreams* was published in French in 1925 (*La Science des rêves*, trans. Meyerson), so the surrealists were only able to read the work in its entirety shortly after the publication of the first *Manifeste du surréalisme* (1924). Prior to 1925, the surrealists would have had access to translated excerpts from *The Interpretation of Dreams* in Régis and Hesnard's *La Psychoanalyse des névroses et des psychoses* (1914).

4   Sigmund Freud, *The Interpretation of Dreams*, trans. Joyce Crick (Oxford: Oxford University Press, 1999) 215.

5   Freud, *The Interpretation of Dreams* 226.

6   Freud, *The Interpretation of Dreams* 235.

7   Freud, *The Interpretation of Dreams* 133.

8   Freud, *The Interpretation of Dreams* 132–33.

9   Freud, *The Interpretation of Dreams* 212.

10   *L'Amour fou*, *André Breton: Oeuvres complètes*, ed. Marguerite Bonnet, 3 vols (Paris: Gallimard, 1992) 2: 706.

11   Oxford: Oxford University Press, 2008.

12   Malt 103–04.

13   Malt 5–6.

14   Malt 103–04.

15   Malt 104–06.

16   'Crise de l'objet', *Le Surréalisme et la Peinture* (*Nouvelle Edition 1928-1965*) (Paris: Gallimard, 1965) 280.

17   In 'Phare de la mariée', *Minotaure* 6 (December 1934): 46, in ed. note to 'Situation surréaliste de l'objet' 1607.

18   'Situation surréaliste de l'objet' 491–92.

19   Breton, 'Situation surréaliste de l'objet' 491.

20   Breton, 'Crise de l'objet' 280.

21   Breton, 'Situation surréaliste de l'objet' 492.

22   Breton, 'Crise de l'objet' 280.

23   Breton, 'Situation surréaliste de l'objet' 474.

24   *Nadja* (Paris: Gallimard, 1964) 62.

25   *L'Amour fou* 697–700.

26   'Situation surréaliste de l'objet' 485.

27   *André Breton: Oeuvres complètes*, ed. Marguerite Bonnet, 3 vols (Paris: Gallimard, 1992) 2: 177.

28   *L'Amour fou* 700.

29   *Premier Manifeste du surréalisme, Manifestes du surréalisme* 32.

30   *Le Paysan de Paris* (Paris: Gallimard, 1926) 187, 216.

31   *Le Paysan de Paris* 187.

32   *Manifeste du surréalisme, Les Manifestes du surréalisme* 15.

33   *Le Paysan de Paris* 246.

34   *Le Paysan de Paris* 11.

35   'Crise de l'objet' 279.

36   *Les Vases communicants* 181.

37   *Les Vases communicants* 158.

38 André Breton, *Qu'est-ce que le surréalisme?*, *André Breton: Oeuvres complètes*, ed. Marguerite Bonnet, 3 vols (Paris: Gallimard, 1992) 2: 256.

39 Dalí qtd. in André Breton, *Anthologie de l'humour noir*, *André Breton: Oeuvres complètes*, ed. Marguerite Bonnet, 3 vols (Paris: Gallimard, 1992) 2: 1151.

40 *Qu'est-ce que le surréalisme?* 256.

41 *L'Amour fou* 685.

42 *Qu'est-ce que le surréalisme?* 258.

43 'Surréalisme et cinéma', *Les surréalistes et le cinéma*, eds. Alain and Odette Virmaux (Paris: Seghers, 1976) 314.

44 Malt 220–21.

45 'Cinéma et surréalisme', *Les surréalistes et le cinéma* 318.

46 John Baxter, *Buñuel* (London: Fourth Estate, 1994) 75–76.

47 *Figures of Desire: A Theory and Analysis of Surrealist Film* (Berkeley and Los Angeles: University of California Press, 1981) xvi–xvii.

48 Williams, *Figures of Desire* xvi–xvii.

49 Williams, *Figures of Desire* 28.

50 Williams, *Figures of Desire* 32–33.

51 Williams, *Figures of Desire* 32–33.

52 Williams, *Figures of Desire* 48–49.

53 Williams, *Figures of Desire* 48–49.

54 Williams, *Figures of Desire* 110–11.

55 Williams, *Figures of Desire* 110–11.

56 Kuenzli 8–9.

57 Williams, *Figures of Desire* 85.

58 Williams, *Figures of Desire* 85, 92.

59 Williams, *Figures of Desire* 89.

60 *Figures of Desire* 78–79. Iampolski notes the surrealists' 'emphasis on concrete form', which allowed them to 'level [...] out the semantic differences between objects that bore any formal resemblance to one another' and 'strengthen the denotative function of the signifier' (168).

61 *Figures of Desire* 69–100. In 'The Critical Grasp: Buñuelian Cinema and Its Critics', Williams acknowledges that for all its descriptive interest there is a 'reductive' quality to this approach: 'in answer to the question what do Buñuel's films finally mean? the Lacanian response is that they mean exactly what Lacan means' (*Dada and Surrealist Film*, ed. Rudolf E. Kuenzli [Cambridge, MA: MIT Press, 1996] 204).

62 *Figures of Desire* xvi–xvii, 14–15.

63 *Dada and Surrealist Film*, ed. Rudolf E. Kuenzli (Cambridge, MA: MIT Press, 1996) 147, 151.

64 145–50.

65 Liebman 151–52. Also ignored is the fact that the crowd surrounding the androgynous woman is not immediately visible, leaving us with her head, seen on its own, as another exception to the rule of 'our' sounds.

66 144, 154.

67 Liebman 145. Iampolski (Chapter 5) offers a dazzling intertextual reading of *Un Chien andalou*, very useful in terms of understanding how particular objects may have been

selected and how the film exemplifies surrealist strategies to renew and liberate expression. While average audience members will of course feel the effect of these strategies, it seems unlikely that they could appreciate precisely how this effect is achieved, or readily pick up on the rich intertextuality Iampolski describes. As such, even if a well-read scholar is able, following close study, to give an unusually satisfying explanation for the presence of objects in this film, the film itself fails to satisfy the need for the surrealist revolution to be generalised.

68   154.

Style and the Hybrid Object in *À Nous la liberté*

Introduction

Before the surrealists began their experiments in cinema, René Clair made his directorial debut with *Entr'acte* in 1924. It was a film that the dadaists commissioned him to make, and has been described as marking the high point and culmination of dada.[1] Actors in the film included Man Ray, Marcel Duchamp and Erik Satie; these were members of the dada group who had not yet taken sides in the disagreement between Tristan Tzara and André Breton that would culminate in the foundation of the surrealist group.[2] As its title suggests, *Entr'acte* was shown in between acts of a performance: a ballet called *Relâche*, whose title in turn suggested, with typical dada playfulness, that there was 'no performance' at the theatre where it was advertised.[3] Dada's leader Francis Picabia invented the film's scenes, and was responsible for its episodic structure and its targeting of solemn tradition.[4] Clair interpreted Picabia's scenes with expressive and creative images that, in dadaist fashion, exploited the full range of cinema's tricks for defamiliarising reality.[5] He also shifted the original emphasis, making it more playful than aggressive, and emphasising movement above all in the film's final funeral-turned-chase scene.[6]

À Nous la liberté, which Clair made under contract for the major German production company Tobis, features a more conventional narrative arc. It follows two friends, Émile and Louis, as they learn from experience that prisoners, factory employees and their bosses are all rigidly controlled by their work and the pressure to conform; in order to find freedom, Émile and Louis must abandon modern life altogether.[7] Although the film does not feature the experimental camera tricks of *Entr'acte*, in other respects it remains characteristic of Clair's approach in the earlier film: it is misleadingly playful in its attack on industrial society, inventive in its aesthetics and highly cinematic in its emphasis on movement.

Released in 1931, the year after the surrealists' practical engagement with cinema ended with Buñuel's *L'Âge d'or*, *À Nous la liberté* was Clair's third sound film. Although it was not highly regarded by the surrealists,[8] *À Nous la liberté* is of interest to the study of hybrid objects in cinema because it came at a transitional moment in film history. The advent of sound would revolutionise cinema, reorientating it towards psychological narrative. By the 1940s and 50s, objects in film were penned in by the mise-en-scène and could only take on meaning in relation to the film's characters. In the early 1930s, however, the conventions of narrative sound cinema had not yet been established: visual methods of storytelling were still dominant, and objects accordingly had an important role to play. For example, in Jean Vigo's *L'Atalante* (1934), the exotic souvenirs in Père Jules' cabin take on a power that amplifies the first mate's own dangerous libidinal energy but which nonetheless stands independently of him; character and object have an equal role to play in elaborating the film's theme of challenges in married life. A film such as Jean Renoir's *Elena et les hommes/Paris Does Strange Things* (1956), by contrast, exemplifies the way in which objects later became entirely dependent on character for their significance. One object, a daisy, is emphasised as early as the film's title sequence, but is meaningless except in relation to the charming princess; it is the characters who embody the themes in this film, and the object exists as a mere physical and semiotic accessory to the characters.

À Nous la liberté was chosen for this study because objects in the film become hybrid not only as a result of a conjunction of historical and technological factors that influenced cinema's development; Clair's own aesthetic choices and expressive concerns also contribute to the creation of hybrid objects. As Clair's career spanned the transition from silent to sound cinema, his work is naturally informed by the tradition of visual storytelling; this is especially the case in *À Nous la liberté*, as one of his early sound films. Objects in *À Nous la liberté* thus take on a hybrid function through their multiple diegetic, thematic and symbolic roles which are typical of objects in a visually-based narrative. However, Clair's style and the theme of this particular film also contribute to objects' hybridity. Objects are instrumental to the film's comedy, most often manifested through slapstick gags and elaborate high-speed comic chases. This comic emphasis on motion helps the object to circulate productively through the diegetic space, accumulating meaning from the different situations in which it appears. The message behind *À Nous la liberté* also determines the emphasis on objects and their disruptive effect as they pass through the film's diegesis; although capitalism's own emphasis on objects is one of the reasons behind the regimented society that the film satirises, the free movement of objects continually disrupts that regimentation.

Finally, the object's hybridity is supported by the formal and generic hybridity of the film itself, which is again the product of both a particular stage in the development of the medium and Clair's own approach to the film. As mentioned, films of the early 1930s can be expected to exhibit characteristics of both sound and silent cinema. In addition, films of the silent and early sound period incorporated a type of performance inspired by circus and low theatre (including operetta, the genre which most influenced Clair). *À Nous la liberté* displays this historical hybridity, even though Clair was sensitive to cinema's specificity and was renowned for his innovative use of the new technology of sound. Moreover, the film is hybrid in that it is both artistic and popular: Clair was able to incorporate his creativity and innovation in this studio-produced film made for a mainstream audience. Finally, *À Nous la liberté* derives generic hybridity from the light-hearted cartoon-like comic approach that Clair uses alongside his serious social criticism, as well as from the element of romance (which Clair said that he added to the film purely in order to please audiences who enjoy the genre[9]). As the object circulates through the film, the film's hybridity increases the types of roles and the layers of resonance that it is able to take on.

The analysis in this chapter will begin with an exploration of style in *À Nous la liberté*, drawing out in particular those features that make the film characteristic of Clair's approach to film-making, but also noting those elements common to early sound cinema in general. I will highlight the way in which style supports the film's satirical theme, and where it contributes to the film's hybridity. In the case of those stylistic features that have the most influence on objects in the film, I will explore this effect by means of specific examples. However, the most detailed example will be reserved for the final section of the chapter, in which I will examine how all the elements of style mentioned in the previous sections come to bear on one important object in one particular sequence of the film.

Style in *À Nous la liberté*

This section will examine seven different elements of Clair's style: music, mise-en-scène, cartoon-style comedy, frame scale, editing, circulation, and symmetrical narrative.

Music

One of the most distinctive and memorable features of *À Nous la liberté* is its music. As explained above, this film is a very early *parlant*, and as a result, not only do objects play a large role alongside the limited dialogue but, most obviously, music fills in where speech is lacking. *À Nous la liberté* evokes operetta through the way in which pieces of music are connected with particular places and situations in the film (the prisoners' working song with the prison, but also with schools and factories later in the film). Some characters even have their own themes: for example, Émile and Louis are jointly associated with the title song, which they perform at the end of the film like actors on stage, facing the camera frontally to sing in a way that draws attention to bare performance as much as the medium by which it is represented, film. One particularly resonant use of sound in the film is that of the marching prisoners' wooden clogs; it recurs twice outside the space of the prison itself, and in both instances it signals that Émile and Louis are recalling their life in prison.

Music both emphasises and contributes to the film's rhythm, yet also serves to undermine this rhythm. The music has an especially marked and fast-paced rhythm, suited to the actions that it accompanies: brisk, repetitive assembly-line work and numerous chases, for example. In such cases, music can be said to reflect and underscore the rhythms of the actions portrayed, even to regulate them. At certain moments in the film, though, music goes beyond being an appropriate accompaniment and actually matches itself exactly to the pace of the action, in a manner unusual in live-action film. It does not strike one as odd to see the factory employees marching to music, even if it is extra-diegetic music, as marching is necessarily rhythmic and often accompanied by music in parades. However, in other cases, there is a sense that the film is indulging in light mickey-mousing (a cartoon-like exact match of music to action): for example, when Émile first sees Jeanne (the film's love interest) at the factory, she seems to move in time to the rhythm of the recruitment machine and the extra-diegetic music that accompanies it. Because spontaneous matching of independent rhythms occurs rarely in real life, such a correspondence in the film points to the deliberate constructedness of the film itself, and more importantly makes the audience feel how unnatural it is for human movement to be determined by mechanical rhythms.

As they denaturalise or otherwise mock the film's serious and regimented pace, cartoon-like effects of music can be as amusing as those in animated comedy itself. When Louis presses a button to summon Jeanne's uncle, a fanfare accompanies the old man's instant appearance at the door of Louis' office. In this example, music creates a disjunction characteristic of cartoon in the expansive grandeur that contrasts with the unimpressive appearance and servile manners of the accountant. In addition, the type of musical instrument used will influence the audience's impression of the music that is played. Throughout the film, the wide variety and sonic qualities of the instruments that intervene are also characteristic of cartoons. While piccolos, chimes and even xylophones are not strictly out of place in military marches, these instruments are used even when the music is of another style, and thus come to stand out in the film. The audience is made more conscious of these particular instruments and their light timbre, which suggests smallness and playfulness; it is a sound quality that creates a mood that contrasts with and pokes fun at the sober rhythms it accompanies. The use of cymbals and the glockenspiel also add a ludic dimension to the film's music; the hollowness of the glockenspiel's sound seems to mock the controlling beat of any strict rhythm. Also, people tend to believe that such instruments are easy to play, and that playing them is therefore a little silly (in the case of tapping the glockenspiel) or extremely satisfying (in the case of clashing the cymbals together), which also makes the sound of these instruments especially comical and enjoyable. Cymbals, glockenspiels and the similarly evocative bass drum can intervene in any piece of music in the film, but when they take part in the musical accompaniment to chases, they contribute particularly to the comedy. Although the film does not quite replicate cartoons' use of musical instruments to create sound effects for falls and collisions, a kick or a slap will often cue the beginning of a new musical segment to accompany a chase, and the mere presence of percussive sounds will amplify the physical comedy of these scenes. Such chases, while they perpetuate a relentless rhythm, nonetheless subvert the mechanised or military rhythms of modern life and offer an alternative: the equally brisk but exuberant rhythms of the liberated human being.

Mise-en-scène

Just as music is used to reproduce and immediately subvert the mechanical and military rhythms that the director perceived in modern life, the film's set design comments on a contemporary utilitarian architectural style by exaggerating its prevalence and proportions; in so doing, it mocks the utilitarian attitude with which the style is associated. The space's emptiness, moreover, turns it into vacuum, inviting chaos.

The prison, the record superstore, the factory and Louis' home (figures 2.1–2.4) all share an improbably similar Bauhaus minimalism. While based on real life, these spaces are so pure and uniform that it is clear that they are sets designed around the film's requirements, and not buildings that exist for use outside the film. The bare cleanliness of the immense spaces defined by the mise-en-scène creates an oppressive sparseness. The architectural forms are devoid of any pattern to break up the monotony, and the spaces that they surround are utterly bare: nothing is out of place, and there is not one piece of clutter or speck of dirt. It is a space that, ideologically, suggests an approach to life that minimises the importance of the individual, and is concerned only with a mass of reliable workers who will create an endless supply of a uniform product. Furthermore, the geometrical logic of the space implies that it will seek to enclose and control all those who enter. In fact, this space is not effective at keeping disruptive forces out, and its control over its occupants is far from perfect, particularly when Émile is introduced, a character who has not yet learnt to conform to the rules of industrial society.

The sets are predominantly composed of large rectangular planes. These shapes reflect light and provoke a flattening effect in the image, because they draw attention to uniform surfaces rather than graduated depths. Although the strong horizontals and verticals of the

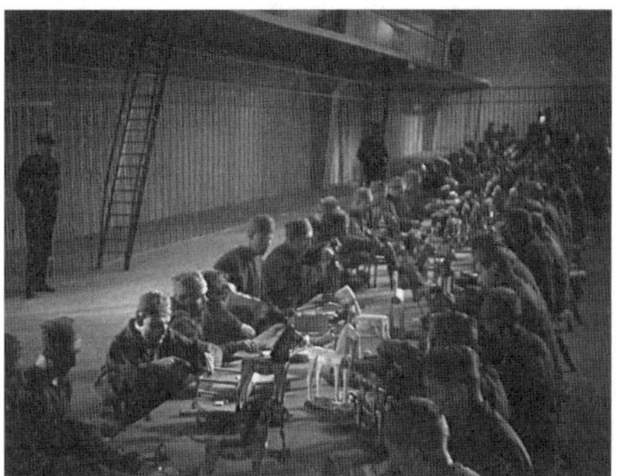

Figure 2.1: The prison in *À Nous la liberté.*

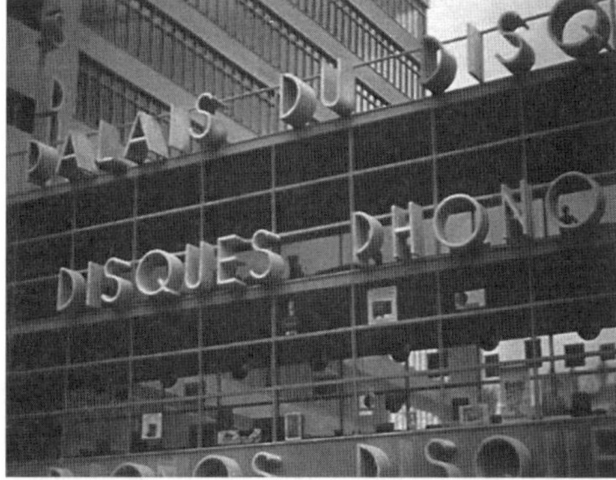

Figure 2.2: The record superstore in *À Nous la liberté.*

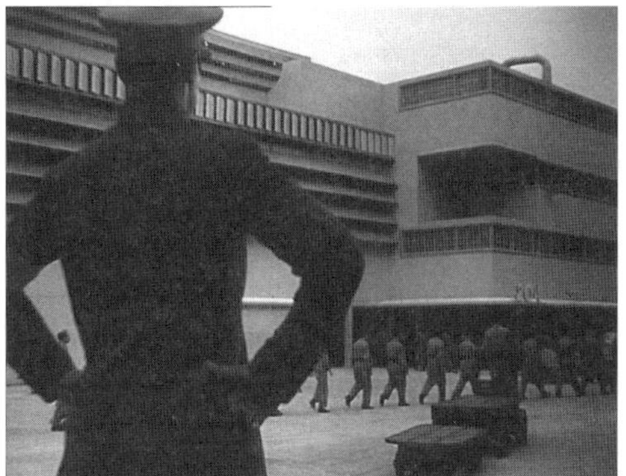

Figure 2.3: The factory in *À Nous la liberté.*

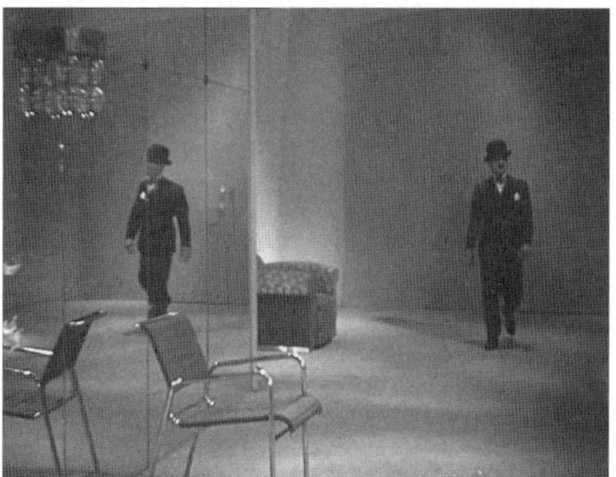

Figure 2.4: Louis' home in *À Nous la liberté.*

buildings are broken up by some diagonals, the effect tends to create sharp corners, rather than suggesting a receding perspective. Image depth would create a background against which human action would appear purposeful; instead, the characters' actions appear as mere agitation or displacement within a geometric space, never as progress. The set design may thus reflect the superficiality of modern consumer society, and the impossibility of making any real progress because of the endless cycles that rule the lives of those operating within its structures. However, the two-dimensionality of the sets is perhaps more important in terms of its contribution to the film's overall hybridity; here again it is operetta that is evoked by the clearly artificial sets. The purity of the space also evokes the purpose-drawn space of animation, just as the comic antics that disrupt that space are cartoon-like.

Cartoon-style comedy

The previous two sections explained how cartoon-like effects in *À Nous la liberté*'s live action contributed to the film's hybridity. Most important, though, is their comically subversive effect on the social organisation that the film portrays; they form a more light-hearted complement to the film's satire on this system. This section will explain the way in which cartoon-style comedy informs the film on a number of levels, from characters and their behaviour to the role of objects.

À Nous la liberté's overall impression of playfulness, exuberance and silliness results from a combination of effects of characterisation, action, and style typical of cartoon. The exaggeration of real-life personality traits results in characters who are clearly typed in their comical appearance and behaviour, which is always predictable and consistent. Even when Louis moves between his normal fun-loving nature and the dignified behaviour necessary for his businessman façade, he is simply alternating between two clear-cut character types, only one of which, moreover, is the real Louis. Like an animated comedy, the film also pokes fun at society's well-defined hierarchy and plays on the audience's joy at seeing it disrupted: in Hanna-Barbera cartoons, Jerry is protected from Tom by Spike the bulldog; in Friz Freling's work, Tweetie Pie is saved from Sylvester by Granny and her umbrella; in Clair's film, the lowly assembly line worker Émile is protected from the angry foremen by Louis, the company president.

As in cartoons, the film's visual, physical humour emphasises feelings and desires that are normally disguised or suppressed for the sake of maintaining social order. Sexual attraction, pride, disgust, anger, fear and its associated impulses of fight or flight: all are given free expression by the characters, although sometimes only when they believe that they are unobserved. To begin with, there is cartoon-like liberation in the exaggerated facial expressions of the characters, such as grins of undisguised delight and winks of complicity shared by Émile and Louis. While it was also characteristic of silent cinema to exaggerate facial expression, *À Nous la liberté* uses a more ostentatious exaggeration that, in combination with other stylistic factors such as cartoon-like music, evokes animated comedy specifically.

Quick switches in behaviour or facial expression are part of comedy in general, but they are especially prevalent in cartoons, where they are so easy to effect. In Clair's film, Louis, his gaze moving back and forth between photographs of Jeanne and her uncle, makes smooth, immediate yet radical alterations in his expression, from delight to disgust, respectively. There are also instantaneous changes in the uncle's behaviour in the presence of Louis, when he is kind and cajoling towards his niece, and in the absence of the company president, when he is commanding and impatient with her; he switches once more to his avuncular self as soon as Louis makes an unexpected reappearance, as he knows that only noble sentiments should be publicly displayed. Both examples are entertaining for their pacing and their exposure of the real feelings that exist behind social façades.

Finally, the film features decisive gestures that echo a childlike tendency to respond to one's own desires without hesitation; while Slavoj Žižek sees these as characteristic of the ontologically infantile nature of silent film,[10] they are equally a staple of cartoons, talkies or otherwise. As in cartoon, such behaviour is always a wily self-indulgence, since the characters all know that the desire in question is socially unacceptable, and the audacity of the gesture results in a moment of shock on the part of its victim, giving the perpetrator the opportunity to evade punishment. In Clair's film, it is most often Émile who delivers a slap to the face or kick to someone's behind before making a quick escape.

Such free expression of desire through action always leads, then, to chases that are also characteristic of cartoon, complete with its near misses, actual collisions and entertaining pile-ups. *À Nous la liberté* is similar to cartoons in that the consequences of its disruptions are never long-lasting. The rapid re-establishment of order in the factory following a chase can be compared with the way in which cartoon characters always survive and quickly recover, unscarred, from the most violent accidents and attacks.

A close-up of an object in Clair's film usually means that it is about to come into play in the narrative, making a significant contribution to the action; this is directly comparable to the use of object close-ups in cartoons, where such a deliberate focus on an object invariably foreshadows the object's importance as a catalyst in events to follow. It is often quite unassuming objects that will be responsible for disproportionately spectacular events, and it is the contrast of small cause/big effect, almost as much as the events themselves, that provides a source of amusement to the audience. Frame scale (otherwise known as camera distance, ranging from close-up to long shot) was also used to foreshadow events in live-action silent cinema, and elaborate slapstick comedy routines and chases frequently hinged on objects (in Chaplin and Mack Sennett, for example). However, the way in which *À Nous la liberté* evokes animated films aesthetically makes it important to consider these examples as part of a larger strategy on Clair's part to give his film the hybrid and light-hearted edge associated with animated comedy.

Cinematography

Silent films were orientated towards action rather than dialogue, and it was therefore common to use long shots in order to give the audience the best possible view of the action. In order to minimise the necessity for inter-titles, it was also common to create narrative cues through close-ups of significant objects and actors' facial expressions. While Clair's choice of frame scale may have been determined to some degree by these conventions of the past, his use of long shots and closer shots also constitutes an individual directorial style that serves both thematic and narrative ends.

Clair's frequent use of long shots does, as in silent film, correspond to frequent chase scenes; however, Clair's long shots are also determined by the immensity of the sets that could not fit inside the frame if the camera distance were smaller. It would become standard practice to use an establishing long shot at the beginning of a sequence to give a clear indication of the space in which the action would evolve, but long shots in *À Nous la liberté* are not confined to this purpose. Instead, they may be used at any point in a sequence with the effect of shrinking the actors, thus supporting the film's theme by showing how industrial society (incarnated by the vast and towering sets) minimises the importance of the individual.

Clair's use of close-ups is another variation on convention insofar as it does not restore centrality to the human figure. While the film does rely on characters' facial expressions, the camera never comes closer than a medium close-up (portrait-bust segment of the actor) in order to capture these expressions. Closer shots of the characters in this film generally vary between the American shot (knees-up) or the medium shot (waist-up); in the entire film, there are in fact only five instances of medium close-ups of the actors. Although these closer shots are neither as close nor as numerous as was typical in other films of the period, every one of these close shots does, nonetheless, serve a conventional function, emphasising the characters' intense emotions and/or comical expressions.

Close-ups of objects in the film are conventional in both number and purpose, yet occupy an even more privileged position than in silent film because of the absence of close-ups of characters' faces. The close-up is reserved almost exclusively for objects, with the occasional exception of hands or feet, which are typically only the subject of a close-up in combination with an object. To distinguish between the genuine close-up and the 'detail', as I will use the term here, the close-up refers to a shot where the camera could not be very much closer to the object without making it unrecognisable; a detail shot is slightly more distant, but the camera does come close enough to the object or body part to show its small details (and notably closer than it ever comes to an actor's face). The detail shot is most commonly used to show an object alongside a hand or foot, a significant combination because it makes reference to the active engagement of the object in the film's development. In silent film, the close-up marked an object as being significant precisely because it would subsequently play an instrumental role in the narrative.

The objects featured in Clair's close-ups do indeed take an active part in the narration: nearly every sequence features at least one close-up or detail of an object, such that these images taken together could provide a step-by-step summary of the film's narrative progression. A chronological list of the film's close-ups and details of objects, organised under headings indicating their relationship to the film's major narrative segments, is provided in Figure 2.5. Objects thus take on an iconic as well as an instrumental role in relation to key moments in the film's narrative.

After the close-up has drawn attention to an object and prepared it for a narrative purpose, thematic resonance may be established through juxtaposition with other objects within the frame or, through montage, with the surrounding environment. The close-up remains a crucial element, however, as it is used to draw attention to the object in the first place, and the juxtaposition with other objects or the surrounding environment continues to depend primarily on specific details of the objects, details that the close-up makes evident.

---

1. Louis and Émile in prison and their attempt to escape:

    - toy horses that the prisoners are making
    - Louis hiding a metal hook
    - cutting through a prison bar
    - Émile's resulting wound on his wrist

2. Louis' rise in status and wealth following his escape:

    - the shoes that he tries on
    - records and their symbolic representation

3. Émile's affinity with nature and love for Jeanne that lead him to the factory and Louis:

    - the flower
    - Jeanne stooping to recover the flower from the ground
    - Jeanne's handkerchief on the assembly line
    - the bank notes that Louis thinks will satisfy Émile when they first meet (and the blood from Émile's cut wrist dripping on them)

4. Louis' attempt to arrange a marriage between Jeanne and Émile:

    - Jeanne's employee badge
    - the notepad on which Louis writes Jeanne's employee number to locate her file
    - the employee file of Jeanne's uncle
    - the button that Louis presses to summon Jeanne's uncle

5. the inauguration of the new factory and Louis' escape with Émile:

    - the lectern insignia
    - the shareholders' hats
    - banknotes flying out of a case
    - coins being thrown at the vagabond Louis' and Émile's feet, and the coins in their hands

---

Figure 2.5: Close-ups and details of objects in relation to narrative in *À Nous la liberté*.

The close-up of blood-spotted cash offers an example of juxtaposition of objects within the frame. The camera initially draws attention to the banknotes and the drops of blood to fulfil a narrative goal: it clearly shows that Louis was completely wrong in his assumption that his old friend Émile would blackmail him. The object, a pile of banknotes, thus serves denotatively to move, via Émile's blood, from Louis' offer of material compensation that is rejected to Émile's offer of friendship that is accepted. As the damage to the paper money is ignored, the value of life and friendship asserts itself against the cash, which recedes into the literal and figurative background. As the object is no longer a simple narrative catalyst but also a thematic cipher, it comes to embody the message that the money that stokes the engine of this capitalist society is worthless when compared with friendship.

À Nous la liberté begins with a powerful juxtaposition of an object and its environment. The film's opening image consists of a close-up of toy horses which, subsequent shots reveal, are located in the space of a prison. The privileged placement of this close-up immediately prompts the audience to wonder why these objects are so important: what essential information do they provide? The wooden horses find their narrative significance as the object of the prisoners' unpaid labour. These toys have the further purpose of justifying the presence of a tool, a hook that will be the subject of the next close-up, and that will in turn serve the narrative by aiding Louis in his escape from prison. The incongruity between the toy horses and the space in which they are located is striking and creates a thematic role for the object. Prisoners, whom one might expect to be rough and tough, are singing about themselves as 'mauvais garçons'/'bad boys' while they make children's toys. The most obvious message is that adults in this film are turned into children by means of social institutions that seek to control them. Less obvious but nonetheless present is a meaning based first in the object in itself: it is a commentary on modern technology, embodied in the juxtaposition of the traditional power source – the horse – rendered inanimate and put on wheels, the basis of the cog-driven machine. The relationship between the object and its environment suggests another related comment on modern methods of production: the job of the artisan is divided into separate stages completed by different people, thus destroying the concept of creation as the unique and spontaneous expression of the individual.

The narrative motivation of objects in the film is as strong as the narrative ideas with which they become associated; moreover, the object's narrative and thematic roles tend to be closely affiliated and therefore mutually reinforce one another. To take the example of the blood-spotted banknotes, while they are admittedly a striking image because they form an unusual combination, the power of the visual message stems from its clarity, as blood has an extremely strong association with family (and, by an easy extension, with very close friendships), while money in its brute form is traditionally despised (or loved with full knowledge of its superficiality). This contrast between the connotations of blood and money makes their visual association compelling, surprising even. However, it is also, crucially, a meaning that is transparent to the audience.

In the case of the toy horses, it was clear that they helped to associate the prisoners with children. Not all audience members are likely to think about the way in which specific characteristics of the object being produced contribute to the film's commentary on modern methods of production; however, the presence of this object does clearly foreground the assembly-line production method that will recur throughout the film as part of its theme.

Editing

À Nous la liberté features two emphatic editing devices: the first of these consists of a juxtaposition of shots that creates emphatic comparisons or contrasts. The most obvious example is the mise-en-abyme, a sequence of shots that come to illustrate and complete the policemen's lesson to Émile on the necessity of work: the image of the officers beginning their moralising phrase is followed by one of a schoolmaster, completing that phrase, part of which will become the refrain of his students ('le travail c'est la liberté'/'work is liberty'); the image of the students doing their work is then followed by one of the factory employees working on the assembly line, similarly monitored by a dour foreman. This device thus draws out comparisons between the different levels of society all controlled by the same ideology. The fact that it seems intrusive confirms the film's hybridity; this scene is one of a limited number in *À Nous la liberté* that destabilises the film as narrative, and nudges it momentarily into the realm of propaganda-style film-making.

The second prominent feature of Clair's approach to editing is his use of an object as a transition. In the sequence that summarises Louis' rise in fortune, Clair uses a special editing technique where the object (in this case a record) functions as a sort of transition between shots, such that the object that fills the frame at the end of one shot is also the object of focus (or at least is present) at the beginning of the following shot. The record works, in addition, as an object framing this sequence's first scene, which shows Louis running a record stall: the record is the focus of both the first and last shots of the scene. Where the record becomes an object of transition is between this scene and the next one, in which Louis has now moved up to the rank of a shop owner; the record on which the last scene ended is, in the new scene, part of the store logo, visible behind Louis, and as in the last scene, this scene ends with a close-up shot of an actual record. In the move from this second scene to the third one (which shows Louis' superstore), the record functions much more clearly as a transition; here again, the actual record from the end of the previous scene is replaced by a record-shaped logo, but here their identical size and shape makes the link between shots much more compelling. This third scene is framed by the record logo in the same way that the first scene was framed by the actual record, and it is this logo that forms a link with the fourth and final scene in the sequence. The logo at the beginning of the fourth scene is not the same size as the giant logo that ends the third scene, but the fourth scene contains an additional use of the record as a transition from one shot to another: the record logo in one shot is matched by a round dial of the exact same size in the following shot.

Clair's editing practice thus draws attention to the record as a formal tool, but it does more than this. The editing also establishes the object's narrative role, and even alludes to its thematic resonance. The record and record-shaped logo's diegetic motivation is clear: they are the means by which Louis moves up in the world and establishes his business empire. The fact that this socio-economic rise is summarised so efficiently by a single sequence, and the formal use of the record as a transition in this sequence also point to a theme embodied in the object: material-based free enterprise allows a penniless criminal to become a rich businessman easily. Moreover, the play between the record and its image in the logo, such that ultimately the logo replaces the record entirely, reflects the increasing abstraction involved in Louis' social ascent: he moves from a stall holder who is in daily contact with his merchandise and his customers' cash, to a factory owner who is usually in an office, concerned with new ideas and projected earnings, while faceless workers are occupied with making and selling the product on which the business is based. The shape of the record and logo, which are matched at one point in the sequence with the dial of the clocking-in machine, also evoke the endless cycle of production.

Circulation

The film's theme of circulation is manifested on a micro level through the formal repetition of circular shapes and on a macro level through the pattern of Louis' socio-economic rise and descent that the film's narrative follows (a level that will be explored in the next section). Patterns of circulation are also emphasised on an intermediate level, in the space of a single sequence. Near the end of the film, for example, the audience is treated to the image of capital literally circulating in the factory yard, in the form of bank notes swept up in a small cyclone with the shareholders chasing after them: Clair characterised this scene as the 'genuine and thematic conclusion' of the film.[11] This is far from the only example of circulation at work: cycles with much less obvious motivation intervene, so that even the protagonists, who are supposed to be paragons of liberty, are involved in cycles from the film's beginning to its end. For example, when Louis first escapes from prison, he immediately becomes involved in an actual bicycle race; Émile, who is much less compliant with capitalism's work cycle, is implicated in even more remarkable patterns of escape, chase and capture throughout the film. Thus while some cycles in the film clearly reflect the vicious circles inherent in modern life, the film also seems wilfully to discover as many additional examples of circulation as possible, exaggerating the degree of circularity that exists in reality. As in the case of the exaggeration inherent in the film's regimented rhythm and architectural minimalism, the effect is to mock the very patterns that this stylistic technique seems to support.

Dudley Andrew's interpretation of the film's style brings him to the opposite conclusion: he believes that Clair's 'own aesthetic conspires with the cold rational modernism he pretends to satirize'.[12] He observes that in *Le Million* (1931), the film that immediately preceded *À Nous la liberté*, 'Clair made good on his intuition that careful attention to the effect of seemingly insignificant objects [...] could create an undeniable momentum'.[13] However, Andrew believes that in *À Nous la liberté*, this momentum 'takes precedence over everything else', with the result that 'characters and actors are largely interchangeable'.[14] In response to Andrew's specific assertion with regard to characters, it is worth pointing out that one-dimensionality was far from being unique to Clair's work: characters in early sound film typically had much less psychological depth than in later films made after classical narrative conventions had been established. Taken together, Andrew's comments on Clair's work suggest that he also sees objects as elements that, once they are set in motion by Clair's film, become undifferentiated anonymous entities. I argue, on the contrary, that it is precisely through their circulation in the film that objects accumulate meanings that are specific to them. Moreover, not only do objects take on multiple diegetic and thematic roles, but their comic function as they circulate through the film does in fact undermine the controlled, circular system that they are caught up in.

The circulation of objects is responsible for a number of comic episodes that disrupt order and control in the factory. Handkerchiefs and flowers make repeated appearances throughout the film, and in the context of just one appearance, may be passed repeatedly from one person to another, in some cases making their way back to the original owner. When Émile loses Jeanne's handkerchief on the assembly line, it moves from one employee to the next and is ultimately thrown out into to the factory yard, where Émile finally retrieves it. However, his pursuit of the handkerchief has created chaos on the assembly line, which does not end when he has regained possession of the handkerchief: his angry fellow employees chase after him, breaking through the rank and file of workers in the factory yard. Similarly, when Émile brings a bouquet to the factory, it serves as a source of distraction as it circulates among five different employees, alternately given as a gift, rejected and picked up again.

The multiple meanings that an object accumulates can create a special type of semiotic disruption that also serves a comic end. As they circulate through the film, objects accumulate a number of different associations, which are always established diegetically through the object's use and through its appearance in various environments. As it is used in different ways and appears in different contexts, however, an object may come to represent ideas and emotions which are usually considered to be opposite. The fact that one object may be related to quite diverse ideas is only brought to the audience's attention when the object shifts between two such meanings in the space of one scene. The ambiguity that the object creates is then used for comic effect.

There are two examples of such ambiguous objects in *À Nous la liberté*. One is the flower, which will be discussed in the final section. The other is a handkerchief which begins as a symbol of caring friendship between Émile and Louis. The line between *philia* and *eros* is slightly blurred, however, when the same object becomes invested with romantic significance as Émile's cherished symbol of Jeanne. These two meanings coexist during one scene, where Émile stops Louis from using Jeanne's handkerchief as a bandage, and Louis must instead tear his own handkerchief to bind Émile's wound. In the same scene, then, the handkerchief stands as a symbol of both romantic and platonic attachment. Even if Émile is particularly strict in marking the difference between Jeanne's and Louis' handkerchiefs, the love that underlies the two objects' respective associations leads the viewer to compare the two types of attachment, particularly given the emotional gaze shared by the two men in this scene. There is, moreover, a subsequent parallel drawn between love and friendship through juxtaposition: shots of Jeanne and her boyfriend gazing into space as though looking at each other while they eat their respective dinners in different locations, are immediately followed by shots of Louis and Émile exchanging jubilant glances across the table at a dinner party. While this parallel was most likely intended as a comic parody of the romantic dinner telepathically shared by Jeanne and her boyfriend, Louis' complete lack of concern for his mistress's disapproval and her infidelity offers further evidence of the strong homosocial bond between Louis and Émile.

By the end of the film, Louis' action of tying a handkerchief around Émile's wrist has been replaced by putting coins in his hand as the two men sing a song that rejects marriage, thus distancing their relationship from the one which Émile had hoped to enjoy with Jeanne. Émile and Louis' itinerant lifestyle is set firmly in contrast to the urban domestic one, rather than hinting at any crossover: soft-hearted concern (in the form of the handkerchief) is finally excised from their friendship, and resourceful co-operation (symbolised by money) replaces it. Nonetheless, the film concludes with Louis pulling Émile out of the way of an approaching car on the road, and Émile then kicks Louis in the backside in order to distract him from memories of his privileged lifestyle: both caring and playful gestures allow a physical element to remain in the rapport between the two men until the very end of the film.

Symmetrical narrative

The analysis of Clair's style so far has established that objects in *À Nous la liberté* always have a strong narrative motivation; this is symptomatic of a narrative that is, overall, strong and rigorously structured. Although the film includes some romantic and comic episodes that seem to digress from the film's principal narrative arc, these too have their place in the overall structure.

The audience will not fail to notice a degree of repetition in the events and objects occurring in this film: the tedious work of the assembly line employees, Émile's persistent efforts to speak to Jeanne, and Louis' progressions and regressions in socio-economic position, for example. Closer analysis reveals how such apparently minor recurrence and parallelism actually fit into an overarching narrative pattern which is perfectly symmetrical. The diagram 'Narrational symmetry in *À Nous la liberté*' (Figure 2.6) maps the chief events in the film's narrative: it begins with the first event at the top left-hand corner of the diagram (1), and features arrows indicating the subsequent flow of events, numbered in sequence up to 15. The diagram serves to demonstrate that if the dinner party scene (8) is taken as the film's turning point, the events on either side of this central scene occur in matched pairs. In other words, when the film is divided by the dinner party scene, every event in the first half of the film will be echoed by an analogous event in the second half. These paired events can be defined as key narrative segments in which similar actions take place.

The paired events are typically situated at parallel points on either side of the central scene, each event at the same distance as its corresponding event both from that central scene and from the beginning (for events 1 to 7) or end of the film (for events 9 to 15); in the diagram, these parallel paired events are joined by horizontal broken lines. However, this film also contains two pairs of events that are not parallel but offset; such pairs are connected by dotted diagonal lines on the diagram. Certainly, this is not a particularly radical departure

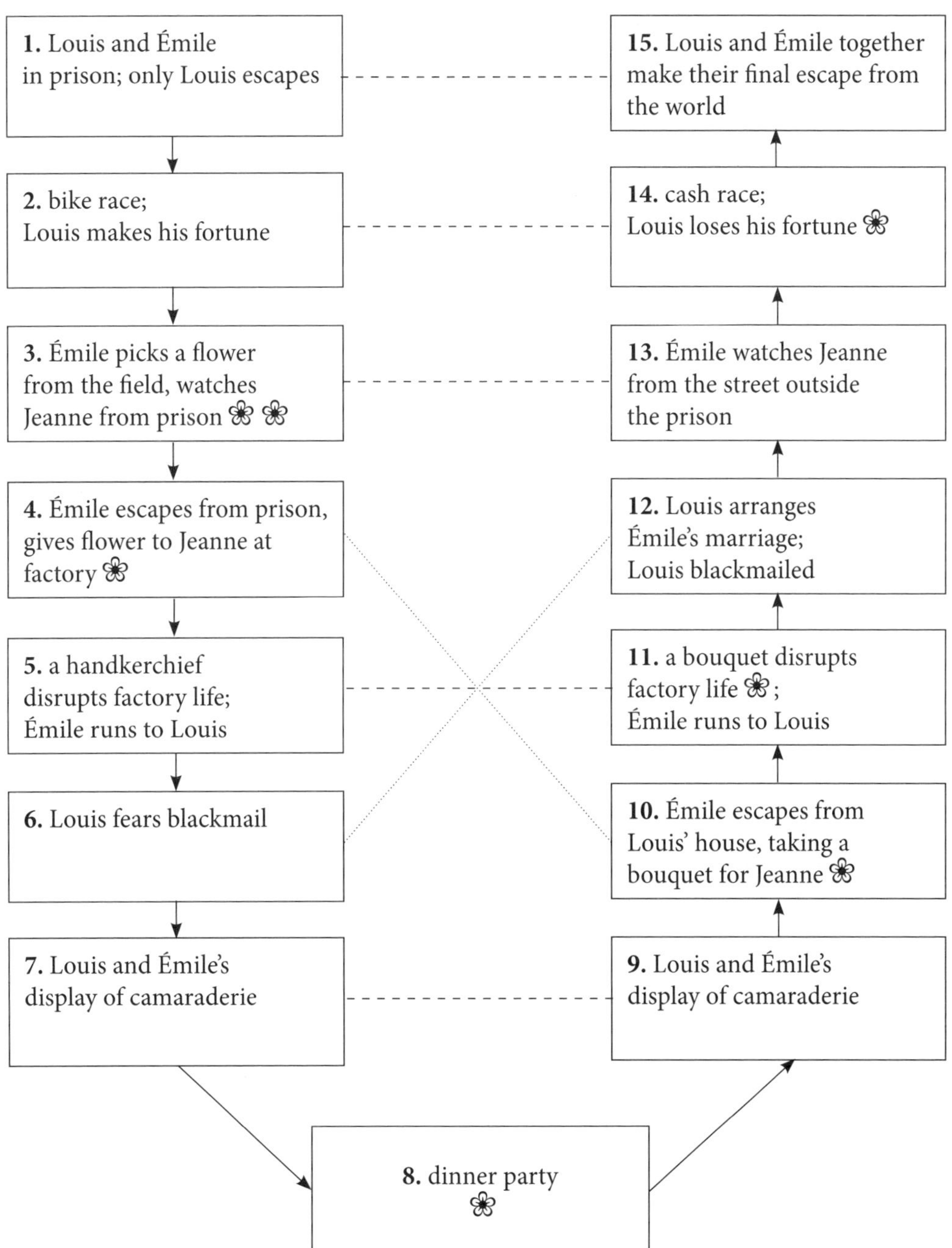

Figure 2.6: Narrational symmetry in *À Nous la liberté*.

from the pattern of parallel events, since these offset pairs of events still do not occur far from each other in the narrative, and if the two offset events in each respective half of the narrative switched places, the entire film would conform to the pattern of parallel events. However, there is good reason for these offset paired events to be placed as they are. First, for the simple sake of variety: if every event had its equivalent occurring at an exactly parallel point in the other half of the film, the pattern would become clearly perceptible to the audience as something mechanical. If the audience began to anticipate the complementary event, the second half would become too predictable. As it stands, however, the repetition is vaguely sensed as a pleasant impression of circularity and completion. Furthermore, the variation is astutely situated, coming soon after the central event: while paired events occurring at a greater distance from the turning point will also be further separated from each other, making the repetition more subtle, repetition will stand out when both events in a pair take place near the central point in the film. This is probably the reason why Clair chose to offset paired events that were almost contiguous to the dinner party. While simple displays of camaraderie between Émile and Louis occurring immediately before and after the dinner party can be understood in the context of the old friends' sustained delight at being reunited, it might seem contrived for Louis to fear being blackmailed and then to find his fears realised so soon afterwards. As he is making just one transposition, Clair ensures that it achieves the desired effects outlined above; rather than simply switching the position of contiguous events, he separates the offset events by one pair of parallel events (5 and 11) and thus achieves more than a minimum of separation between each offset event and its complement. The second half of the film does nonetheless retrace the events of the first half, even if they do not always occur in the exact reverse order, and this means that the film has a circular structure, which echoes the cyclical patterns of modern capitalist culture satirised by the film.

The diagram also indicates the recurrence of one important object, a flower, which will be subject to a close analysis in the final section of this chapter. Marked by a flower symbol on the diagram, this object's appearances in the film do not lend themselves to pairing, unlike the film's events. There is, nevertheless, symmetry involved in the significant appearances that the flower makes in the narrative: three times in the first half of the film, once in the central dinner party scene, and another three times in the film's final half.

Object analysis

The last section of this chapter will examine the way in which all the stylistic elements mentioned so far work together to emphasise one particular object in the space of one sequence. Specifically, it will highlight the way in which style brings the object to the audience's attention, and its influence in associating multiple meanings with that object.

The object that will be studied is the flower, and as indicated by the flower symbol in Figure 2.6, there are seven sequences in *À Nous la liberté* in which flowers play a significant role. The scene in which Émile is alone in jail stands out for the degree of emphasis that it places on the flower; it is therefore this sequence that will receive the most attention in the following analysis. The flower's appearances in other sequences will be mentioned insofar as the associations that it takes on elsewhere relate to the object's meaning in this sequence.

Description of the sequence

Before considering the stylistic means used to draw attention to the object, it is necessary to have a clear idea of the events exactly as they occur in this sequence. Émile finds himself imprisoned for the second time. The flower in his shirt pocket, sunshine at the window, and light-hearted song coming from somewhere outside all remind him of the freedom that has been taken away from him again. Unable to bear his imprisonment, he decides to hang himself from the bars of his cell window. As he prepares the rope, he sees the apparent source of the song: a pretty young woman at the window opposite.

In order to make the sequence's visual qualities more explicit, and facilitate references to specific moments, a shot-by-shot summary of the scene follows:[15]

1) FS (HA) Émile at cell door demanding freedom, then giving up
2) FS Émile lying down, then sitting restlessly on platform in cell
3) MS Émile turning his attention to flower, taking it from pocket and gazing at it
4) CU (POV) flower held between Émile's fingers (figure 2.7)
5) MCU Émile smiling at flower (off), then turning his gaze upward to window (off)
6) CU (POV) cell window with bars, as sun begins to shine and singing begins
7) AS Émile turning his gaze from window to flower (figure 2.8), then back to window again; he gets up
8) MS Émile moving to cell window, taking rope from trouser pocket, then looking out window and smiling
9) LS (POV) Jeanne at her bedroom window
10) AS (LA) Jeanne adjusting flower garlands at window (figure 2.9)
11) MS record player beside window (seen from inside the room)
12) MCU (LA) Émile in sunlight, dreamily listening to song (figure 2.10)
13) AS (LA) Jeanne at window, adjusting garlands, apparently singing
14) MS Émile at cell window, preparing to hang himself
15) AS (LA) Jeanne at window; her uncle comes along, separates garlands to look out window, then departs.

Music

Song is used to introduce Jeanne, a character who will exert a strong influence over the meaning of the flower in this sequence. The flower begins the sequence as a symbol of nature, but its dominant meaning switches to love during the course of the sequence, and music is the catalyst in the switch. Émile's contemplation of his boutonnière is interrupted by Jeanne's

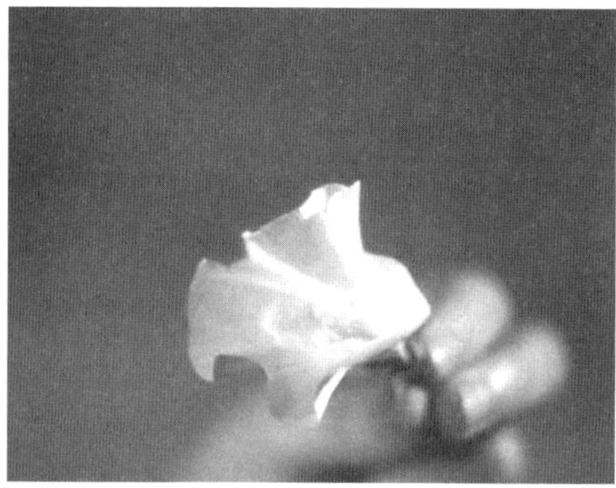

Figure 2.7: Close-up of the flower in *À Nous la liberté*.

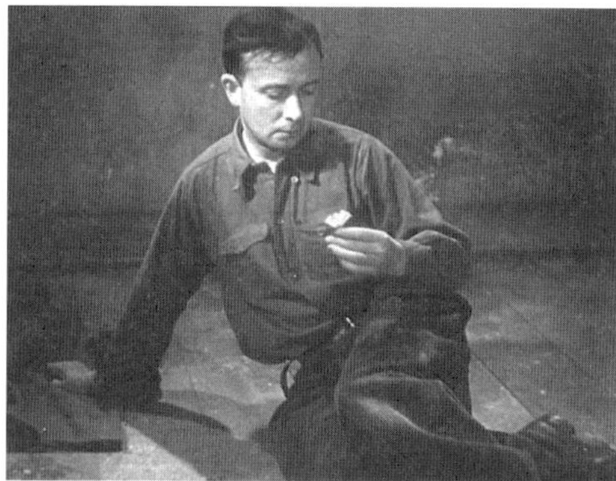

Figure 2.8: Émile gazes at the flower in *À Nous la liberté*.

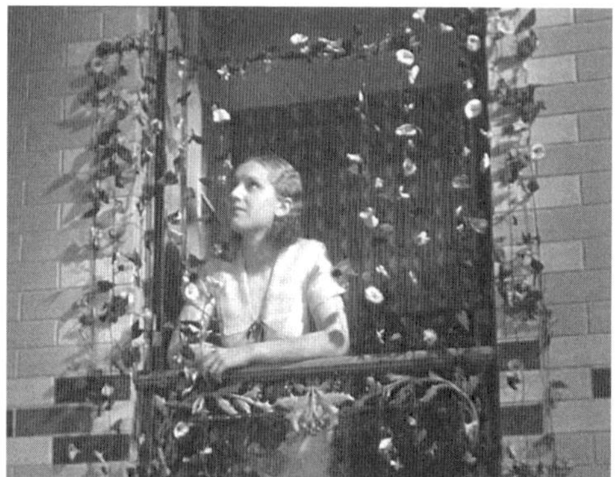

Figure 2.9: Jeanne and the flower garlands at her window in *À Nous la liberté*.

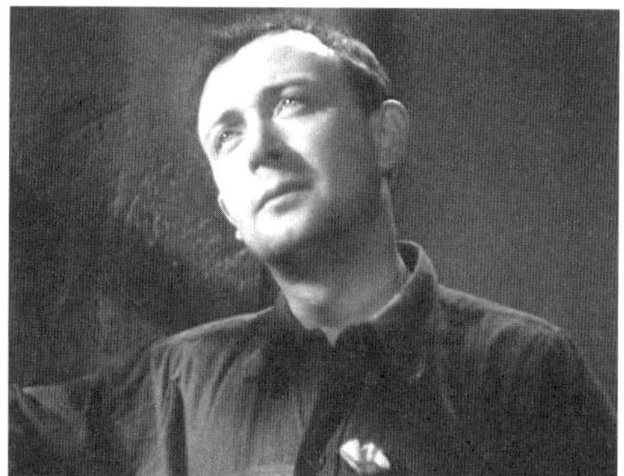

Figure 2.10: Émile listens to his neighbour's song in *À Nous la liberté*.

singing which leads him to discover her at the window opposite, tending to the same type of flower. His impression that she is singing is false, however, as it is revealed later in the sequence that she is only lip-synching to a song playing on the record player in her room. This introduces an element of artificiality to the scene, which may also have a direct relation to the flowers themselves, as will be discussed later.

The carefree song that Jeanne seems to sing initially supports the previous scene's association of flowers with freedom. However, an additional, more subtle meaning is carried by one segment of the tune: its initial rising swell is reminiscent of the obedient schoolboys' chorus which equated work and liberty in the previous scene, and both songs are similar to the penitent singing of the prison inmates in the film's first scene. This introduces a new, and seemingly contradictory, association to the flower, one of imprisonment by social control.

Mise-en-scène

Through its contrast with the open field in the previous scene, the prison cell initially serves to emphasise the flower's associations with nature and freedom. However, the mise-en-scène subsequently serves to link the flowers with imprisonment.

In the previous scene, a visual opposition between nature and industry, or freedom and imprisonment, was set up: the field where Émile was napping in the foreground represented liberty, and the factory in the background stood for confinement. Here, it seems that the spaces have reversed, with Émile's cell in the foreground the space of imprisonment, and Jeanne's bedroom in the background the space of freedom: the bars of Émile's cell window replace the ominous verticals of the factory chimneys, while the strands of morning glories at Jeanne's window evoke the vines growing up the fence posts in the field. Yet if Émile's and Jeanne's respective situations are considered more carefully, the opposition is not quite so clear: Émile will escape from prison by the end of this scene, while Jeanne is never free from the surveillance of her uncle or boss. The use of flowers in this scene supports this alternate association, as the way in which the flower garlands are strung in front of Jeanne's window bears a direct resemblance to the vertical bars of the prison window.

The mise-en-scène also suggests that the flower may be associated not with nature but its opposite, artificiality. Although the unusual appearance of the flowers in front of Jeanne's window initially serves to draw them to the audience's attention and suggests a romantic connection with Émile whose flower is of the same variety, Jeanne's flowers may in fact be quite different. The number of blossoms and the regularity with which they appear on the garlands suggest that they are not in fact real, but false; this provides a visual reiteration of Émile's false impression that Jeanne is singing. It was perhaps to preserve the opposition between Émile's real flower and Jeanne's imitation ones that Clair decided to remove the special effect that had Émile's boutonnière sing the film's theme song to him.[16]

Cartoon-style comedy

There are no slapstick gags or chases in this scene which would connect the object's function with cartoon. Comic effects in this scene are chiefly limited to effects of character. The most cartoon-like character here is Jeanne's uncle, a doddering old man who is mystified by his niece's window decoration, which he parts in order to peer uselessly out of the window. There is an ambiguity of meaning underlying this comic effect, however. In the earlier example of the handkerchief, humour resulted from the object's ambiguous shifting between romantic and platonic associations. In this scene, humour may distract from the ambiguity between the garland's role as a decoration and its symbolism of Jeanne's imprisonment. Jeanne's uncle in fact acts as a monitoring presence, a jailer even; when he parts the strands of flowers to peer out of the window, his gaze of bemusement at the decoration is followed by one of keen surveillance, as he checks whether there are any suitors outside. There is light-hearted comedy in the disjunction between Émile's impression that Jeanne is singing and the fact that the voice is actually coming from a record player.

There is more irony than comedy in the disjunction between Émile's belief that Jeanne is living in an idyllic space of freedom and the fact that she is at least as much a prisoner as he is: the object's significance here is therefore more influenced by satire than by cartoon-style comedy.

Cinematography

This sequence is significant for its number of close shots: the close-up of the morning glory is in fact among the closest shots in the entire film. It is a distance perfectly motivated by the narrative: the shot is book-ended by moderately close shots of Émile's gaze, so that the close-up of the flower is justified as a believable rendering of his point of view. The nature of Émile's gaze, which effectively surrounds the shot of the flower, determines its meaning: it clearly symbolises the freedom that he was just demanding and the natural surroundings that he misses so much.

The camerawork also helps to associate the flower with love by connecting it with Jeanne and her window decoration. The close-up allows the audience to take note of the details of Émile's flower in order to realise that Jeanne is tending to flowers of the same kind, thereby reinforcing the connection between the two characters. The way in which the close-up reveals the flower's details may also allow a comparison between the flowers and the young woman herself: there is a similarity between Jeanne's light summer dress and the delicate texture of the flower petals.

Editing

Montage was important in establishing the significance of the flower in its close-up shot, associating it with freedom and nature. These associations are reinforced by the series of shots that follows this close-up: a shot of the window of the cell, where the sun begins to shine, placed immediately after a shot of Émile turning his gaze from the morning glory (off) towards that window (also off) (5 and 6 on the shot-by-shot summary).

Circulation

The flower makes seven significant appearances in the film, and these appearances are distributed equally between the first and second halves of the film, with one appearance in the central dinner party scene (Figure 2.6). While repetition of an object is likely to make it stand out, differences in the type of flower, the way it is used, and its importance to the narrative mean that most members of the audience will probably not notice each occasion that flowers appear. Every viewer will notice that Émile twice offers Jeanne a floral gift at the factory (once in the first half of the film, and again in the second half): these are comic scenes in which the object is disruptive because it introduces human emotion to the rational and disciplined space of the factory. However, not all viewers are likely to notice that Émile wears two boutonnières in the film: the first, though simple, is of great emotional importance (the one that he takes to prison), whereas the second, more elaborate one that he wears at Louis' dinner party is purely decorative. Finally, it is most unlikely that on a first viewing one would note the similarity between the flowery bars in front of Jeanne's window and the garland of flowers that is cut at the inauguration of the new factory. Nonetheless, it may be argued that this last parallel, however subtle, was one deliberately evoked by the director, as a rather more conventional ribbon could have been used as easily as a flower garland, and the shot composition as well as the dialogue draws special attention to the object. Furthermore, the association between the two appearances of flowers is symbolically apt: the cutting of this floral barrier gives Jeanne a measure of freedom, as it is in this sequence that she is finally seen side-by-side with her boyfriend.

Contrary to Dudley Andrew's argument, then, it is not circulation in itself that makes the object important; the flower makes many appearances in the film, but the audience is unlikely to take note of every occasion that it appears. It is only when the object takes on meaning in relation to its context that it becomes important. The example of the flower showed that objects in this film most frequently take on meaning in relation to human emotion; this further undermines Andrew's claim that reason dominates in this film, structurally if not thematically. The rational system in which the object circulates is physically undermined by this circulation: the emotional associations that the object accumulates as it passes through the film create comic disruptions to the film's order, aesthetically as well as thematically.

Conclusion

In *À Nous la liberté*, style underlined the utilitarianism, rigid rhythms and repetitive cycles of the capitalist industrial society that Clair wanted to satirise; it also effected the satire by exaggerating these characteristics to the point of comedy. This strong comic element often evoked cartoon, a source of hybridity in the film which contributed to challenging the socio-economic order it portrayed; it also served to lighten what otherwise risked becoming an earnestly political satire.

Style defined a range of circulation for objects in *À Nous la liberté*. Implicated in Clair's stylistic strategy of replication and subversion, objects too at first appeared to contribute to the endless cycles and materialism of modern life. They were caught up in cyclical patterns on a variety of stylistic levels, and frame scale in particular served to privilege objects over humans. As objects circulated through the film, however, they took on multiple diegetic and thematic roles which ultimately allowed the object to comically disrupt, both physically and semiotically, the structures of control that governed the story space, the narrative and the image. Moreover, the object often derived its thematic resonance through its relationship with human characters in a context of emotion. Ultimately, then, characters and objects functioned together to liberate both the individual and the object from the strict physical and semiotic controls represented by Taylorisation.

Clair's personal approach to film-making determined to a large extent the way in which the film manifested its theme through style, and thus the way in which style allowed the object to take on a disruptive hybrid function. However, part of Clair's style and much of the film's overall hybridity were characteristic of a historical moment which was, cinematically speaking, quite privileged in terms of the roles it made available to objects. Films were becoming more narrative, they now had the new expressive register opened to them by sound, and as cinema began to move in a new direction, objects could continue to play a prominent role in the small time that remained before new conventions came into effect. Of course, not all films of the early 1930s offered such prominent and diverse roles to the object as *À Nous la liberté*; nonetheless, the time at which the surrealists gave up on film-making may in fact, without their realising it, have coincided with a brief golden age for objects in cinema.

Notes

1 Georges Sadoul, *Le cinéma français (1890–1962)* (Paris: Flammarion, 1962) 37.
2 Kuenzli 5.
3 Steven Kovács, *From Enchantment to Rage: The Story of Surrealist Cinema* (Cranbury, NJ: Associated University Presses, 1980) 85.
4 Kuenzli 4–5.
5 Kuenzli 5.
6 Kuenzli 5–6.
7 Dudley Andrew, *Mists of Regret: Culture and Sensibility in Classic French Film* (Princeton: Princeton University Press, 1995) 62.
8 Michael Richardson, *Surrealism and Cinema* (Oxford: Berg, 2006) 175.
9 Pierre Billard, *Le Mystère René Clair* (Paris: Plon, 1998) 188.
10 *The Pervert's Guide to Cinema*, dir. Sophie Fiennes, 2006.
11 Qtd. in Andrew, *Mists of Regret* 59.
12 *Mists of Regret* 60.
13 *Mists of Regret* 59.
14 *Mists of Regret* 60–61.
15 Key to abbreviations, in alphabetical order: AS=American shot; CU=close-up; FS=full shot; HA=high angle; LA=low angle; LS=long shot; MCU=medium close-up; MS=medium shot; POV=point of view.
16 Michael Atkinson, 'À *Nous la liberté*', Criterion Collection web site (http://www.criterion.com), 19 August 2002, viewed 7 November 2007.

Chapter 3

The Everyday and the Hybrid Object in the Czech New Wave
and Jan Švankmajer

Introduction

The former Czechoslovakia has a strong history of surrealism; unlike French surrealism, the official Prague surrealist group has continued in its activities to this day. The country also has a strong history of film-making, including its own New Wave, which came into being in the 1960s but has frequently been overlooked in favour of the French New Wave and other western European cinematic movements of the same period. As this chapter's historical contextualisation will explain, both culture and history determined that objects would play an important role in Czech New Wave cinema.

The 1960s was cinema's modernist period; the films that will be examined in this chapter will therefore differ in distinct ways from *À Nous la liberté*, in terms of the development of the cinematic medium as well as for their cultural difference. The previous chapter explained that objects in Clair's film owed something of their role to silent film practice; before the advent of sound, film had to make broad use of objects' expressive and narrative capacities. However, the special role that objects play in *À Nous la liberté* is also motivated by Clair's own expressive objectives; by exaggerating silent film's tendency to privilege objects, he highlighted what he saw as modern society's excessive materialism. He further critiqued this materialism by allowing objects, as they circulated within his film, to take on a number of different meanings dependent on their appearance in different contexts of human emotion. However, the significance of this effect is of more theoretical than historical interest: key to this study is the fact that the creation of hybrid objects in Clair's film was influenced by generic hybridity, that is, a combination of comedy (especially its slapstick form) and romance.

Czech New Wave films were also marked by a certain degree of generic hybridity. As will be explained, Czech New Wave film-makers were far from being a cohesive stylistic group, and the films that will be studied here span a diverse range, from documentary-style to fantasy. Within individual films, too, documentary and experimental approaches were routinely combined, rather less obtrusively than Clair's insertion of romance in his satire. Unlike *À Nous la liberté*, Czech New Wave films incorporate only a small amount of slapstick comedy, but humour is nonetheless an important aspect of Czech New Wave film-making: it formed part of their subtle dissidence to the political regime. Within the diegesis of the films themselves, a frequently erotic humour acts as a disruptive force to the films' otherwise sophisticated style. This humour also comes as a disruptive force to meaning: objects not only take meaning from the diverse contexts in which they appear as they circulate through the film (albeit much less frenetically than in *À Nous la liberté*), but their meaning is also multiplied as a support to the film's comedy.

The following sections will first explain the background against which the Czech New Wave came into being: the political support and challenges it received as the 1960s progressed. The history of the Czech version of surrealism will also be discussed, and its indirect cultural influence on the Czech New Wave film-makers.

The context of a cultural renewal

The circumstances in which the Czech New Wave came into being explain why it was also known as the 'Czech Film Miracle'. Against the background of Communist Czechoslovakia where the public had become accustomed to formulaic and didactic films of Socialist Realism, it seemed miraculous when, in the 1960s, an increasing number of thoughtful, innovative and entertaining films began to be made.[1] In fact, the political and historical context that made this artistic renaissance so surprising was also responsible for establishing the conditions that allowed such creativity.[2]

Facilities and support

Almost all of the Czech New Wave directors were young men and women who had just graduated from FAMU (Filmová a televizní fakulta Akademie múzických umění v Praze/ Film and TV School of the Academy of Performing Arts in Prague), the national film school that had been founded in 1946.[3] As students at FAMU, these aspiring film-makers were able to learn from experienced directors and writers such as Otakar Vávra[4] and Milan Kundera.[5] The school also provided them with access to key historical and contemporary works in world cinema.[6] In addition, FAMU gave young directors the opportunity to form friendships and a professional network with their peers, which would be an important source of support for the Czech New Wave.[7]

Graduates of FAMU could proceed to work at Barrandov Studios in Prague. As early as the 1930s, when this film-making facility was founded, the Czechs had wanted to nationalise their film industry. In 1946, Barrandov Studios finally became publicly owned, and films made there were fully funded by the government.[8] Although this also gave the Communist authorities the right to decide which films would and would not be made, the Czech New Wave directors often saw this as a challenge. They learnt to predict how far the censors would allow them to push official boundaries, which, moreover, were becoming more flexible as the 1960s progressed. Czech New Wave film-maker Jiří Menzel identified the 1960s as the 'most happy period' for him as a director:

> It was such an ideal time, ideal atmosphere, ideal place to make films. On the one side, there was an ideological ease and plenty of topics for films, but on the other side there wasn't total freedom, so there was a stimulus for creativity to break the ideological barrier [...].

Economical[ly] [...] nobody was responsible for anything. That was good for young debuting directors because nobody risked anything. There was a demand for our films. The whole cultural atmosphere was ideal for filmmaking.[9]

The Czech New Wave directors benefited, then, from the convergence of strong educational, technical and financial support for making films.[10] At the same time, they were allowed more and more freedom to determine what the nature of those films would be:[11] from 1963, Czech Communist Party moderates and public pressure began pushing for a liberalisation of culture.[12] When Alexander Dubček was chosen as the new secretary of the party in January 1968,[13] the months that followed were known as the 'Prague Spring' because of the immediate cultural thaw and large-scale public celebration. By August of the same year, however, the Soviet Union sent tanks into Czechoslovakia to reassert control.[14] When the subsequent 'normalisation' (systematic firing of those with liberal political views) reached the film industry, some directors saw their past or current work banned, and many were themselves banned from making films for several years, or even indefinitely.[15]

The political and creative impetus of the Czech New Wave
Though the Czech New Wave directors were a stylistically diverse group who had no manifesto and did not consider themselves to form a movement, they were united in their rejection of the Socialist Realism model.[16] The so-called realism of Soviet Socialist film-making corresponds to Georg Lukács' definition of films that were goal-oriented,[17] contained no subtle symbolism and thus were considered to be easily understood by the masses. The Czech New Wave directors used their films to represent a more familiar reality: filming 'pour eux-mêmes, avec leur vécu, leurs incertitudes, leurs experiences, leurs souffrances'/'for themselves, using what they were living through, their uncertainties, their experiences, their suffering',[18] they tended to focus on the contemporary day-to-day existence of individuals rather than the idealised future of a collective group. In this sense, all Czech New Wave films can be described as realist in that they seek to reflect everyday reality, whether they do this in a documentary-inspired style that generally aims for objectivity, or in a more fantastic or experimental style that seeks to create a more subjective 'personal vision' of contemporary life.[19] Although formal innovation and departures from conventional narrative forms had been discouraged by the censors, directors gained more freedom for this type of experimentation as the 1960s progressed.[20]

Whatever stylistic approach was adopted, what was crucial was this ability to represent contemporary everyday life, particularly the domestic sphere: under totalitarianism, it was only at home that people could speak freely.[21] This context had a doubly subversive quality because the humour that so often characterises domestic settings could be turned to political satire. Whereas Soviet Socialist Realism didactically and humourlessly represented the past or an idealised future, Czech New Wave narratives exposed the ambiguities, challenges, absurdities and disappointments of life in the present; by inviting viewers to come to their own conclusions,[22] Czech New Wave films implicitly contributed to creating debate about the political transformation that the country needed.[23]

Czech surrealism from its beginnings to the 1960s

Like the other films studied in this book, the films of the Czech New Wave bore only an indirect relationship to their country's surrealist movement. In light of the fact that Czech surrealism will be less familiar to most readers than French surrealism, and in order to provide this study of the Czech New Wave with a more complete historical and cultural background than that offered by the previous section alone, this section will introduce the Czech surrealist movement and its nationally specific origins.

Poetism

The avant-garde movement in 1920s Czechoslovakia was known as devětsil. Like French surrealism's forerunner, dada, devětsil reacted to the barbarity of World War I by rejecting Western culture and technology.[24] Devětsil did not share dada's nihilism, however, as it found a viable alternative to that which it had rejected: leftist politics, folk art, and traditional lifestyles with their emphasis on simple pleasures.[25]

Devětsil's orientation changed radically within two years of its foundation. By 1922, the movement's leader Karel Teige and poet Vítězslav Nezval began to promote constructivist approaches that privileged the very technology devětsil had initially rejected.[26] What remained unchanged, however, was the group's focus on real-life concerns: where devětsil had initially embraced reality by turning to simple pleasures and popular art forms, a similar concern for everyday reality was subsequently reflected in the modern utilitarian approach of constructivism.

In 1924, a new movement called poetism grew out of devětsil, and ultimately replaced it as the centre of the country's avant-garde. Poetism constituted a freer, more playful and imaginative complement to constructivism's austere discipline.[27] Although the birth of poetism coincided with the foundation of the surrealist movement in Paris, poetism was not the Czech version of surrealism: the Prague surrealist group would not be established until ten years later.[28] Poetism was the precursor of Czech surrealism and, like the larger devětsil movement, poetism shared a few common features with dada; however, poetism was distinguished as being a specifically Czech movement with its own unique character.[29] In *Poetismus*, the group's first manifesto, Teige described poetism as follows:

> playful, unheroic, unphilosophical, mischievous and fantastic [...] Poetism seeks to turn life into a magnificent entertainment, an eccentric carnival, a harlequinade of feeling and imagination, an intoxicating film track, a marvellous kaleidoscope.[30]

Poetism shared dada's sense of humour (which it considered 'a form of poetry') and its desire to provide liberation from reason, but the similarities clearly ended there.[31] In contrast with dadaist nihilism, the poetists' revolt consisted of turning away from the sombre war years and embracing the beauty and pleasure of existence.[32] Dada and Bretonian surrealism had a common negativity in their attitude to the status quo; poetism, on the other hand, was closer to Apollinaire's early definition of surrealism and to the modernism of devětsil, which, in the manner of the *esprit nouveau*, was marked by its enthusiasm for contemporary cosmopolitan urbanity.[33] The poetists' hedonism, with its emphasis on physical pleasures, can also be seen as a continuation of devětsil's allegiance to physical reality.

Petr Král has attempted to account for the specific character of poetism by contextualising it in terms of Czech history. He suggests that poetism's positive outlook, on the one hand, can be explained by the fact that the end of the First World War resulted in Czechoslovakia gaining its independence from the Austro-Hungarian Empire. It makes sense, then, that the country's spirit of optimism should be reflected in an artistic and intellectual movement that looked towards the future and wanted to redefine its identity in a modern, international context in contrast to its traditional rural roots. On the other hand, the Czechs were aware that their country was a small one that would never play a decisive role in the world; this also helps to explain poetism's connection with reality, exemplified not only by the poetists' appreciation of life's sensual pleasures, but also by their unpretentious sense of humour that was very much attuned to the popular and the absurd.[34]

As mentioned in the quotation from its manifesto, poetism was characterised by its imagination and sense of the fantastic. Although these elements seem to connect poetism with Breton's surrealism, poetism was distinguished by its attachment to physical reality, and this was reflected in the difference between poetist and surrealist approaches to poetry.[35] The French surrealists saw language and experience as separate realms, and used language to transform reality: their poetry emphasised, as Breton put it, 'arbitrary' connections which they felt contained the greatest shock value in order to jolt readers out of their habitual relationship with reality.[36] The poetists, on the other hand, believed that language should follow experience, and be used as a tool to translate the marvellous that already existed in reality.[37] Their poetry emphasised possible connections arising from the individual's subjective and pleasurable experience of reality by means of the senses.[38] The poetists looked to the imagination as a means of heightening their sensual experience of the world, rather than as a means of investigation of the unconscious as the French surrealists did.[39] In fact, the poetists were initially suspicious of psychoanalysis, and only accepted it wholeheartedly once they became surrealists.[40] The poetists' suspicions may have stemmed from their commitment to Communism, which frowned on Freud for his emphasis on the unconscious and its mysterious control over the individual; psychoanalysis undermined the Communist notion of man as a perfectible inhabitant of a collectively oriented world.[41] However, the poetists' attitude was also symptomatic of the general artistic orientation of poetism, which looked outward as much as inward. Teige, notably, had reservations about joining the international movement led by the French surrealists; one reason was their focus on automatic writing, which in Teige's view emphasised unconscious at the expense of conscious experience.[42]

Czech surrealism: the difference between Paris and Prague

The constructivist element had initially made devětsil irreconcilable with French surrealism.[43] However, the *Druhý manifest poetismu/Second Manifesto of Poetism* (1927–28) reflected the poetists' growing interest in psychoanalysis and the creativity of the unconscious.[44] Meanwhile, the Paris surrealists' second manifesto in 1929 communicated the French group's commitment to dialectical materialism[45] and developing fascination with physical objects.[46] Clearly, there was increasing overlap in the interests of the poetists and the French surrealist group. Following a meeting in Paris with Breton, Nezval founded the Czech group of surrealists in 1934; as leader, Nezval officially declared the group's loyalty to the Communist Party, while maintaining their right to artistic freedom.[47] Nezval remained the group's leader until the late 1930s when he left to join the Stalinists. Teige then took over leadership until his death in 1951, at which point Vratislav Effenberger became head of the group. Coinciding with the 1968 Prague Spring, the Czech surrealist group published a joint manifesto with the French surrealist group (not long before the latter was dissolved): 'The Platform of Prague' asserted that surrealism continued to be an active force, and expressed the movement's allegiance to a more liberal form of socialism.[48]

Czech surrealism remained distinct in certain ways from French surrealism, in part as a result of the groups' respective origins in poetism and dada.[49] However, scholars such as Petr Král and current members of the Czech surrealist group such as Jan Švankmajer also point to historical circumstances as responsible for changes in the Czech surrealists' outlook. Although in many (and arguably the most basic) respects Czech surrealism shared the same concerns as French surrealism, there were a number of features which made it distinct from both poetism and international surrealism.

During the inter-war period, Czech surrealism maintained its similarity to poetism.[50] However, with the experience of oppression from the Nazis during World War II and the Stalinists after the war, the Czech surrealists' attitude began to change.[51] Finding their activities and public presence radically limited, they began to take on a pessimism and rage more characteristic of dada.[52] The French surrealists had meanwhile returned to a life of freedom after the war, and thus not only maintained their lyricism but became more idealistic in their outlook.[53] Even as poetists, the Czechs had tempered their romantic tendencies with a realist attitude; with their experience of Nazism and Stalinism, however, the Czech surrealists more decisively rejected utopian ideas, and not only political ones.[54] Jonathan L. Owen suggests that post-war Czech surrealism has a greater affinity with the ideas of Georges Bataille who, rejecting the Bretonian belief in the unconscious as purely a force for good, left Breton's surrealist group to explore the darker side of the unconscious, with its 'reassertion of the bodily, of the coarsely material, at the expense of ideas and ideals'.[55] The post-war Czech surrealists became suspicious of any claims to absolute truth, and applied this to their own movement in a manner that was unique in international surrealism: rather than establishing one ideology for their group as the French surrealists did, they allowed many different ideas to coexist.[56] By the 1950s and 60s, they had ceased even to call themselves surrealists, but were nonetheless united as a group by their refusal to accept reality as it stood.[57]

Characteristic of the Czech surrealists' new rage and pessimism was the way in which they replaced their former lyricism with an aggressive black humour.[58] They developed a theory of 'concrete irrationality' that combined poetry and black humour: a confrontation between individual subjectivity and the outside world was used to point to the presence of the irrational in physical reality.[59] This discovery of the irrational in everyday life sometimes resulted in poetry in which 'les gestes et les objets les plus banals [...] participent d'un cauchemar à la fois monstrueux et grotesque'/'the most commonplace gestures and objects [...] take part in a nightmare that is both monstrous and grotesque'.[60] For the Czech surrealists, the idea of the irrational no longer had the positive connotations it held for the poetists, or which it still held for the French surrealists; the Czech surrealists had come to know the oppressive form of irrationality incarnated in authoritarian state bureaucracy, which had taken reason to such an extreme that it resulted in a nightmarish meeting with its opposite.[61]

Like the poetists, the Czech surrealist group was distinguished from the French by its affinity for the real over the sur-real, but their new relationship to reality was different from that of poetism.[62] They continued to emphasise experience over language, contrary to the practice of the French surrealists.[63] However, for the Czech surrealists, this experience of reality had become a consolation and an escape from an otherwise unbearable existence, rather than the uplifting practice through which the poetists had embraced the world as it stood.[64] Their work insisted on the heaviness of reality; they even became drawn to its most abject parts, as they found any physically concrete quality more reassuring than the state's abstractions.[65] Nonetheless, they did not see material reality as fixed: in an apparent extension of the poetist practice of tracing the infinite series of association that the individual mind could make based on its surroundings, the Czech surrealists engaged in 'critique by absurdity', which revealed the endless flux of meaning that characterised reality.[66] The sense of instability could be disturbing, but not in a pessimistic way; it translated the sense of concern about contemporary reality that united the Czech surrealists more than any one theory, but also reflected a belief in the richness of physical reality that persisted in spite of their cynicism.[67] Even with its post-war disillusionment, surrealism remained first and foremost, as Král puts it, 'un examen émerveillé du quotidien'/'an enraptured examination of the everyday'.[68]

The contribution of Czech surrealism and its forerunners to cinema
The cinema-related work of the Prague surrealists and their forerunners was, like that of the French surrealist group, mainly limited to scripts for films that were never made (or were impossible to make) and poetry influenced by film.[69] Members of devětsil became involved with writing and directing in the 1930s, but no poetist film was ever made.[70] Effenberger's

1948 surrealist film, *Étude d'un fragment de réalité*, is now lost.[71] Jan Švankmajer is by far the best-known and most successful Czech surrealist director.

French and Czech surrealists have both made a relatively restricted contribution to film-making on a practical level. However, poetism and Czech surrealism had much less ambivalent feelings towards physical reality. This meant that they had less difficulty than the French surrealists in developing a theoretical framework for surrealism in cinema. In the 1920s, Teige laid the basis for Czech surrealism's theory of cinema through his writing on the specificity of the medium. Inspired by Louis Delluc's notion of *photogénie*, Teige described cinema as a form that would capture 'la poésie de la réalité quotidienne, prise sur le vif par l'objectif de la caméra'/'the poetry of everyday reality, captured live by the camera lens'.[72] Effenberger, too, before taking leadership of the Czech surrealist group, wrote *A propos de l'esthétique du film* (1947), a book of film theory that became well-known and highly regarded.[73] Whereas the French surrealists were constantly changing their minds about the best way to use cinema as a tool for communicating surrealism to the public, the Czechs were always certain that the key was to exploit cinema's ability to capture physical reality, which always retained its primacy in their work.[74] Although they shared the French surrealists' fascination with the idea of using film to convey dream states, they never found cinema's basis in physical reality to be a drawback. Indeed, it has been suggested that the reason that the Czech surrealists wrote scripts for films that were impossible to make was as a response to a political climate that would not allow them to make the films they wanted to,[75] rather than any reflection of a lack of faith in film as a medium to express their ideas. While they agreed with Breton that film should reflect the '"fonctionnement réel de la pensée"'/'"the real way in which thought functions"', they felt that it should nonetheless be based on a documentary-style version of reality.[76]

Effenberger's lost film offered an 'interpretation [of the] "states of mind" of an adolescent boy during half an hour in the afternoon, and had 'chaque fait quotidien se tranforme en réalité magique'/'each everyday fact transform itself into a magical reality'.[77] Effenberger believed that cinema's strength lay not only in the ideas and opinions of the film-maker but in the medium's own '"vérisme" et son objectivité fonciers, qui donnent davantage la parole aux choses mêmes qu'à une volonté romantique de les transfomer'/'"realism" and essential objectivity which, rather than indulging a romantic desire to transform objects, tend to allow them to speak for themselves'.[78] By allowing objects to speak for themselves in this way, Effenberger hoped that film would be able to 'dégager la vraie nature du réel'/'draw out the true nature of reality', thus furthering the investigation of physical reality, which was one of the Czech surrealists' primary preoccupations.[79] In order to achieve this, Effenberger wanted the images in his own film to be based simply on 'des blocs entiers du réel'/'whole blocks of reality': their 'aspect "insolite"'/'"strange" appearance' was to be derived only from 'leurs superposition et montage'/'superimposing and editing them together', and as a result, he hoped that objects in his film would 'acquièrent une présence hypnotique tels quels'/'acquire a hypnotic appearance just as they were'.[80] The Czech surrealists' attitude to film was, then, similar to their use of language, as discussed earlier: it was seen as a tool for communicating the 'magic' that they saw already present in reality, rather than a means of transforming reality in order to make it 'magical'. Moreover, they recognised the special power of cinema over other forms of communication to express this 'magic':

> Sa supériorité [...] tient au fait qu'il enregistre directement et durablement une certaine réalité, là où le verbe – écrit ou proféré – n'est que le signe de celle-ci, et la peinture, sa transcription. Le cinéma repose sur les deux sens humains les plus suggestifs – le visuel et l'auditif – et il peut interpréter la réalité de façon immédiate. [...] Sous forme d'oeuvre achevée, il exerce sur la perception humaine une influence exceptionnelle par la valeur documentaire du réel présenté. Il peut induire son interprétation sans devenir didactique.
>
> Its superiority [...] lies in its ability to directly and durably record a certain reality, while writing – written or spoken – only symbolises reality, and painting transcribes it. Cinema relies on the two most evocative human senses – vision and hearing – and it can interpret reality with immediacy [...] As a completed piece of work, it has an exceptional influence on human perception through the documentary quality of the reality it presents. It can lead towards an interpretation without becoming didactic.[81]

The Czech surrealists' appreciation of cinema, then, was based on the overwhelming impression of immediacy in its recording of reality, such that the film-maker's perspective on that reality could be unobtrusively suggested.

The contrast between French and Czech surrealists' attitudes to cinema can be illustrated by the types of Czech New Wave films that the respective groups singled out for praise. While the Paris group most admired Věra Chytilová's *Daisies* (1966), which used experimental techniques to alter reality, Effenberger criticised Chytilová for 'mere eclecticism' and 'decorative cynicism' in her work.[82] The Prague surrealists preferred the documentary-style approach of Miloš Forman and Ivan Passer, or even the 'onirisme'/'dream-like quality' of Jan Němec's films that nonetheless 'inclut [...] un sens des réalités crus'/'incorporated [...] a sense of raw reality'.[83]

Owen argues that there was a 'profound and fundamental [...] bond forged by 1960s Czechoslovak cinema with the avant-garde, and especially Surrealism'.[84] This may be overstating it, particularly given that the Czech surrealists themselves felt that those outside their movement adopted surrealism superficially as just one of a range of styles to add to the appeal of their work.[85] To call Czech New Wave films surrealist is to risk falling into the trap of 'surrealist influence' which has led to increasingly loose definitions of the term 'surrealist cinema'. In the case of the Czech New Wave, though, Owen has a particularly strong argument for surrealist influence.[86] By the Sixties the French surrealist group was moribund; meanwhile the Czech surrealists, who had remained productive despite being forced underground (first by the Nazis, then by the Stalinist regime), were finally able to surface during Czechoslovakia's cultural thaw.[87] Along with artists, intellectuals and young people in general, the Czech New Wave directors enthusiastically embraced surrealism and other art, literature and philosophies, domestic and international, that had previously been suppressed.[88]

For the purposes of this study, it is enough to say that surrealism had some influence on Czech New Wave cinema. Moreover, the opinions of the Czech surrealists will not be normative in this chapter any more than those of the French surrealists in other chapters. Like Clair in relation to the Paris surrealist group, the Czech New Wave directors were contemporaries of the Czech surrealists. There are definite points of comparison that result from existing in a similar cultural and historical context, as the following section will explore.

Common concerns of Czech surrealism and the Czech New Wave

There are three main points of similarity between the Czech New Wave directors' approach to cinema and general characteristics of the 1960s Czech surrealist movement: their desire to engage with physical reality; their subversive use of humour; and the dynamic between subjectivity and objectivity.

As explained earlier, the surrealists had always had a fascination with the physical world, and their experience of totalitarianism and its abstractions reinforced their commitment to tangible reality. Czech New Wave films, too, from the most documentary-influenced to the most experimental, all exhibit a strong connection to physical reality, whether it is portrayed in cinéma-vérité style, or evoked by emphasis on the tactile dimension of the reality that is presented. Both the Czech New Wave directors and the Czech surrealists wanted to show reality to be other than that which the authorities declared it to be: specifically, they wanted to reveal the multi-layered complexity of contemporary existence.[89] Although the directors were treated with far less suspicion than the surrealists, it was, as mentioned, a considerable step forward for them to be allowed to portray everyday situations.

Humour played an important role in creating a more nuanced portrait of reality. For the surrealists, who had been consistently persecuted by the ruling powers both during and after the war, it was a black humour that was most commonly used to highlight the absurd and the irrational. Czech New Wave films also feature black humour, especially in order to make more pointed political statements. Effenberger admired Forman's approach to satirising contemporary reality, praising the director's 'feeling for contemporary forms of aggressive humour, and for the critical functions of absurdity'.[90] More typical of Czech New Wave films, though, is an irreverent form of humour, playfully subversive in a manner characteristic of poetism and pre-war Czech surrealism.

The question of the subjectivity–objectivity dynamic is one that has not been directly addressed in the preceding account of Czech surrealism; however, it is a question that will be relevant in relation to the hybrid object in film and the audience's relationship to that object. The contrasts that the previous section highlighted between French and Czech surrealism implied a basic difference which was not explicitly formulated: namely, that the Czech surrealists seemed naturally to achieve a balance between subjectivity and objectivity, while the French surrealists were fixated on the distinction between the two, and on demolishing that distinction. As a result, the French group tended to gravitate towards extremes. In their more transcendental mode, they suggested that all elements of physical reality are connected to each other by means of invisible links that have objective existence, independent of human perception, but which the unconscious might lead one to perceive. Typically, however, the French surrealists located the source of the marvellous entirely within the individual's unconscious, and looked to art as a means of creating an objective (that is, material) representation of subjective perceptions. The Czech surrealists, by contrast, did not seem to feel the same need to dwell on the distinction between subjectivity and objectivity; they were content to use language and art to convey their individual experience of the marvellous without troubling over how much of that marvellous existed objectively outside the mind and how much was dependent on the poet's or artist's subjectivity. The subjectivity–objectivity dynamic in Czech New Wave films is similarly unselfconscious, but will be discussed in more detail in the context of the hybrid object, which will be the primary focus of the rest of this chapter.

Hybrid objects and the Czech New Wave

Hybrid objects in the films of the Czech New Wave will be physical objects that take on a disruptive function in the film. This disruptive function will be determined by the multiple layers of resonance that the objects acquire by means of their narrative, thematic and visual roles in the film, often in combination with a humorous dimension.

As an introduction to the hybrid objects that will be encountered in this chapter, there is an important distinction to be made between them and the hybrid objects examined in the previous chapter. In *À Nous la liberté*, objects circulated through the film, building up meaning from the various contexts in which they appeared, and producing meaning by being out of place. Hybrid objects in Czech New Wave films will work differently, not least because they will appear in a wide variety of films: narratives with a tendency towards documentary realism (by the directors Miloš Forman, Ivan Passer and Jiří Menzel), narratives incorporating a dream-like or fantastic dimension (by Jan Němec and Jaromil Jireš) and films that keep only the bare bones of narrative and concentrate more on experimentation with form (by Věra Chytilová and Jan Švankmajer). Although it is difficult to identify characteristics that hold true for objects across such a range of different approaches to film-making, there are clear differences between these films and Clair's film. First, the objects that appear in these films often do recur multiple times: if not the object itself, then objects of a similar category will make several appearances. As the Czech New Wave films tend to focus on the everyday and are more contemplative, the repetition will not occur at such a frenetic rate as in Clair; this, combined with the fact that it may be a related object rather than the same one that recurs, means that the repetition of objects will be more subtle.

Related but not confined to this subtlety of repetition are more nuanced possibilities of meaning than in *À Nous la liberté*. Where characters in Clair were one-dimensional, in Czech New Wave films character psychology will typically be explored in detail. As a result, the question of character subjectivity will arise in these films, and the main characters' personal preoccupations will intervene to inflect object meaning. Like the Czech surrealists, however, who had little interest in using Freud to turn the physical world into a collection of symbols,[91] the Czech New Wave directors avoid any symbolism that leads away from the physical characteristics of the object. Rather, the meanings that will be explored in relation to character psychology will simply call into play those meanings that are already associated with the objects in question by means of their use in the diegesis and their everyday or cultural signification. As in the Czech surrealists' work, then, the dynamic between subjectivity and objectivity is balanced.

In terms of the audience's relationship to the film, only the most experimental of the Czech New Wave films will demand subjective interpretation. In most cases, objects themselves generate a fairly transparent meaning as they circulate within the films; the role of the audience, then, is simply to take note of and appreciate the multiplicity of meaning that may be present in one object. Moreover, as this multiplicity derives from a diegesis that reproduces a recognisable reality, and objects are thus placed in a familiar context, the audience is able to engage with the objects and easily perceive their contextual meaning; this appreciation of the multiple layers of meaning in familiar objects may also, then, be extended to an appreciation of the complexity of everyday reality, something that the Czech New Wave film-makers were keen to communicate, as were the Czech surrealists themselves.

Whereas objects in Clair's film often achieved their comic effect by being placed in an environment where they did not usually appear, in Czech New Wave films comic effects are often achieved by means of hybrid objects in themselves, or through their juxtaposition with other objects. The effect of the object or its juxtaposition is frequently given a moment to make its impression upon the audience when it first appears; this typically occurs at the beginning of a sequence when an object or juxtaposition of objects appears without an immediate explanation. The more documentary-oriented films will end this moment with a verbal explanation for the object (even if this explanation does not account for the entirety of the object's meaning); films tending more towards fantasy and experimentation often avoid offering any single rationale for the object's appearance.

Like *À Nous la liberté*, a number of Czech New Wave films feature an element of satire, although political content generally had to be indirect in order to be approved by the censors. As mentioned earlier, unlike *À Nous la liberté*, Czech New Wave films feature only a limited amount of slapstick comedy. It is much more common for hybrid objects in Czech New Wave films to develop humorous situations based on the erotic, creating a lowbrow humour that increased the popular appeal of these artistically ambitious films. Once again pointing to a common cultural background with the Czech surrealists, it seems that the Czech New Wave directors, rather than looking to a more cerebral examination of the unconscious as a means of subverting the status quo, took on a naturalistic approach to subversion. By turning towards the physical dimension associated with the country's rural tradition, they found a source of transgression in irreverent humour based on eroticism. This humour, moreover, contributed to creating multiple layers of meaning in the objects involved in this comedy.

The analysis of the hybrid object and its contribution to the creation of comedy in Czech New Wave films will proceed in order through a selection of key films representing the documentary-oriented, the more fantastic or the more experimental approaches to film-making. It will trace similarities and differences in the roles played by the object in these different types of film. The analysis will take note of which objects receive emphasis through repetition, and examine how they develop multiple layers of meaning in relation to narrative, theme, visual treatment, and contribution to comedy, and how the audience may be expected to assimilate these meanings. It will also examine the way in which, through this multiple meaning, in particular that derived from a naturalistic/erotic humour, hybrid objects in Czech New Wave films take on a subversive function.

Miloš Forman's **Lásky jedné plavovlásky/A Blonde in Love** *(1965) and Ivan Passer's* **Intimní osvětlení/Intimate Lighting** *(1965)*

Miloš Forman, Ivan Passer and Jaroslav Papoušek were collectively known as 'the Forman School'. They regularly collaborated on each other's films, and shared a concern with the realistic portrayal of contemporary life that the liberalisation of the 1960s allowed.[92] Passer identifies the break with Soviet Socialist Realism's prescriptive model as the greatest source of inspiration for himself and his contemporaries:

> I believe that our films were a reaction to the official aesthetic of social realism, where nothing on the screen reflected reality as we knew it. We found it exciting to shoot reality the way it really was, to film people who were not actors.[93]

Although many Czech New Wave films had tendencies towards documentary realism, the Forman School's films were most consistent in their focus on everyday life; often featuring non-professional actors in familiar settings, they were distinguished by their debt to Italian neo-realism.[94] Nonetheless, compared with neo-realist films, those of the Forman School were 'more conscious (and less simplistic) [in their] critiques of society'; their portrayal of contemporary life was both funnier and more scathing,[95] and produced a characteristically Czech black humour. This element of black humour, absent from Italian neo-realism, may in fact account for the Forman School's more nuanced approach to social criticism.

Forman and his colleagues were able to criticise without condemning: they showed people as they were, complete with both admirable and less admirable characteristics. Moreover, though censorship had been relaxed, it still existed, and a less clear-cut position helped a film both politically and artistically. Passer himself notes that censorship 'forces film-makers to find a language which the censors don't pick up on immediately and because of that the language becomes ambivalent – it is able to express more than just definitions'.[96] Such ambiguity of meaning will work in favour of hybrid objects, which rely on meaning that is multiple rather than unique.

The way in which the Forman School's films point to the multiple layers of physical reality in general, not just in relation to objects, was highlighted by the Czech surrealists who admired the Forman School's films for the way in which they 'découvrent la face cachée du réel, son comique ou sa monstruosité latents à même ses accidents, ses bégaiements et flottements quotidiens'/'discover the hidden face of reality, its comical or monstrous qualities lying just beneath everyday accidents, mistakes and hesitations'.[97]

The following study of two films from the Forman School will concentrate specifically on the way in which hybrid objects may reveal such ruptures in the seemingly uniform, comprehensible surface of everyday existence.

Forman's *A Blonde in Love* follows the love life of adolescent factory employee Andula, who lives in a girls' hostel in a small town. The film opens with a warm and intimate scene between Andula and her friend as they lie in bed together discussing Andula's boyfriend Tonda. The opening of the next scene creates a startling contrast with the first as it shifts to the brightness of a snowy forest in daylight, with no people present. The camera pans and comes to rest on another surprise: the film's first hybrid object. It is a necktie knotted around a tree (figure 3.1), an object that is not only out of place but creates an unusual juxtaposition, inviting the viewer to compare the tree trunk to a human neck. When a passing forester sees that Andula was responsible for placing the tie around the tree, his objections have a ridiculous basis and make a mockery of inane official regulation that seems designed to crush spontaneity. The explanation for this surreal juxtaposition of tie and tree only comes in the next scene, which returns to the girls' hostel. Andula confides to her friend that she had placed the tie on the tree as a present for Tonda, but not only did he never receive it, in the attempt to give it to him Andula considered replacing him with the forester. In retrospect, the scene in the forest is more comical: the forester's exchange with Andula became playfully flirtatious towards the end of the scene, and as the necktie formed the pretext for their conversation, it points to the fact that an object can have multiple functions, from being a gift for one lover to inviting a chance encounter with another. Moreover, the manner in which the tie itself is situated in the natural context of the forest can be seen as having an erotic as well as a comic effect, as the tree trunk takes on a phallic resonance. (André Breton himself unwittingly gives his Nosferatu tie a phallic resonance by mentioning it only a few pages after he reveals his dislike of women seeing him naked without an erection).[98]

The same tie makes a second appearance near the end of the film, when Andula makes an unannounced visit to her new love interest, Milda, in Prague. Milda's mother discovers the tie when she secretly opens Andula's suitcase (figure 3.2), hoping to learn more about her; the tie is again an object out of place, as it is an unusual item of clothing to find in a girl's suitcase. While the audience may assume that Andula is planning to give Milda the gift that she never gave to her last boyfriend, the camera's focus on the mother's face suggests an alternate point of view: she may think that it is something that Milda left behind when he slept with Andula, and thus interpret it as evidence of the sexual nature of their relationship.

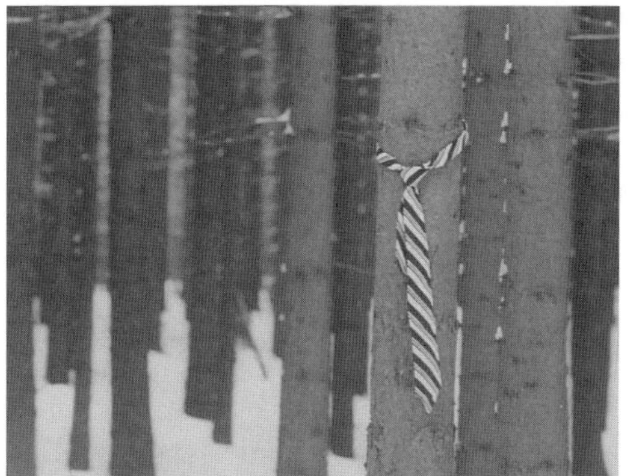

Figure 3.1: A tree wears a tie in *A Blonde in Love*.

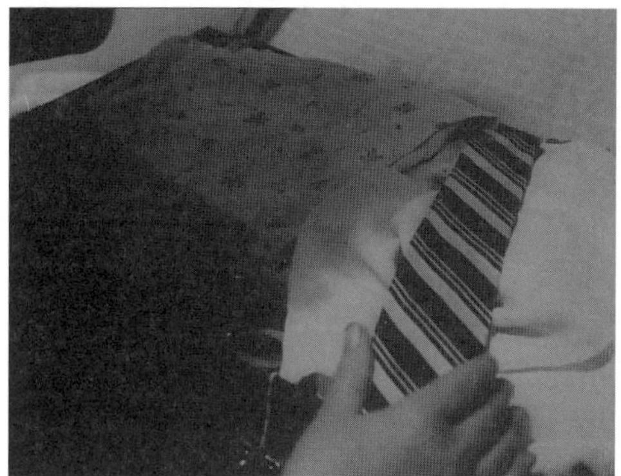

Figure 3.2: A tie is discovered in Andula's suitcase in *A Blonde in Love*.

There is again, in association with this tie, a stark and comical contrast, this time between the mainly tranquil, loving and intimate night that Andula and Milda did indeed spend together before, and Andula's stay at Milda's parents' house, where she is treated as an unwelcome guest and must sleep alone while the family bickers endlessly.

An object that recurs more frequently in the film is a ring. It is not involved in unusual juxtapositions with other objects but, like the tie, it points to the multiple meanings that a familiar object may take on, depending on a character's personal preoccupations. The conversation between Andula and her friend in the first scene revolves around the ring that Tonda gave Andula as a present. A comic element of doubt is introduced to the ring's traditional connotation of a serious relationship. The friend asks 'Is it real gold?' and Andula replies with a youthfully naive assurance of its authenticity. In relation to this first scene, the ring's second appearance questions its connotations much more radically. This time, Andula is lying in bed with Milda, and as they notice each other's rings, both claim that they were presents from their mothers. Although it is possible that Andula was lying about having a boyfriend in the first scene, as until this point the audience has only seen a photograph of Tonda, it is more likely that she is lying to Milda, just as he may be lying to her.

The film more directly undermines the assumption that a ring signifies commitment on two other occasions when rings are foregrounded. The first comes just before Andula and Milda spend the night together. As women outnumber men in the town where she lives, Andula's employer organises a dance and asks the army to send some soldiers. As it is mainly middle-aged reservists who arrive for the dance, many of them are married. Keen to seduce some younger women, however, one of them tries discreetly to remove his wedding band, but winds up having to chase it around the dance floor when it falls out of his pocket. This comical episode shows how one may attempt to take advantage of the fact that a ring as a symbol of commitment may be temporarily suspended by taking it off. After she has slept with Milda, Andula makes a more definitive statement by ceasing to wear the ring that Tonda gave her. However, childishly embarrassed when Tonda confronts her about the missing ring, Andula denies the object's symbolism. She forces Tonda to admit that the ring is hers, and argues that she therefore has the right to decide when she wants to wear it.

In Passer's *Intimate Lighting*, the repetition of objects is less clear. Rather than a single object making repeated appearances, it is objects of a similar category that recur. Even more than *A Blonde in Love*, the film highlights the difference between life in Prague and life in the countryside. It does so through a narrative centred on the urban Petr and his young girlfriend Štěpa's visit to Petr's former classmate Bambas, a family man who lives in the country. With even less narrative momentum than *A Blonde in Love*, rather than focusing on events the film gives a sense of the atmosphere and experience of the visit, both for the visitors and their hosts. The springs in *Intimate Lighting*'s mechanism are its interpersonal dynamics, chief of which is the contrast between the two old friends, who are both musicians. While Petr's urban life offers hope in the form of artistic opportunities and unfixed relationships, Bambas feels like a failure, slightly bored by his predictable family life and extremely frustrated in his cultural aspirations. However, the stereotype of young, sophisticated urbanites mocking and despising country dwellers who are not even aware of their backwardness is modulated by the sense of a mutual exchange of gazes: these country dwellers are sympathetic and self-aware, taking a largely good-humoured and philosophical approach to every undignified aspect of life.

With an even greater sense of documentary realism than *A Blonde in Love*, *Intimate Lighting* is a film in which the objects present are fully justified by the context. As hybrid objects, however, they also take on a symbolic resonance that is clear yet not contrived. The additional layers of meaning that objects acquire derive both from the circumstances in which they appear and from the obvious preoccupations of the characters which constitute the film's theme.

As this film showcases the tension that arises from the social pressure felt by both guests and hosts to conform with grace to their roles, one of the themes that naturally arises is the difficulty of maintaining a dignified façade. Chickens and their related foodstuff consistently intervene to disrupt any attempts to put up such a front.[99] As live animals, chickens thwart Bambas's attempt to keep his car clean and presentable. The first time he opens the garage doors, there is a chicken standing on top of the car, a surrealist juxtaposition, certainly, but not at all gratuitous. However much Bambas loves his family, his car is tacitly associated with the freedom of his previous life as a bachelor, a part of himself that he would like to keep sacrosanct and separate from his family life. However, the chickens invariably find their way into his garage, making it (as Bambas bitterly observes) 'more like a hen house', and the fact that they do so in order to 'hatch' reinforces the symbolic confrontation of Bambas's freedom and individual self versus his family obligations. Bambas angrily tries to chase the chickens out of the garage, while his mother-in-law protests that he is scaring them, and that 'they'll stop laying eggs'. This minor confrontation highlights differing perspectives on the chickens. Bambas's overreaction shows that he sees the chickens as more than a minor inconvenience, as they also stand as constant proof of the lack of privacy in his life; the grandmother, meanwhile, is focused on the chickens as living creatures and, above all, valuable livestock.

It is the grandmother's perception of the animals that is emphasised most at the end of the scene when a chicken is run over as Bambas impatiently drives the car while the chicken is still underneath it; the scene's final shot pans down from the rear of the car to follow an egg rolling back into the garage until it bumps into the chicken that lies with a broken neck. The sadness here is only for the lost domestic animal, rather than having any sinister undertones of a desire in Bambas to do away with his family. Indeed, the cut from the chicken to the funeral procession that begins the next scene serves to mock the sadness the viewer may feel for the dead chicken, as the montage creates a brief but fallacious impression that it is the chicken that is being mourned. When the image of the chicken on the car recurs later in the film, its juxtaposition with an immediately preceding shot once again evokes the symbolism of Bambas's frustration. The rather lyrical silhouettes of Bambas and Petr are caught by car headlights as they drunkenly head off together to pursue a dream of a free life on the road. The next shot comes as a contrast, as it combines car and chicken to create the very image of Bambas's perpetual defeat (figure 3.3): the only vehicle is in the garage; as it is now morning, its headlights appear weak; the silhouettes of the two men have been replaced by the more prosaic and terribly familiar silhouette of the chicken on top of the car.

Elsewhere in the film, chickens and eggs as food serve as catalysts to undermine the gravity of ritual and hospitality. For example, when the family and their visitors sit down for their first meal together, which is a roast chicken, Bambas's wife attempts to give the guests the best cuts. However, she is foiled by her father's and son's greediness and Štěpa's generosity. The guests wind up faced with the parson's nose, which they have to share, and as Bambas's children squabble over the coveted chicken leg, it flies through the air and lands in the middle of the table, upsetting a glass of beer, and ends the family dinner before it even begins. However, Bambas cannot be more embarrassed than Petr, who must apologise for his childish girlfriend as she begins laughing uncontrollably at the situation. In this instance, the chicken's association with rural life brings a natural, erotic dimension to the humour, giving the object a sexual resonance: the grandfather shows his desire for Štěpa's

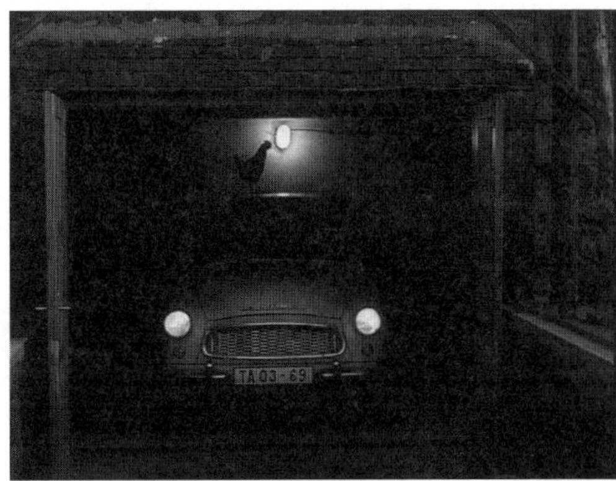

Figure 3.3: The inescapable chicken atop Bambas's car in *Intimate Lighting.*

leg of chicken, and it is he who presents her with the parson's nose. The next time the adults assemble at the table is at the end of the film, and this time it is to drink some home-made eggnog (which has already been the subject of an unclear but bitter dispute between the grandparents); having gone through the ceremony of proposing a toast, they all lift their glasses and find that the thick drink will not budge. 'A bit of patience, that's what we need', says the grandmother, and as the film ends, there is a shift from a full shot (figure 3.4) to a long shot of the group with their glasses still resolutely glued to their lips and their heads tilted back. The eggnog is the embodiment of the adjective '*domácí*' ('home-made'), a quality lauded elsewhere in the film: special food that here, in its consumption, recalls the patience required in its preparation. At the same time, the presence of this object creates a humorous acknowledgement of how ridiculous such perseverance may appear to outsiders.

Both Forman and Passer's films offer a comic yet realistic portrait of contemporary reality; indeed, it may be said that it is comic precisely because it is so realistic, the comedy of *A Blonde in Love* deriving from the convincing combination of the ingenuity of desire and the naiveté of adolescence, while *Intimate Lighting* highlighted the patience and good humour demanded by rural family life. Objects played an important narrative role in creating

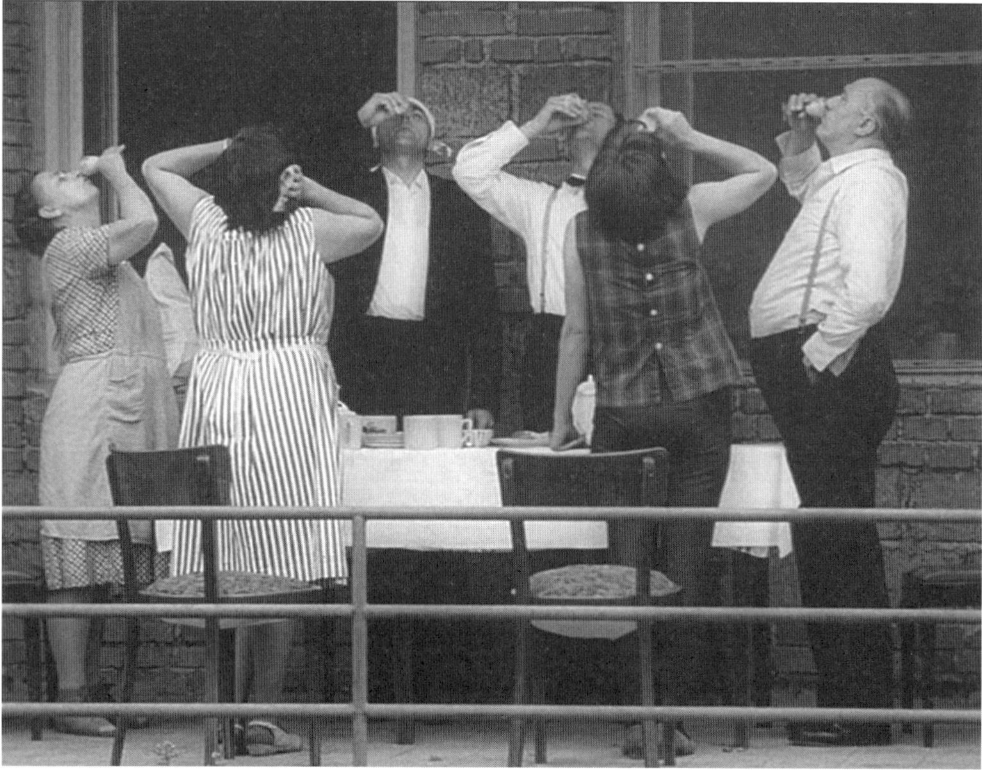

Figure 3.4: Drinking eggnog requires patience in *Intimate Lighting*.

comedy within the diegeses of these films, from the declarations and disavowals surrounding rings in *A Blonde in Love* to the consistently comic effects of chickens and eggnog in *Intimate Lighting*. The meanings associated with these objects were communicated by their narrative function, their thematic resonance (specifically through the characters' own preoccupations which influenced the meaning that the objects held for them) and their visual treatment. By maintaining a documentary feel to the films, then, Forman and Passer showed that objects in everyday life naturally acquire multiple resonances dependent on their use, on individual point of view, and on comic and erotic connotations that derive from these.

Jiří Menzel's Ostře sledované vlaky/Closely Observed Trains *(1966)*

Like *A Blonde in Love*, *Closely Observed Trains* revolves around youthful erotic adventures and misadventures; however in this film, the main character, Miloš, is male and his sexual awakening is set not in the 1960s but during the Nazi occupation of Czechoslovakia. This film portrays life in a small town, in particular its railway station where Miloš has just started a new job.

Closely Observed Trains can be grouped along with the films studied so far in this chapter in that it shows the influence of documentary. It differs, though, in that the narrative drive in Menzel's film is much stronger, while narration in the Forman School's films is meandering, and gives the impression of observing reality's own structures rather than imposing structure on reality from outside. Nonetheless, Menzel does not allow traditional narrative form to limit his personal style; indeed, Peter Hames asserts that Menzel 'inject[s] surrealist imagery into a conventional form'.[100] It seems, however, that Hames is thinking of French surrealism rather than the Czech version. Although his praise of Menzel's sensitivity to the '"magical" qualities of individual objects'[101] suggests a connection to reality characteristic of the Czech surrealists, Hames's subsequent observations demonstrate that he considers Menzel's film more in terms of French surrealism's preoccupation with the unconscious. He says that the surrealist-influenced 'poetic charge' in *Closely Observed Trains* is created through 'the consistent eroticisation of the images that reflect Miloš' situation'.[102] Hames's conception of surrealism in Menzel's film provides an illustrative contrast with my own approach because it implies that the mise-en-scène recreates (whether figuratively or literally) the way in which Miloš projects his conscious and unconscious desires onto his surroundings. I will argue, on the contrary, that objects are not restricted to symbolising one character's state of mind, but that they reflect erotic awareness, something common to all characters in the film, as one dimension of their meaning and the source of their comic effect.[103]

Even more than Forman's and Passer's films, *Closely Observed Trains* shows that an obsession with sex is far from being restricted to the young. Everyone at the train station is associated with eroticism in some way, and this erotic dimension is just as obvious in the objects that appear in the film as in the characters' own flirtations and sexual exploits. Station property is put to illicit use in two different ways: first, the station's own Lothario, signalman Hubička, while working the night shift with the young telegrapher, captures her and imprints the station's rubber stamps on her bottom. These stamps are brought to the audience's attention earlier in the film when the local inspector for the Nazi party makes a visit to the station and uses them, as they were intended, to seal an official document. The connection between illicit and official uses is made not only through the rubber stamps themselves but also through Hubička's action of breathing on the surface of the stamps to moisten them in order to make them work. Even in the official use of the stamps, then, there is a suggestion of eroticism: the juxtaposition of the cold, inanimate metal of the stamps and Hubička's warm breath emphasises the vital force and sensuality of the latter. Moreover, during this scene the inspector himself is distracted, while he is in the middle of a serious explanation of Nazi military manoeuvres on a map, by the telegrapher who uses a pencil to scratch between her breasts, another example of a piece of office equipment being put to an alternate, erotic use (and notably by the other character who will be involved in the illicit use of the stamps).[104]

The other piece of station equipment that has its official use subverted is the stationmaster's sofa. This piece of furniture is an object of much greater veneration than the rubber stamps (even if Hubička's misuse of the stamps was punished with an official reprimand for 'abuse and disgrace of the German language'). When the sofa makes its first appearance in the film, Menzel takes the unusual step of filming it in medium shot all by itself, without any human figure in the frame. A similarly object-oriented image precedes the shot of the sofa: a low-angle shot of the clock on the mantel, above which hangs a framed painting of trains. The two images of sofa and mantel area together, then, introduce and summarise the old-fashioned formality of the stationmaster's office. Later in the film, the tradition and prestige represented by the sofa is expressed verbally by the stationmaster, who says that he inherited it from the last stationmaster; its age and the high quality of its leather evoke the glory of the old Austro-Hungarian Empire. When Hubička and, later, Miloš use the sofa for lovemaking and each makes a tear in it, they show their irreverence towards the sofa, both as the prized property of the station and its master, and as a symbol of dignified traditions of empire and officialdom.

To understand the stationmaster's fury at the damage to his sofa, it is important to see it in the context of a sexual and social hierarchy. Past his prime, married to a plain and placid woman, and having so far achieved only the modest distinction of being in charge of a village train station, the stationmaster has a strong attachment to the work hierarchy and its symbols of office; avid for any form of distinction, he cherishes hopes of promotion, and scours his family history for traces of blue blood. His desire to command respect is dangerous because it makes him willing to ingratiate himself with anyone of rank. He fawns shamelessly over the local countess, incarnation of the old powers; at the same time, he acquiesces readily to the de facto authority of the Nazi occupiers. The stationmaster's character is more comic than despicable, however, as it becomes clear that he is hypocritical in his allegiance to those of rank. When a woman whom Hubička calls his 'cousin' comes to visit (the very woman with whom he will make the first rip in the sofa), the stationmaster enjoys flirting with her as much as Hubička does. However, when the stationmaster must unwillingly obey his wife who summons him away for dinner, his attitude changes. Clearly disgruntled at being excluded, he leans out of the window to shout biblical imprecations ('Armageddon!') against the very dalliances he himself would like to be enjoying. The tear that Hubička subsequently makes in the stationmaster's sofa is thus a double insult: he not only rubs the stationmaster's face in his sexual success, but in doing so also shows his disrespect for the one area in which the stationmaster is superior, the work hierarchy. Although the stationmaster does not feel the same sexual rivalry with the meek young Miloš, the second rip in the sofa nonetheless constitutes another attack on his authority, as it proves that he has little control over his staff.

The visual treatment of the tear in the sofa also emphasises its erotic resonance. The first tear is revealed by a succession of shots of the sofa, again without any human figure in the frame, recalling the earlier shots that introduced the undamaged sofa as emblem of the stateliness and tradition of the stationmaster's office. The later succession of shots moves from a medium shot to medium close-up of the sofa, and finally to an almost obscene close-up of the rip itself. This closest shot reveals thick strands of horsehair that protrude like pubic hair from the triangular, orifice-like tear in the soft leather of the sofa. The stationmaster's podgy fingers then slide into the frame to feel the stuffing as cautiously as if it were a living thing (figure 3.5). The shot that reveals the second tear shows a similarly yonic opening alongside the first one, which has in the meantime been repaired (figure 3.6). The attempt to cover up the first tear (and, by extension, the sexual act that produced it) is thwarted, however, both by the clumsy, ugly stitches that draw attention to the damage, and by the new tear that seems to symbolise an irrepressible sexuality, an opening that cannot be sealed.

Like *Intimate Lighting*, *Closely Observed Trains* creates hybrid objects from animals. There is a surprising number of animals in and around the station, so much so that Hubička, when he takes Miloš on a tour of his new workplace, remarks to him, 'What a station, eh? More like a farm'. This statement recalls Bambas's complaint that his garage is 'more like a henhouse', and in *Closely Observed Trains*, pigeons serve a similar role to *Intimate Lighting*'s chickens in bringing people amusingly down to earth. The stationmaster is awkward and

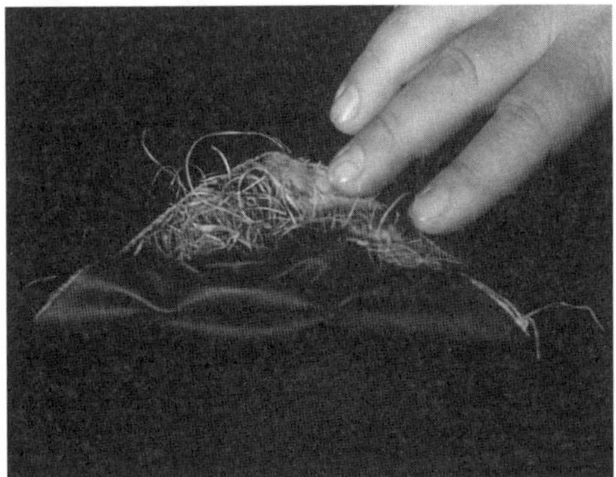

Figure 3.5: Investigating the first tear in the sofa in *Closely Observed Trains.*

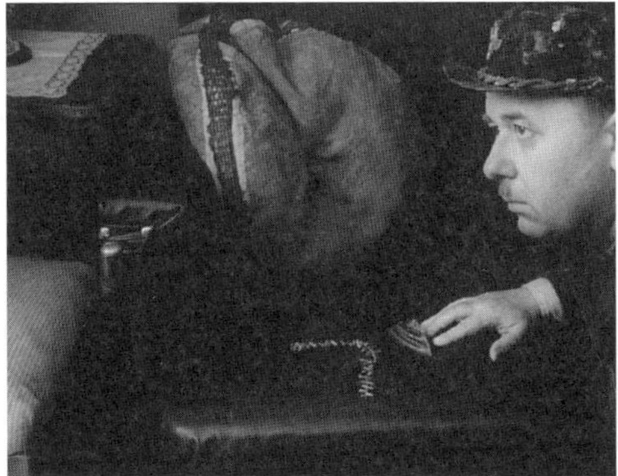

Figure 3.6: The stationmaster discovers the second tear in his sofa in *Closely Observed Trains.*

nervous around horses, although he wishes he were a skilful rider so that he could impress the countess and support his pretensions to nobility. He is a pigeon-fancier at heart, a natural affinity that underlines his squarely middle-class identity. It is, unfortunately, an affinity that will have a negative impact on his career aspirations. One day, the Nazi officials make a surprise visit and catch him wearing his old uniform that he keeps for tending the pigeons. As one of the officials picks a feather from the stationmaster's guano-spotted suit, he says, 'So you want to become an inspector.... Wouldn't you prefer breeding geese?'. This devastating remark in response to the inanimate traces left by the pigeons highlights their connection with nature as well as their sexual dimension, which combine to create a comic effect that undermines officialdom itself and the stationmaster's ambitions within its hierarchy. The officer's evocation of a farmyard animal effectively knocks the stationmaster even lower down the hierarchy, associating him with rural labour (breeding geese) rather than leisure pursuits (keeping pigeons).

The stationmaster's matronly wife is also associated with animals, and their sexual resonance is highlighted much more insistently than is the case for her husband's connection to pigeons. In fact, the way in which the stationmaster's wife interacts with rabbits and geese highlights a dominant sexuality that is surprising in light of her mild, matronly appearance. When Miloš first meets the stationmaster's wife she is tending rabbits, and in a subsequent scene soon after, she kills one of them. She takes the rabbit by its hind legs, smiles as she strokes the writhing animal to calm it down, and then a medium close-up shows her hand giving the rabbit a firm blow to the back of its neck, bluntly silencing its screams. The calm dominance of this gesture is emphasised by its contrast with the reaction of the old railway employee who is supposed to be helping her: he runs away with his hands over his ears, unable to stand the rabbit's terrified squealing. Shortly afterwards, the same old employee is slightly more at ease holding up the now floppy and lifeless rabbit by its feet. The fact that the director makes a point of showing the rabbit both turgid before and flaccid after death suggests that the rabbit is one of many phallic symbols in the film. When, having called her husband away from the flirtation he was enjoying with Hubička's cousin, the stationmaster's wife asks whether she should fry the rabbit, her innocent question nonetheless associates her power over the rabbit with her control of her husband's sex life. The rabbit's association with the stationmaster himself is reinforced in a much later scene when the stationmaster, speaking of the shame that Miloš has brought on the station, says 'this is how you skin me alive'; in order to illustrate his metaphor more vividly, the stationmaster points to the dead rabbit that his wife and the old employee are in the process of skinning. The way in which the rabbit is used moves beyond the simple clichéd connection between rabbits and sex, which is based on the success with which they reproduce; though their association with sexuality may be a factor, attention is focused more on the rabbit's physical characteristics (tense or limp), and on the way in which the stationmaster's wife treats the animal. While moving beyond cliché, the sexual dimension of the animal's association with the stationmaster's wife does create a rather disturbing rupture in the audience's perception of her as a gentle mother figure, as does the calm manner in which she inflicts violence upon the animal and its body (killing, skinning, frying).

The stationmaster's wife is again associated with a dominant, subtly aggressive sexuality through her treatment of a goose, in the scene where Miloš approaches her to ask for advice about his sexual problem. In the intimate space of an underground cellar, the stationmaster's wife sits astride a goose and strokes its neck. Miloš finds this arousing as the goose's neck evokes a phallus, but at the same time a mildly sadistic dimension is created by the woman's actions and her verbal exchange with Miloš; though it was to be expected that she would refuse to help him sexually, she also pretends not to know what Miloš is talking about, making it more difficult for him to explain his problem. Furthermore, the reason why she is caressing the goose's neck is to force it to eat more and become fat, and thus the apparently gentle action has the same ultimate motive as her stroking of the rabbit: the animal is destined to be killed and eaten. As a representative of nature, the goose creates another disruption in the audience's perception of the stationmaster's wife, underlining the carnal current running beneath her social façade even as she attempts to deny her knowledge of it.

However strong their comic dimension, animals (as representatives of the natural world) as well as station equipment (as part of the official realm) take on a sexual resonance that does more than, as Hames would have it, 'reflect Miloš' situation', and even goes beyond amplifying all of the characters' erotic awareness. The sexual dimension to these hybrid objects has an additional function in that it creates a rupture in official regulation and everyday decorum; in doing so, it mirrors the film's other major theme of resistance to the Nazi occupiers and to any other ruling power that, by taking rules and regulations to absurd and repressive extremes, would attempt to deny the primary importance of the simple sensual enjoyment of life.

Jan Němec's O slavnosti a hostech/The Party and the Guests *(1966)*

In a narrative that follows a group of friends who have been invited to an open-air banquet in the countryside, *The Party and the Guests* (henceforward abbreviated to *The Party*) allegorises the power dynamics of authoritarian government. The host of the party at first seems affable but eventually demonstrates an irritable and controlling side when one of the guests leaves early. The host's adoptive son and his gang play a frightening trick on the group of friends, bullying them and taking them prisoner before the banquet even starts.

The Party introduces a sense of unreality through nightmarishly absurd events and situations which distance it from the quality of documentary realism that has characterised the films studied so far in this chapter. Němec believed that 'the director must create his own world [...] a world independent of reality, as it appears at the time',[105] and in doing so looked to Chaplin, Bresson and, most notably, Buñuel as examples.[106] The effect is that Němec's films are not completely disconnected from reality, but nor are they slaves to it. The director's aim was that viewers should cease to be concerned with realism and instead focus on 'what the director really tries to convey'.[107] The allegory in *The Party* was conveyed clearly enough for the film to be banned immediately after its release, and Němec himself was banned from Barrandov Studios soon afterwards.[108]

Hames has remarked upon the way in which Němec's films 'encourage you to interact' with them,[109] and this is in large part due to the fact that they provide key elements of a familiar everyday reality and highlight ambiguity within that reality. This ambiguity, which exists in events, dialogue and, most importantly for this study, objects, can be seen as both rupturing the surface of reality and making that reality more convincing. Objects in *The Party* take on a dual meaning, which chiefly contributes to a darkly humorous reflection of the discrepancy between official façades of order and reason and practical states of chaos and corruption in authoritarian systems. Certain ambiguities of this satire on a specific political system highlight a more general hypocrisy in human relationships. This ambiguity may be unrealistic in the context of the film, and constitute an exaggeration of the reality of both authoritarian systems and human interaction; there is, however, a basic, haunting truth in the notion that the meaning of words, situations and objects can be shifting and unstable.

Past studies of this film have tended to focus on dialogue rather than image,[110] but the two in fact work in a similar manner, and objects are thematically at least as important as dialogue. The film's writer, Ester Krumbachová, used 'dialogue [...] to convey its absurdity, or alternatively, a reality beyond the apparent meaning of words'[111]. There is, however, also (to adopt Krumbachová's terms) an absurdity in the characters' relationship with objects, based on a disturbing reality that exists beyond objects' apparent meaning. There are two different types of ambiguity relating to objects in this film: ambiguity with a clearly political resonance, and ambiguity with a more general relevance to human relationships. The fact that the film presents the general ambiguity before moving on to the political one adds to the film's criticism of society by suggesting that the more dangerous political ambiguity naturally developed from the seemingly innocuous social one.

To begin, as Němec does, with the more familiar type of ambiguity, material things in the film seem initially to be no more than pleasurable accessories to life, as (one likes to think that) they are in reality. The film opens with an extreme long shot of the group of friends in a country setting, having their own private picnic before the official banquet. This first scene evokes old-fashioned Romantic images of urban dwellers enjoying a day in the country, as Renoir père would have painted them. The women's arms and legs are bare; both men and women flirt, recall other happy occasions, dream about the future, and enjoy the present moment. Almost all of the shots are medium close-ups showing just the shoulders and face of the guests, adding to the intimacy and joyful sensuality of the moment. However, the cake that they are eating also has its own close-up (figure 3.7), and such shots of food are carefully arranged, leading one scholar to compare the images to Dutch still-life painting.[112] The camera assiduously follows the slices of cake as they are passed around, and then dwells in medium close-up on the actors, emphasising the moment of eating; food thus begins to take part in the sensuality of the moment, and continues to do so in subsequent shots. When one man compliments a woman on the excellent cake she baked, her cleavage is on show as she laughs. One of the men brings alcohol back from the river, and a detail shot shows him playfully placing one of the cold bottles against his neighbour's bare arm, making her cry out. She later steals one of the men's shot glasses and the camera shows her face in profile,

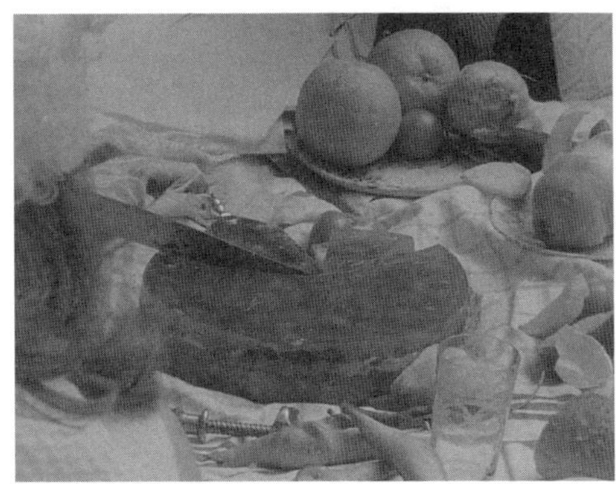

Figure 3.7: A close-up of the cake in *The Party and the Guests*.

close-up, as she drinks it down; soon after, the camera follows one of the men as he drains his glass and reclines for a nap in a single movement. Another woman in close-up lazily stretches out a piece of gum she is chewing. By this point, the viewer may have noticed that the sensuality of the scene, like much of the conversation, is not only influenced by objects, but actually relies on them. The woman who at the beginning declared, 'I like good fun, good company, and good food', by the end of this relatively short scene has already shifted the emphasis of her desires: 'I like nice, well-looked-after things', she states complacently.

The next scene also evokes Impressionist paintings, of bathers this time, as the women, aesthetically arranged along the river, wash in preparation for the party (figure 3.8). Here again, the film differs radically from traditional depictions, in that the focus of the sensuality is based not on the women's bodies but on material things: the conversation revolves around the perfume one woman's husband gave her as a gift, or concerns about whether they will

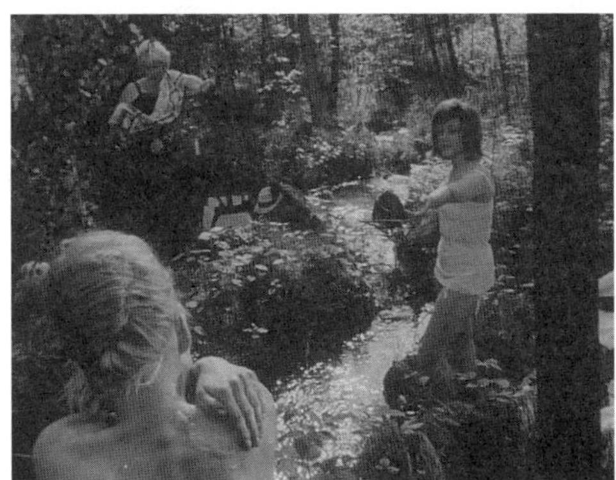

Figure 3.8: The women bathe after the picnic in *The Party and the Guests*.

ruin their high heels on their country walk. The camera trails the bar of soap as it is passed around; it focuses on the fastening of a stocking to a garter belt rather than the leg that supports them; it follows a dress as it is slipped over a woman's head, as though unconcerned with her body.

If these first two scenes emphasise objects in an unusual way, the audience may still feel indulgent towards the characters' apparent materialism, not yet having understood its full extent or significance. By the final scene of the film, viewers will discover the true shallowness of the majority of these characters. When the search party decides to take along a vicious dog to follow the scent of the missing guest, that guest's wife is only concerned that the dog might tear her husband's new suit. Similarly, another guest whose bag was damaged as part of the joke declares in false-deadpan before all the guests, 'Stuff the bag. I don't give a damn about it. But what about my knife and lighter?' Though he concludes by saying, 'I'm not bothered about those either. It's the principle I'm bothered about', this last assertion, arriving so late, rings hollow. The host's promise to replace the knife and lighter is received with applause, and the guest and his principle are placated.

Němec's treatment of objects thus leads to a change in the audience's understanding of their significance in the context of the film. This mirrors the audience's developing perception of characters and situations, as they discover the inhumanity that exists behind façades of playful or considerate behaviour. Objects in this film, then, become hybrid in an ingenious and disturbing way: those objects that at first seem relatively insignificant actually have more power over the characters than higher principles such as justice and humanity. The fact that the viewer does not immediately suspect the exaggerated importance of objects, an importance that nonetheless existed all along, makes the power of the objects all the more sinister in retrospect.

Shortly after the first and second scenes that hint at the unexpected extent of the characters' material obsessions, Němec introduces a duality more directly relevant to the film's political satire of ideals versus realities. He does so by evoking in close succession both threatening and innocuous means of employing specific objects. Verbal and visual methods are used to associate objects with a threatening meaning in addition to their innocuous one. For example, the host's adoptive son, as part of his so-called joke, has a desk set up in the middle of a forest clearing, and sits behind it with a black folder, the contents of which are unknown. An undercurrent of aggression soon quells any amusement the viewer might feel at the absurdity; the ridiculous ease with which an office is set up outdoors ceases to be the focus, as the terror of an unexplained detention and possibly violent interrogation dominates. When the host arrives to rescue the victims of the joke, he demands that the desk be put back in its original location as part of the banqueting table, and seizes the black folder which turns out to be the guest list. Although it may seem at that point that the objects have returned to their everyday significance as unthreatening items, the viewer quickly discovers that even when the desk becomes part of an open-air banqueting table and the black folder contains the names of 'honoured guests', the innocuous meaning no longer exists except as a façade for the threatening reality, because the situation is still one of coercion. This is confirmed by the dual meanings that are mobilised in another object when the host notices that one of the guests has left the banquet. A search party is formed, and it is suggested that a gun should be fired when the missing guest is found so that the other guests know to stop looking for him. The overtly stated use of the gun, then, is to harmlessly signal a piece of information. However, just before the search party was formed, and before any gun was seen, the host's son spontaneously expressed a desire to shoot himself, and enjoyed describing his fantasy in lurid detail. If it were ever possible for a gun to make an innocent appearance in a film, the images that the son has evoked make it impossible in this case: the reference to a gun turns the search party into a hunt. The threat of violence is reinforced physically as well as verbally shortly after the search party has left, as the guest who has become the favourite of the host and his son idly aims the gun across the lake while he addresses an interrogation-like series of questions to the missing guest's wife.

This latter set of examples has a political resonance in that it demonstrates how individuals who are in control may, through an unspecified threat, activate a terrifying significance in objects, even if the stated use of those objects is innocuous. A peaceful and reasonable façade is maintained by pretending that the stated significance of objects is the real one, while never explicitly acknowledging the very real existence of threat. The obvious political relevance in these examples is that if one does not speak out and identify the reality of a situation, a manipulative and violent regime may claim legitimacy by creating a false façade of harmony. However, the film also suggests that a disturbing degree of selfishness underlies the façades of harmony that people like to maintain in social situations in general, and that political corruption is simply an example of this same discrepancy on a larger and more menacing scale.

To conclude this study of *The Party*, it is worthwhile considering the significance of the director's choice of a natural setting for the film. The juxtaposition of the world of nature and man-made objects created both lyrical and absurdly menacing scenes in the examples studied. A natural context initially seemed an essential dimension of the sensual pleasure in the opening scene's picnic, yet objects were slowly revealed to be even more essential to the characters' pleasure than the natural environment or even their fellow human beings. Whereas the sensuality associated with nature was a positive disruptive force in *Closely Observed Trains*, one that brought people together in spite of any oppressive regime, the solipsism of the characters in *The Party* causes them to turn destructively in on themselves, away from the liberating force of nature. In fact, when the friends begin their interaction with the host and his son, the lyricism of nature, to which the film's opening alluded, is decisively revealed to be powerless as a disruptive force to the structures of so-called civilisation. The host's son effortlessly sets up his office in a forest clearing with nothing more than a desk, a black folder and a few thugs who can force his victims to respect the imaginary walls of their prison. Rather than being a positive force against oppression, nature begins to reflect and support the animalistic qualities of a corrupt civilisation: the natural environment offers no quarter from the brutality of the regime, only a wilderness in which a man may be hunted like an animal.

Jaromil Jireš's Valerie a týden divů/Valerie and her Week of Wonders *(1970)*

Of all the feature-length films studied in this chapter, *Valerie and her Week of Wonders* (henceforward abbreviated to *Valerie*) is most directly related to surrealism. It is based on a novel written by Czech surrealist leader Vítězslav Nezval in 1935. The film adaptation reflects the fact that Nezval's *Valerie a týden divů*, as an early surrealist novel, is closely related to surrealism's precursor, poetism.[113] As explained in this chapter's introduction, poetism was similar to surrealism in many ways; however, it differed in its 'freshness' and (complementing its predilection for the urban and the modern) its marked 'nostalgia' for the countryside.[114] The youthful spirit and lyrical rural setting of Jireš's film are the embodiment, then, of distinctly poetist characteristics; the strength of its allegiance to physical reality alongside its fantastic transformations and illogic, however, make the film equally characteristic of Czech surrealism. Nature will be of most relevance to this study in terms of its influence on object meaning, particularly in comparison with the significance of nature in *The Party*, the other film that along with *Valerie* forms an intermediary group of films in this chapter, those more fantastic in their approach.

The film's eponymous heroine is a 13-year-old girl who lives with her grandmother in a village. Soon after the film begins, Valerie menstruates for the first time and the wonders to which the film's title occurs may be interpreted as the product of a meeting between a still childishly vivid imagination and a young woman's sexual awakening. Almost all of the film's scenes in fact pair their marvellous dimension with an element of sensuality or, more often, sexual threat. Although this film differs from the others studied in this chapter in that it is not humorous, like the other films it does contextualise its eroticism in relation to the natural world. The beginning of Valerie's sexual awareness as marked by her menstruation is connected to nature visually, for example, by the drops of blood that fall on some daisies as she walks through the yard of her grandmother's house. The young minstrel who is Valerie's protector has a relationship with her that is at times fraternal but which also grazes the romantic; he is connected to nature by his name, 'Orlík', which means 'Eagle'. The film's lyrical approach to the natural world makes it a complement to Valerie's own youthful beauty. At the same time, nature also serves as a backdrop to sinister characters and their evil intentions: there is a sense that the natural world provides hiding places for hidden dangers, such as vampires who feast on chickens' blood. This dangerous dimension of nature is confirmed most vividly by the other character with an animal name, 'Tchoř' or 'Weasel'; the opposite to Orlík, Tchoř is the most horrifying character in the film, and is actually able to take on the aggressive, insinuating animal's form.

The film's wonders include various illogical and magical events, such as frightening transformations of the type mentioned above. All of the characters except Valerie have multiple identities, at least one of which tends to be threatening. Adding to the sense of unreality is the fact that chronology and cause-effect relationships in the film are unclear; Hames appropriately characterises *Valerie*'s narrative as being very much 'post-*Last Year in Marienbad*, post-8½'.[115] This confusion of chronology, general absence of logical causation, and the multiple identities of characters make the experience of the film similar to that of a dream: the viewer is, as a dreamer (and as Valerie herself), able to accept events as they occur and follow their progression with relatively calm interest. A basic unity of place (Valerie's home, the village, and the surrounding countryside), character (the same individuals who take on different personas) and motivation (Valerie's will to preserve her virginity and her life) allow the audience to orientate themselves. Objects are also important in anchoring the narrative in the physical world: a pair of pearl earrings, for example, appears both in those scenes that are most dream-like or fantastic, and in those scenes that seem more plausibly realistic. The pearl earrings thus provide proof of a certain continuity between real and fantasy worlds, while their grounding in physical reality encourages the viewer to engage with them and figure out their meaning. In spite of their physical existence, the meaning of these pearl earrings is complicated as a result of their ubiquity; they become the film's most consistently foregrounded and hybrid object.

Valerie's pearl earrings are the object that receives most emphasis, both as a symbolic motif and as a narrative catalyst. Although the fact that they are valuable quickly becomes clear, the exact nature of their interest is never made explicit. Instead, a general sense of their significance is established through their visual treatment and association with different characters early in the film, and only later does one specific power that they hold become clear.

The pearl earrings are the only object to feature twice in the title sequence, occurring symmetrically at two privileged points: in the sequence's second image, which comes immediately after the title of the film, and in the second last image, just before the director's name. In both cases the earrings are filmed in close-up as Valerie holds them suspended, one in each hand, a gesture of contemplation or admiration that will be repeated in the course of the film. The pearl earrings immediately receive further emphasis as a focal point of the film's first and second scenes. Orlík steals the earrings from Valerie's ears while she is asleep in the first scene. In the second, he returns the earrings, and through the dialogue, the audience and Valerie learn that the theft had been ordered by the constable (one of Tchoř's personas). Valerie, happy to have her earrings back, performs the title sequence gesture of holding them up in front of her before she puts them back on. As she watches Orlík and the constable, the oval window of the carriage in which she is sitting frames her (figure 3.9) and provides a link with a portrait of her mother that will appear soon afterward.

When the earrings next become the focus of attention, Valerie is in the dining room with her grandmother. She takes off her earrings and a close-up shows her again holding one in each hand to admire them. Her grandmother comments on her 'playing' with her earrings and the camera follows the grandmother as she moves towards a portrait of Valerie's mother. Here, the pearl earrings that the mother is wearing and the oval frame of the portrait reinforce the link with Valerie when she was framed by the carriage window in the earlier scene; further, when the mother returns at the end of the film, she too will be framed by the oval carriage window (figure 3.10), and Valerie will put the earrings on her mother's ears. Surprisingly, in this dining room scene the grandmother 'warn[s]' Valerie to 'get rid

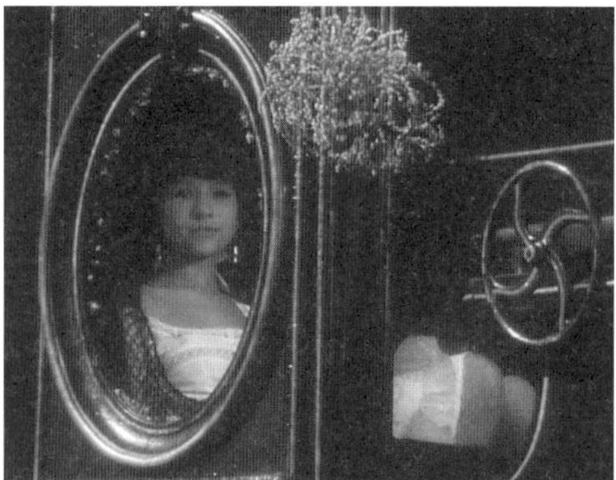

Figure 3.9: Valerie framed by the carriage window in *Valerie and her Week of Wonders.*

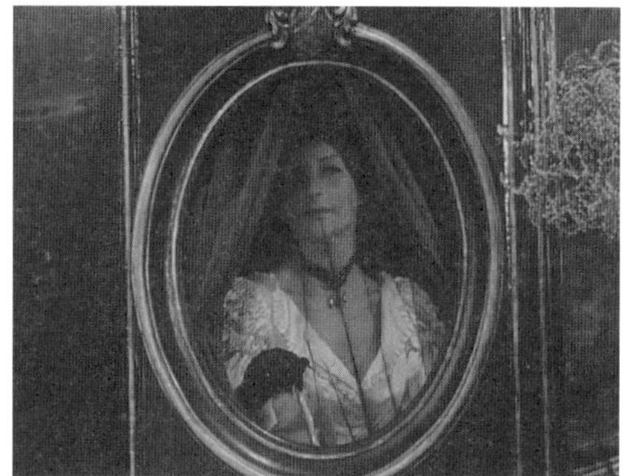

Figure 3.10: Valerie's mother framed by the carriage window in *Valerie and her Week of Wonders.*

of [those] earrings', which belonged to her mother. When Valerie, curious, asks whether there is 'some secret' in the earrings, her grandmother lightly replies 'oh no', and says that she bought them, along with the house, from a constable. This scene thus encourages a conventional understanding of the earrings' heirloom value through their connection with Valerie's mother, only to immediately undermine this meaning by the grandmother's paradoxical instruction to 'get rid of' rather than treasure them. This instruction in itself suggests a new significance to the earrings (that they contain a 'secret' reason that they should be discarded), but this too is denied by the grandmother, as she reveals their prosaic origin, that she bought them from a constable. Although this new information could help to explain why that same constable ordered Orlík to steal the earrings in the first scene, the reason is not made explicit, and the earrings' significance remains undefined.

The other important dimension of the earrings is that, in spite of the grandmother's disavowal, they do in fact contain a 'secret' ('*tajemství*'). This is the exact term that Orlík uses later in the film when, the vampiric persona of Valerie's grandmother having stolen the earrings, he again returns them to Valerie; this time, however, he gives her only their powerful essence in the form of two small pearls, and leaves the original earrings 'empty'. These pearls bring an additional level of symbolism to the earrings; indeed, the fact that the earrings have two parts, a beautiful external form and a 'magical' internal one, embodies the notion that an object has more than one layer of meaning. In order to escape from danger, Valerie has only to swallow one of the magical pearls from the earrings, and she will either appear to be dead or else be transported away from that danger; later, having escaped, she spits out the pearl, which can be used again.

Through visual emphasis and as an instrument to advance the narrative, the pearl earrings are thus brought to the audience's attention as a significant object. The object becomes hybrid as the audience is offered a number of different hints as to its meaning; with the exception of the earrings' association with Valerie's mother and the pearls' transformative powers, none of these hints allows for a clear understanding of the object's significance. Crucially, however, its grounding in a familiar and realistic world (as an item of jewellery that a young and imaginative girl may have inherited from her mother, and that her grandmother may know more about) offers an initial lure to the audience to attempt to trace the pearl earrings' meaning, rather than casting them aside as an object that is impossible to understand. Jireš's early emphasis on the pearl earrings' physical beauty, like the general emphasis that he places on nature throughout his film, anchors the earrings in a material context that encourages the audience to interact with them, thus also leading them to tolerate the pearl earrings' ultimate ambiguity of meaning and accept it as part of their 'magical' nature, that they should never be fully understood. In this sense *Valerie* goes further than any of the films studied so far, in which objects were associated with meanings that were multiple but, finally, restricted in number. Jireš's refusal to limit the number of meanings associated with an object, or to make every one of those meanings clear, preserves the object's 'magical' quality and links him with the directors of the next and final group of films.

Věra Chytilová's Sedmikrásky/Daisies *(1966)*

In addition to being considered one of the founding film-makers of the Czech New Wave,[116] Věra Chytilová was its most experimental director.[117] To give just a few examples of the techniques she employs, *Daisies* features sudden changes from black-and-white to tinted or colour film stock, fast-forwarded segments and non-naturalistic sound effects. Like *Un Chien andalou*, the film also subverts conventions of continuity editing to create an impression of the impossible: by linking two shots, it makes it appear as though characters can step from their apartment directly into a distant landscape. This formal daring is an inseparable dimension of any message in her films. 'I want to give new meaning to a film with my editing', Chytilová declared, firmly associating formal properties with rhetorical objectives: 'I want to put things together in a new way'.[118] In *Daisies*, the director's own philosophy of film-making was complemented by that of her cinematographer, Jaroslav Kučera, who wanted the film image to escape from a strictly objective vocation; instead, he believed it should acquire the same power of 'subjective meaning' as other modern arts such as poetry, music and painting.[119] The audience's role in creating the film's meaning is thus, as in *Valerie*, crucial and yet comes with freedom as the film is by no means restricted to one or even a set of correct interpretations.

Although many Czech New Wave directors moved away from conventional narrative and documentary-inspired realism in favour of formal experiment,[120] Chytilová's approach was nonetheless remarkably 'disjunctive' by comparison with that of her contemporaries; Hames has suggested that the practical purpose of this fragmentation was to 'encourage a critical attitude towards the reality presented'.[121] Chytilová's formal experimentation can be compared to the camera tricks that Jireš used to create 'magical' effects in *Valerie*; in both cases, techniques that take away from cinema's impression of documenting physical reality in a direct manner are used to draw audiences in and encourage them to change the way in which they usually think about that reality. In *Daisies* as in *Valerie*, however, the artifice that the director imposes on the film image is balanced by an attention to the natural world that emphasises its physical properties, and that gives the audience a familiar reality with which to orientate themselves. Moreover, in *Daisies* the sensual characteristics of the natural world create an eroticism with a comic effect that contributes overwhelmingly to undermining the established socio-sexual order. In this respect, *Daisies* is more similar to the documentary-inspired films of Forman, Passer and Menzel than Němec and Jireš's more fantastic films; in the latter, the eroticism associated with nature was not humorous, and played an ambivalent role in relation to the status quo.

Daisies' desultory narrative follows two adolescent sisters who take the commonplace cliché that 'everything is going bad' as licence to behave as badly as they like. They play disruptive or destructive games that undermine traditional values of respect for people and property. The naturalist emphasis that acts as a complement to the film's formal experiment is achieved in part through a choice of locations that underline physical rather than intellectual aspects of human existence. The places featured most prominently are restaurants and a banquet hall (seven times), where enjoyment of food moves from the gourmet to the grotesque. The next most common locations allude to sensual acts or bodily functions: public toilets (five times), where the girls are seen emerging from cubicles or attending to their appearance; their bedroom (six times), where the girls engage in physical games, eat sexually suggestive foods and parade in dishabille; and a pier (five times), where the film begins, and where the girls are seen wearing bikinis and enjoying the sunshine, sometimes watching men.

A large part of the destruction that takes place in the film is a result of the girls' insatiable love of food, a greed that has enough social stigma attached to it to stand in for sexual appetite in women. It is thus through its use of food that the film's emphasis on the physical world also evokes its sensual or even erotic dimension; further, this eroticism has a comic effect that is subversive to social order. Towards the end of the film, when the sisters destroy a carefully laid out banquet before the guests' arrival, they take pleasure in eating with their hands, or simply squeezing food between their fingers and throwing it at each other. Another example of the subversiveness associated with their attitude to food is the girls' dinner dates that become a sort of one-meal-stand with the girls in the position of control: they take advantage of the gourmet pleasures offered to them by their suitors and, once the bill is paid, rid themselves of the men as quickly as possible. Pointing out the purely sexual motivation of older men who take young women out for dinner, Chytilová subverts the model so that the girls simultaneously define the nature of their own sensual pleasure and make use of men before men can make use of them. Having undermined the practice of polite conversation by asking the older suitor inappropriate questions, one of the girls squirts cream into his face as she takes an enormous mouthful of cake, thus emphasising the erotic element in their enjoyment of food with a comical effect.

A later scene that takes place in the girls' bedroom seems to foreground the erotic aspect of food with far less subtlety, evoking a clichéd sexual symbolism: it features a variety of food items, every one of which is either phallic (sausages, bread rolls, pickles, bananas, and general references to meat) or else evokes feminine fertility (eggs and fruit). The fact that the girls are burning, cutting or impaling the phallic food items seems no more than an easy way of indicating their lack of sympathy for men, already shown by the way in which they are ignoring the voice of a suitor on the telephone as he begs one of the sisters to return to him. A greater degree of hybridity is developed in relation to these food items, however, as the girls treat objects evoking female fecundity in the same violent manner (one even attempts to cut the other's toe with scissors or pierce her pelvic area with a fork). It is ultimately not entirely clear whether there is any real aggression in the girls' play with these evocative food items, or whether they are simply pointing out the generally aggressive and destructive nature of both digestion and reproduction.

Hames has noted that *Daisies* features numerous 'allusions with variations on cliché',[122] and this practice has a strong influence on the creation of hybrid objects in the film, as was demonstrated in the previous scene. The sequence in the film that comes closest to being a 'seduction scene' also begins with a cliché: butterflies feature prominently, as in Czech culture they symbolise sex.[123] Yet this very symbolism is denaturalised: the excessive emphasis placed on the butterflies is an unnecessary amplification of a scene in which sexual intent is already manifest. The scene takes place between one sister and a man about twice her age, and begins with his clichéd declarations of love ('you're so earthly, yet so heavenly!') in voice-over with images of his collection of butterfly specimens. His adoration quickly turns to frustration, however, and he resorts to playing a lively tune on the piano; at this point, further shots of dead butterflies appear in a frenzied montage that matches the pace of the music, while two intercut shots show the girl taking down the straps of her brassiere. When he finally approaches the girl and his emotion continues to intensify, the piano music and montage of butterflies return; this time they are much closer shots that show the detail of individual butterflies' wings as if to reflect the fact that the man is closer to the object of his admiration. The naked girl holds up cases of butterflies in an apparently simple allusion to the erogenous zones she is hiding beneath them (figure 3.11).

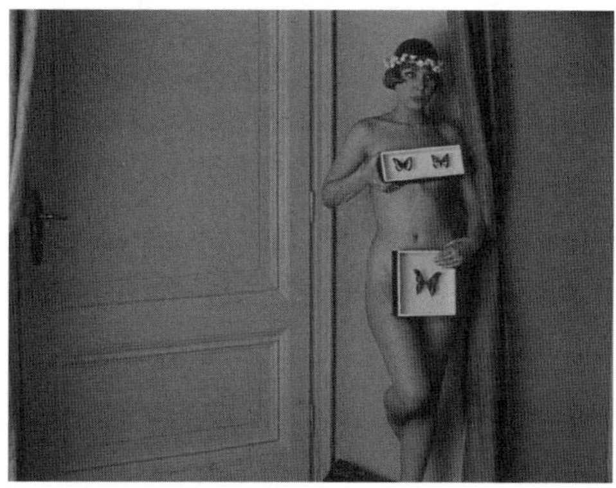

Figure 3.11: Hiding behind butterfly cases in *Daisies*.

Yet the butterfly is not only a symbol for sex or erotic passion in this scene; the butterflies as objects actually come between the man and the girl he supposedly desires. When he finally comes close to her, instead of taking away the butterfly case covering her pubic area, he removes the butterfly, leaving the case where it is. This is not, moreover, a modest metaphor for the sexual act; when the girl moves away in surprise and bumps the butterfly case on the wall behind her, she is able to escape the man's embrace because he is more concerned with saving the butterflies than pursuing her. There is, in fact, uncertainty about the object of the man's admiration from the beginning of the scene: his voiced-over admiration seems to refer to the butterflies that fill the frame, while the girl to whom he is actually speaking is only revealed later. By the end of the scene, the ambiguity of reference has returned, as it seems possible that the man is most concerned with butterflies as beautiful objects to be collected, rather than the sexual activity that the butterflies symbolise. His obsession with the butterflies serves as an apt metaphor for the notion that the man's idealised impression of the object of his affection does not correspond to who she really is. Buñuel makes a similar notion the premise of *Cet obscur objet du désir/That Obscure Object of Desire* (1977), using two actresses to play the same, impossibly capricious female character in order to symbolise the fact that Fernando Rey's character never sees his mistress for who she really is. Chytilová satirises any fixed ideal of the feminine by means of a male character who ignores the real woman in front of him in order to admire beautiful but dead butterflies.

Chytilová similarly satirises fixed images in the media through cut-out images evoking a cliché that is then undermined. The first instance of such an object is a rose that one sister is seen cutting out of a magazine. Its symbolic charge comes from the montage in which it is involved just before it is cut out: the other sister answers the phone with the blackly humorous words, 'Rehabilitation centre. Die, die, die!'; she then repeats the joke by dialling a number and uttering the final exclamation another three times, each word this time accompanied by a glossily professional image of a rose or bouquet of roses, the diegetic source of which has not yet been revealed. The scene seems to downplay the youth, beauty and innocence with which the film (playing on traditional stereotype) most frequently associates flowers, and instead reminds the audience of flowers' association with funerals, with short-lived beauty and hence mortality. However, death is also evoked by the finality of the fixed media image, as oppressive as the feminine ideal associated with the (dead) butterfly specimen. Chytilová had temporarily worked as a model early in her career, but her FAMU graduation film, *Strop/The Ceiling* (1963), expressed her disillusion with the modelling world.[124] *Daisies* also involves reference to the fashion world,[125] and when Chytilová makes use of photographs from magazines, it is most likely a comment on the consequences of turning real people and objects into static images that then become commodities. Chytilová also pokes fun at the supposed substance behind commercial images in the earlier example of the phallic food scene: unable to satisfy their appetites with real food, one of the girls happily stuffs her mouth with a picture of food that has been cut out of a magazine. Later, the sisters concoct a suggestively fertile soup of milk, eggs and a small cut-out image of a muscular young man; adding this image to the soup is both a humorous and a mildly violent act, as a little picture

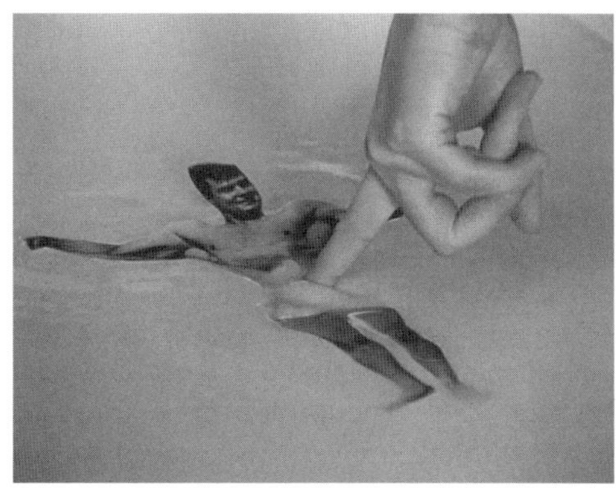

Figure 3.12: Drowning a cut-out paper man in *Daisies.*

of a man is obviously not the equivalent of a real man, yet the iconic power of the image is enough to make it slightly sinister to push the cut-out man beneath the surface of the liquid, as though drowning him (figure 3.12). The power that culture ascribes to beautiful images is once more playfully undermined when one sister tries to make a cut-out of the other; rather than restricting herself to cutting the fabric on which her sister is lying, she cuts into her clothing and the girls begin a duel with scissors. Camera tricks give the impression that one sister has lost her arm and the other her head, but the girls' jokingly exaggerated reactions maintain a consistently humorous tone. Whether as film images or paper dolls, the girls refuse to conform to feminine standards of physical perfection, serenity and beauty, instead making ugly grimaces as they cheerfully dismember each other. It is the same refusal of conventional beauty that confronts the audience in the film's opening scene: the bikini-clad girls may look like beautiful dolls, but their limbs make squeaking noises when they move, and the girls spoil their beauty with ugly gestures or sounds, as one puts her finger up her nose and the other blows an off-key note on a trumpet.

Daisies' use of humour is a key element, not only to engage the audience through its entertainment value but also to undermine cliché, particularly in relation to established gender roles. As explained, the source of this humour was an eroticism that derived from the sensual experience of the natural world. The girls' refusal to conform to restrictive definitions of femininity is often expressed through this very insistence on the physical, on highlighting sensuality or even eroticism in the very places where its presence is traditionally meant to be ignored.

The film has, as explained, an experimental structure, which one commentator has said imitates music or poetry rather than conventional narrative:[126] the meaning associated with a certain category of object such as food, butterflies or the cut-out image is thus built up not only in the space of one scene but through a series of repeated appearances of these objects. By alluding to familiar, easily accessible meanings, typically based on cliché, the film offers an entry point for the audience to begin thinking about the object in question. However, each appearance of the object also moves beyond clichéd meaning by suggesting other possible interpretations; whether the alternate interpretation is suggested by exploring an aspect of the object in question that is less frequently considered (such as the oppressive nature of the fixed ideal, or the eroticism of consuming food), or whether meaning is expanded by juxtaposing two clichés (such as flowers as symbols of youth and beauty or of death), the significance of the object is thereby shown to be not only hybrid but based on associations that may be in conflict. While suggesting these meanings, however, the film does not offer one correct way of interpretation, instead leaving much of this task up to the audience. It was Chytilová's express intention that there should be an 'active [...] interplay'[127] between the audience and the film and that each audience member should be 'free to interpret the film in his own way'.[128] While many of the films studied so far highlighted a hybridity in the object, few (with the exception of *Valerie*) have opened up meaning to the viewer's subjectivity in quite as radical a way as *Daisies*.

Hybrid objects and Jan Švankmajer's short films of the 1960s

As Jan Švankmajer began directing in 1964, his first films coincided with those of the Czech New Wave film-makers. Although Švankmajer was not a part of the Czech New Wave, as a contemporary of these directors he was, like them, a 'dissiden[t]',[129] and some of his 1960s shorts 'share [...] [the] atmosphere' as well as the 'socio-political context' of Czech New Wave films.[130] Such a connection is relevant when it comes to political readings, which his films certainly permit.

The general liberalisation in 1960s Czechoslovakia did not only result in the emergence of new artistic styles and movements, such as the Czech New Wave; pre-existing movements that had been forced underground by political circumstances were able to re-emerge, and one of these was the Prague surrealist group.[131] Švankmajer joined the group in 1970 but says that he thought of himself as a surrealist much earlier.[132] He acknowledges, however, that his understanding of surrealism was only a 'superficial' one before he actually joined their ranks.[133] This admission offers all the more reason for hybrid objects in his films to be considered in their own right rather than understood in direct relation to Czech surrealism.

I have grouped Švankmajer along with Chytilová at the end of this study of Czech 1960s film-making because of all the directors mentioned here, they are the two who take greatest advantage of the medium's ability to manipulate the representation of reality. Where Chytilová's manipulations tended to take place in post-production, however, Švankmajer relies on stopping the camera during filming in order to create his effects. Through his use of stop-motion animation, Švankmajer is able to make everyday objects appear to come to life. While making the impossible possible arguably undermines the realism of his films, like the other film-makers studied in this chapter Švankmajer shows great sensitivity to the physical characteristics of the objects in his films; in this way his imaginative transformations are balanced by an emphasis on the material reality of the objects that he transforms. Indeed,

Švankmajer himself has said that 'the more deeply a person probes the fantastic, the more he needs to be realistic in form'.[134] Specific techniques through which Švankmajer shows his respect for the material reality of objects, the reason for his use of these techniques and the effect that they have on the audience will each be explored in relation to four of his 1960s short films.

Tactility: Tichý týden v domě/A Quiet Week in the House *(1969)*

Švankmajer films objects in a way that brings out their tactile dimension,[135] a practice influenced by his work as an artist in the *Český informel* (Czech informal) style of the 1950s and 60s, which featured explorations of texture.[136] *A Quiet Week in the House* (henceforward abbreviated to *A Quiet Week*), for instance, involves a variety of different textures with the result that each one is set off against its opposite. These textures are emphasised through a combination of visual and sonic dimensions, as the director does all he can to evoke the reality of each object through the two senses to which film is able to appeal: the camera is placed close enough to the objects to reveal their texture in detail, and where possible sound effects also suggest what it would feel like to touch the objects. There is the hardness of the metal wind-up toy and the malleability of the clay that crushes it; the soft flesh of the pigs' trotters versus the smooth, sinuous wire wrapped around them; water is absorbed by a bouquet of flowers, then the flowers become dry and set on fire; a wet tongue enters a meat grinder and is transformed into dry curls of newspaper.

Švankmajer believes that 'the sense of touch [...] becomes highly sensitive in moments of psychic tension'; in other words, tactile qualities are associated with a particular immediacy in relation to the emotions, not least because touch is one of the senses that has greatest importance in early life.[137] The emphasis of textures in Švankmajer's films makes such a powerful impression on the audience, then, not only because it evokes the sense of touch and anchors the objects in physical reality; it also appeals to the viewer on an emotional rather than an intellectual level, an effect that will similarly be created by some of Švankmajer's other techniques.

Object form: Picknick mit Weissmann/Picnic with Weissmann *(1968)*

The other way in which Švankmajer increases the realism of his films is by animating objects based on their specific formal characteristics. Švankmajer says that 'he does not "rape" the objects he uses but always selects some natural properties, which he then imaginatively develops'.[138]

In *Picnic with Weissmann*, objects go on a picnic. Chess pieces play against each other on a chessboard, and playing cards flip themselves over on a table. Records roll out of their sleeves onto the turntable of a record player that winds itself and lowers its own needle. A set of clothes lies on a divan and eats a plate of fruit (figure 3.13): the plums roll up the sleeve of the shirt, and their stones drop out of the opposite sleeve, while the coat hanger holding the shirt turns from side to side like a human head. Chairs play football and go for a walk, and the camera also walks about on the legs of its tripod, sets itself up and takes pictures of its

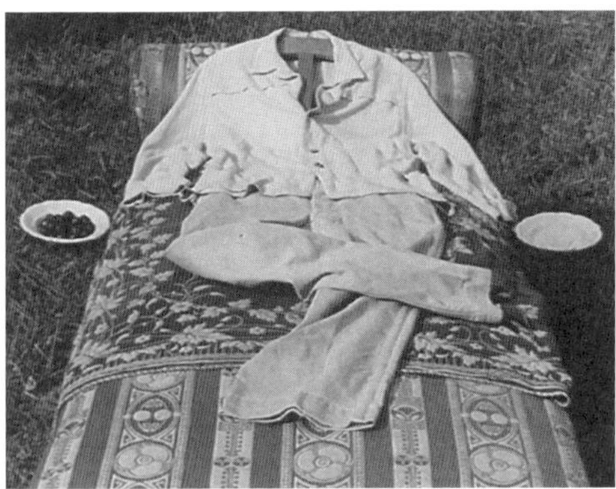

Figure 3.13: A set of clothes eats a plate of plums in *Picnic with Weissmann.*

fellow objects. A dustpan digs a grave for the human 'Weissmann' named in the film's title, who is only revealed at the end, when a wardrobe opens its doors and drops his lifeless body into the completed hole in the ground.

It is surprising to see some of these objects making, on their own, the same movements as they would if humans were manipulating them (the chess pieces and the playing cards, as well as the record player that winds itself). Much more haunting, however, is the majority of objects in the film which move in ways that they rarely do when humans are present, but which are all the more convincing because they correspond to the objects' form. By basing objects' independent movement on their shape (round objects roll, objects with legs 'walk', a coat hanger's hook moves like a head to the 'body' defined by the clothes) Švankmajer leads the audience to imagine how these objects would move if they could; combined with the fact that he animates real objects, it creates a powerful degree of verisimilitude that draws the audience in despite their rational objections.

Mechanical objects and the uncanny: **Spiel mit Steinen/A Game with Stones (1965)**

Švankmajer's early animated films rarely feature more than one human actor: in *A Quiet Week* there was just one man whose life revolved around spying through a keyhole on the mysterious actions of objects. In *Picnic with Weissmann*, Weissmann was initially separated from the objects by being shut inside one of them; he had even less of a role to play, as he was dead and only appeared at the film's conclusion. In *A Game with Stones*, no people appear at all: the camera effectively acts as a stand-in for a human perspective, making the film's viewer the unwilling lone human observer. This minimisation of human actors emphasises, conversely, the importance of objects, but more importantly, in combination with other effects it also creates a sense of the uncanny.

Švankmajer has a clever tendency to include mechanical objects that the audience is accustomed to see moving on their own. His animation then consists simply of extending this familiar power of movement in an object so that the object also becomes capable of setting itself in motion independently. This technique was used once in each of the previous films mentioned (the mechanical chicken in *A Quiet Week* and the record player in *Picnic with Weissmann* were both able to wind themselves up). The director may also, as in the case of *A Game with Stones*, push the boundaries of believability further, extending the power of independent movement to any objects connected with the mechanical one, even if they are not normally governed by clockwork. The film centres on a strange machine composed of a clock, a music box, a tap and a pot. When the clock strikes, the tap attached to it turns and stones fall from it like drops of water, clattering into the pot hanging below; the stones then move about in a dance to the sound of the music box.

Freud's definition of the uncanny is the sense of unease and even fear that is created when the line between animate and inanimate objects is blurred. The sense of the uncanny has a tendency to overrule rational objections about what is or is not logical, as it is an emotional rather than an intellectual response. It was noted earlier that Švankmajer's films appeal to the emotions by evoking the tactile dimension. The emotional power of the uncanny is created in his films through a combination of features: on its own, the stop-motion animation of real objects is not, I believe, enough to create a sense of the uncanny, at least not a very strong one, as their movement may be seen as amusing rather than frightening, and reason may still intervene to remind the audience that the movement is a mere camera effect. A fear that more effectively overrules reason is created by isolating humans from each other and by making the movement of objects unpredictable and even dangerous.

The isolation of human actors in *A Quiet Week* and *Picnic with Weissmann* is taken to extreme in *A Game with Stones*. It is quickly made clear that the viewer is the only human present in a vaguely threatening space: the camera, standing in for the physical presence of the viewer, enters a room that is bare apart from the bizarre clock, and the room is explored in close-up detail that reveals a dead spider and cracks in the white plaster wall, but no living creature. The audience is alone with the strange machine, and their irrational fear (or fear of the irrational) is like that of a child left alone with an overactive imagination.

Through sonic and visual means, Švankmajer enhances the sense of menace already established by isolation. A ticking sound starts with the film's title sequence, before any animation has taken place. As the camera enters the room where the clock is located, the door opens with an ominous creak. The clock's ticking speeds up as the moment approaches when it will strike for the first time, and the editing begins to match this brisk pace, all of which adds to the audience's anxious anticipation of what the machine will do when its other parts are set in motion. When the clock does strike, its sound is startlingly loud; the tap turns with a jarring squeak, and the stones make a loud noise as they land in the pot. The dulcet tones of the music box and the lyricism of the forms created by the stones as they 'dance' (figure 3.14) do not erase the sense of menace that has been so powerfully established; if anything, they contribute to the sense of menace as the audience begins to feel that this beauty of sound and image is being used to distract from a more pressing danger.

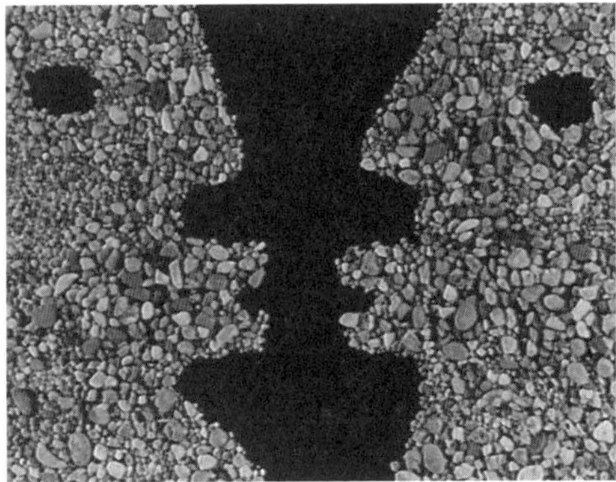

Figure 3.14: Lyrical forms in *A Game with Stones.*

The uncanny blurring of the boundary between animate and inanimate in *A Game with Stones* comes, of course, from the objects associated with the clock. While the movement of the clock and the functioning of its machinery is familiar, a tap that moves on its own seems strange, even if the structure of the machine suggests that it could also be governed by clockwork. The movement of the stones, however, takes the audience into the realm of the impossible. Moreover, unlike the working of the clock, the movement of the stones is unpredictable; although the stones always dance, their interactions become more violent as they begin breaking each other and, finally, the pot.[139] This unexpected behaviour preserves the initial sense of danger even after the machine's functioning becomes familiar, and adds to the fear created by the uncanny. Not only does stone, one of the most reliably inanimate materials of all, come to life; when it does come to life, its most dangerous quality, its hardness, is emphasised. Part of the film's menace also comes from the sense that the stones' hardness could be used to attack humans as easily as it has been turned against other objects, particularly when objects outnumber people.

Black humour and the life of objects: Byt/The Flat *(1968)*

Ancient Hermetic teachings are a major influence for Švankmajer, who strongly agrees with the premise that objects have their own 'life' and 'memory': they can 'witness' anything that occurs in their presence and, most importantly, 'absorb' the thoughts and emotions of any person who touches them.[140] Švankmajer says that he thus 'collect[s]' objects based on what he 'feel[s] they contain'.[141] Although the Czech surrealists' attitude towards objects was not as extreme as Hermeticism's in terms of considering objects as having their own life, it did rely on a similar notion of a dialectic relationship between humans and the world around them. The motion of objects in Švankmajer's films can be understood as symbolising the strength of objects' latent power: the nature of the deeds that objects perform offers clues to their interior life, to a past that has determined their unique personality, complete with desires, grudges and a sense of humour.

In *The Flat*, the uncanny creates both horror and black humour. A man is trapped inside a room where everyday objects turn against him, to the point of threatening his life by denying his most basic needs: the door is sewn shut by a snake-like piece of wire so that he cannot escape; holes appear in his spoon so he cannot eat his soup; a glass of beer becomes minuscule the moment it reaches his lips; the bed disintegrates into wood shavings, so that sleeping means suffocation; when the man turns on a tap to fill a bowl with water to wash his face, rocks come out instead and break the bowl (recalling *A Game with Stones*); water does, however, come out of the stove, and extinguishes the match that he held ready to light it for heat; wire makes another appearance, sewing the man's clothes to the wall, floor or furniture when they come in contact with it, and forcing him to strip to his underwear in order to move away. Point-of-view shots put the audience in the unenviable position of the protagonist-victim, and complementary reverse shots show his horrified, bemused or impassive reactions to the objects' unconventional behaviour. Point-of-view or otherwise, shots tend overwhelmingly to be close-up or extreme close-up and put the audience, even more than the protagonist sometimes, in the most intimate contact possible with the frighteningly unpredictable objects.

While *The Flat* has an undeniable element of horror, in spite of the audience's sympathy for the protagonist it is impossible not to laugh at some of the film's slapstick-style gags that invariably occur at his expense. When the protagonist drops an uncharacteristically tough-shelled egg on the table, it falls right through and lands on his toe, making him hop about with pain. When he stands on a chair in order to reach something, the chair's legs immediately shrink, and when he picks up the chair to examine it, the legs spring back to their original length, giving him a terrible poke in the eye. Such events are reminiscent of misfortunes with conventionally behaving objects, the last example in particular recalling Lumière's *L'Arroseur arrosé/The Sprinkler Sprinkled* (1895). Because they are impossible, these events also suggest cartoon, yet the fact that they occur in a live-action film means that they mobilise different reactions in the viewer, in addition to the schadenfreude typically evoked by cartoon or slapstick.

First, there is a strong element of black humour: unlike a cartoon character, the protagonist could really be hurt by the objects, or even die from the violence and privation they inflict. Furthermore, it is not simply that objects in *The Flat* behave differently than expected; it is as though they are taking their revenge on humans, and this sense of inanimate objects making deliberate choices draws out the terror of the uncanny. These objects do not accidentally malfunction, nor does the protagonist make any obvious mistakes in his interactions with them; the objects seem to have secretly calculated that to have the worst effect on their victim, they must abandon their usual behaviour, so that they consistently thwart the protagonist's expectations. As humans, our sympathies ultimately lie with the downtrodden human protagonist, trapped in a Kafkaesque apartment with disturbing significance for a society temporarily emerging from totalitarianism. However, when the audience's sympathy leaves room for delight, it is not only because they sometimes take a dark pleasure in the suffering of the protagonist; at some level they are led to feel a complementary sympathy for the objects, and thus they share a defiant pleasure when they see objects, which are usually the slaves of man, refuse their servitude.

Through stop-motion animation, Švankmajer's films allow objects to come to life. The reason why his work is so powerful, however, is that even as the objects themselves do the impossible, the director's techniques insist on their material reality. Image and sound are used to evoke objects' texture, and the objects' movement corresponds to their physical characteristics, and thus seems to be a plausible representation of how they might really move if they could. The films regularly include objects that function based on clockwork, again offering a real precedent for the independent motion of objects. As Švankmajer himself believes that objects, like humans, have their own interior life that is influenced by their experiences, the movement of objects in his films may be seen as metaphorically representing objects' genuine inner reality, according to him. This emphasis of the real alongside the fantastic makes the objects' movement plausible, and creates a sense of the uncanny in Švankmajer's work, a terror that is relieved only slightly by black humour.

The idea that emotional effects predominate over any intellectual message in Švankmajer's short films has been made evident by the way in which this section has been able to focus overwhelmingly on the impact of the way in which objects are presented rather than their associated meaning.[142] Yet there is certainly an objective behind the films that goes beyond terrifying or amusing the viewer. Taken independently of their context, the films seem to suggest that objects' meaning is mysterious and cannot be fully understood. This is communicated most strongly by the often inexplicable combinations of objects in *A Quiet Week* and slightly less by a lack of clear rationale behind the strange clock in *A Game with Stones*. In *Picnic with Weissmann* and *The Flat*, however, it is only the objects' ability to move that is mysterious; the reason for their behaviour seems sometimes to be human (such as enjoying themselves at a picnic or exacting revenge), at other times just a neutral or animalistic reflex (to perform a set task such as burying Weissmann, or to attack the inhabitant of the flat). The films all suggest that everyday reality should be treated with caution, as the principles which govern that reality may be turned upside down without notice. It is here that the films' meaning also becomes political, and of special relevance to the context in which they were made.

Politically, *A Game with Stones* and *A Quiet Week* again stand apart from *Picnic with Weissmann* and *The Flat*; made in 1965 and 1966 respectively, the first two films involve an undefined sense of threat and may reflect a moment when Communism was becoming less rigid. The spy in *A Quiet Week* is curious rather than ominous, and the objects, while violent in their interactions, never turn against the human spy, and often point directly to issues such as freedom of speech; similarly, while the objects in *A Game with Stones* seem potentially dangerous, no attack against humans is ever actualised. By contrast, in *Picnic with Weissmann* and *The Flat*, both made in 1968, the threat posed by objects is far more clear and direct, perhaps reflecting the director's awareness of the imminent return of an oppressive totalitarianism. In *Picnic with Weissmann*, Weissmann is already dead and the audience may assume that the objects that prepare to bury him at the end of their cheerful picnic were responsible for his death. In *The Flat*, it is clear that the objects are a threat to the human protagonist's life. This film also ends with the opening of a wardrobe, and the protagonist finds not a body but a profusion of names scratched into the wall behind. This could be interpreted in a chilling way as a list of other unlucky prisoners of the flat, now mysteriously absent. However, a closer look reveals the names André Breton, Benjamin Péret (written large as 'B. Peret'), 'S. Dali', 'A. Jarry', as well as Jan Švankmajer himself ('J.Š', written inside a heart, alongside the initials of his wife and daughter). This suggests an affinity through surrealism rather than suffering, where the names identify those who have profoundly experienced the irrational side of everyday life. By writing his name alongside theirs, the protagonist officially joins their ranks.

Conclusion

Hybrid objects clearly play a prominent role in Czech New Wave films, and take on roles as diverse as the range of films in which they have been traced. In *A Blonde in Love* and *Intimate Lighting*, they demonstrate the degree to which a character's point of view can modulate the meaning of a familiar object, making it less stable than is commonly supposed, typically with humorous results. In *Closely Observed Trains*, it is less a specific character's point of view than a generalised erotic humour that multiplies the object's meaning; as a result of this erotic humour, objects in Menzel's film are able to take on a role of resistance. In *Daisies*, too, hybrid objects tend to subvert the established order; however, it is not only through erotic humour that their meaning is multiplied, but through a confrontation of clichés. Objects with more than one meaning do not always take on such a positive function, however; in *The Party*, the unstated significance of objects was a sinister one that in spite of (in fact, because of) being unformulated, influenced the characters' relationships in an insidious but very real way. In Švankmajer's short films, too, objects are often threatening; although unlike objects in Němec's film, objects in Švankmajer's work can be mysterious, the work of both directors demonstrates that when objects take part in an allegorical portrayal of an oppressive political system, hybrid objects can, rather than resisting the oppression, themselves contribute to it. The main hybrid object in *Valerie* was one of the most mysterious of all objects examined here. Although some of the object's associations put Valerie in danger, the mysteries of the object were seen as intriguing and magical, and therefore positive rather than threatening.

The Czech New Wave was united by its creative impulse much more than by any overt political engagement. As mentioned in the introduction, the portrayal of day-to-day life was in itself political; a focus on the everyday was, moreover, a culturally influenced tendency that was manifest in the work of both the poetists and the Czech surrealists through a clear fascination with physical reality. Accordingly, this chapter highlighted the fact that Czech New Wave films, from the most documentary-influenced to the most fantastic or experimental in form, all retain a grounding in reality through an emphasis on its physical characteristics: visual detail, rich sound, evocations of taste, smell and especially texture. This connection with an objective reality offers a more universal context in which objects remain grounded, even if some of their associated meanings have a more subjective basis.

An important dimension of the realistic grounding of Czech New Wave films is their sensitivity to the nation's rural history. With the exception of some of Švankmajer's shorts in which he sought to create a claustrophobic atmosphere, every one of the films studied retains a pronounced connection with nature: both Forman School films trace a contrast between rural and urban life; *Closely Observed Trains* is set in a village train station surrounded by farmland; *The Party* takes place entirely in the countryside, as does *Valerie*, though the latter film's portrayal of nature is more decidedly lyrical; *Daisies* features a number of rural scenes, though with a typically less romantic attitude than *Valerie*; Švankmajer's *Picnic with Weissmann* may have a macabre ending, but most of the film emphasises the enjoyment of nature. However, this affinity for country life is more than a simple cultural characteristic: as has been repeatedly noted in this chapter, nature serves a specific role in relation to objects. The films' association with the natural world privileges an irreverent and slightly lowbrow erotic humour that brings an additional layer of resonance to any objects it involves. Moreover, objects that take part in such suggestive visual jokes also take on a subversive role in relation to the reigning order. Even if they do not have conventionally happy endings, films that privilege such naturalistic irreverence come across as markedly more optimistic than films by directors such as Němec and Švankmajer who prefer black humour. In Czech surrealism, these different approaches to the comic formed part of a historical evolution in response to increasing political oppression: while a more playful humour was characteristic of the poetists and Czech surrealists before World War II, black humour was typical of the post-war surrealist attitude.

These two dominant features of Czech New Wave films, their humour and their grounding in physical reality, are also relevant to the audience's relationship to the films. Although a more sexual humour is bound to broaden the appeal of an otherwise artistically sophisticated Czech New Wave film, even a subtler black humour will intrigue a wide audience. The way in which humour works in relation to objects will also develop the audience's perception of the multiple ways in which objects may be interpreted, as humour often hinges on differing perspectives on an object. The fact that all Czech New Wave films connect with physical reality (by means of natural settings, documentary realism or a sensitivity to objects' textures, for example) creates a familiar context for objects; this is important because it lends plausibility to the diverse and sometimes subjective or 'magical' meanings that may be associated with an object. Similarly, if the object's meaning is only hinted at or left open to interpretation, anchoring that object in an everyday environment will offer the audience a starting point from which they may move on to other, less common associations. Such an active individual engagement with everyday life and its multiple meaning was crucial to both the French surrealists' definition of the surrealist object and to the Czech surrealists' discovery of the hidden wonders inherent in physical reality. As Effenberger put it, 'Imagination does not mean turning away from reality but its antithesis: reaching through to the dynamic core of reality'.[143] This dynamic core that the Czech surrealists sought was characterised not by an object's established meaning, but by the shifting and multiple meanings that individuals will perceive in their interaction with an object.

Notes

1 Hames, *New Wave* vii.
2 Hames, *New Wave* 273; Owen 221–22; Stanislava Přádná, 'Les Personnalités de la Nouvelle Vague', *Le Cinéma tchèque et slovaque*, eds. Eva Zaoralová and Jean-Loup Passek (Paris: Pompidou, 1996) 127.
3 Hames, *New Wave* 26, 28.
4 Robert Buchar, *Czech New Wave Filmmakers in Interviews* (Jefferson, NC: McFarland, 2004) 115.
5 Hames, *New Wave* 28; Galina Kopaněvová, 'Un Quart de siècle de métamorphoses', *Le Cinéma tchèque et slovaque*, eds. Eva Zaoralová and Jean-Loup Passek (Paris: Pompidou, 1996) 105, 107.
6 Hames, *New Wave* 28.
7 Jan Svěrák qtd. in Buchar 100.
8 Hames, *New Wave* 26.
9 Qtd. in Buchar 38.
10 Hames, *New Wave* 26, 28.
11 Buchar 38.
12 Hames, *New Wave* 2.
13 Zdenek Zaoral, 'Histoire, culture et cinéma', *Le Cinéma tchèque et slovaque*, eds. Eva Zaoralová and Jean-Loup Passek (Paris: Pompidou, 1996) 49–50.
14 Hames, *New Wave* 2.
15 Buchar 13–14.
16 Hames, *New Wave* 4. This diversity is consistently highlighted, for example by Czech New Wave directors Vávra and Passer (in Buchar 116 and 144–45 respectively), and scholars such as Martin Šmatlák ('La Spécificité du cinéma slovaque' in *Le Cinéma tchèque et slovaque*, eds. Eva Zaoralová and Jean-Loup Passek [Paris: Pompidou, 1996] 148) and Přádná (127).
17 Zdena Škapová, 'La Cinématographie tchèque: littérature et cinéma, et plus particulièrement dans les années soixante', *Le Cinéma tchèque et slovaque*, eds. Eva Zaoralová and Jean-Loup Passek (Paris: Pompidou, 1996) 119.
18 Přádná 127.
19 Šmatlák 147.
20 Hames, *New Wave* 271–72.
21 Škapová 119.
22 Kopaněvová 107, 109, 111.
23 Hames, *New Wave* 271.
24 František Šmejkal, 'Devětsil: An Introduction', *Devětsil: The Czech Avant-Garde of the 1920s and 30s*, ed. Rostislav Švácha (Oxford and London: Museum of Modern Art and The Design Museum, 1990) 10.

25 Šmejkal, 'Devětsil: An Introduction' 10.

26 Šmejkal, 'Devětsil: An Introduction' 12, 18.

27 Hames, *Theme and Tradition* 169.

28 It is interesting to note, however, that Teige thought that the poetist manifesto, which in fact predated the French surrealists' first manifesto, already put forward many of the same ideas (Owen 26).

29 Michal Bregant, 'Le cinéma d'avant-garde: entre le rêve et l'utopie', *Le Cinéma tchèque et slovaque*, eds. Eva Zaoralová and Jean-Loup Passek (Paris: Pompidou, 1996) 75.

30 Qtd. in Hames, *New Wave* 202.

31 Petr Král, *Le Surréalisme en Tchécoslovaquie* (Paris: Gallimard, 1983) 14.

32 Král, *Le Surréalisme* 14–15, 17.

33 Král, *Le Surréalisme* 13–14; Bregant 75.

34 Král, *Le Surréalisme* 14–15.

35 Král, *Le Surréalisme* 17–18.

36 Král, *Le Surréalisme* 17–20, 42.

37 Král, *Le Surréalisme* 42.

38 Král, *Le Surréalisme* 17–18.

39 Král, *Le Surréalisme* 40–41.

40 Owen 5, 28.

41 Owen 19.

42 Owen 30.

43 František Šmejkal, 'From Lyrical Metaphors to Symbols of Fate: Czech Surrealism of the 1930s', eds. Jaroslav Anděl et al., *Czech Modernism 1900–1945* (Houston: The Museum of Fine Arts Houston, 1989) 66.

44 Peter Hames, 'The Film Experiment', *The Cinema of Jan Švankmajer: Dark Alchemy*, 2nd edn, ed. Peter Hames (London: Wallflower, 2008) 10.

45 Šmejkal, 'From Lyrical Metaphors' 66.

46 Král, *Le Surréalisme* 19.

47 František Šmejkal, 'After Devětsil: Surrealism in Czechoslovakia', *Devětsil: The Czech Avant-Garde of the 1920s and 30s*, ed. Rostislav Švácha (Oxford and London: Museum of Modern Art and The Design Museum, 1990) 88.

48 Owen 35.

49 Švankmajer in Peter Hames, 'Interview with Jan Švankmajer', *The Cinema of Jan Švankmajer: Dark Alchemy*, 2nd edn, ed. Peter Hames (London: Wallflower, 2008) 109–10.

50 Švankmajer in Hames, 'Interview with Jan Švankmajer' 110.

51 Švankmajer in Hames, 'Interview with Jan Švankmajer' 110.

52 Král, *Le Surréalisme* 31.

53 Král, *Le Surréalisme* 29, 45.

54 Petr Král, 'D'un Imaginaire réaliste', *Le cinéma des surréalistes tchèques*, ed. Petr Král (Cognac: Temps qu'il fait, 2002) 3–4; Král, *Le Surréalisme* 28–29.

55 Owen 78.

56 Král, *Le Surréalisme* 25–26.

57 Král, *Le Surréalisme* 25–26, 55; Hames, 'The Film Experiment' 34.

58 Švankmajer in Hames, 'Interview with Jan Švankmajer' 110; Král, *Le Surréalisme* 29.

59 Král, *Le Surréalisme* 30, 44.

60 Král, *Le Surréalisme* 44.

61 Král, *Le Surréalisme* 26.

62 Král, *Le Surréalisme* 47.

63 Král, *Le Surréalisme* 41.

64 Král, *Le Surréalisme* 40–41.

65 Král, *Le Surréalisme* 30–32, 41, 49–50.

66 Král, *Le Surréalisme* 33–34, 44.

67 Král, *Le Surréalisme* 28–29, 33–34, 44.

68 Král, *Le Surréalisme* 18.

69 Hames, *New Wave* 18; Bregant 76, 83.

70 Owen 27.

71 Král, 'D'un Imaginaire réaliste' 4; Bregant 83.

72 Bregant 76.

73 Bregant 83.

74 Král, 'D'un Imaginaire réaliste' 3–4.

75 Bregant 83.

76 Král, 'D'un Imaginaire réaliste' 4.

77 Bregant 83.

78 Král, 'D'un Imaginaire réaliste' 4.

79 Král, 'D'un Imaginaire réaliste' 4.

80 Král, 'D'un Imaginaire réaliste' 4.

81 Vratislav Effenberger, 'Notes sur le cinéma (extraits)', *Le Cinéma des surréalistes tchèques*, ed. Petr Král (Cognac: Temps qu'il fait, 2002) 14.

82 Josef Škvorecký, *All the Bright Young Men and Women: A Personal History of the Czech Cinema,* trans. Michael Schonberg (Toronto: Peter Martin, 1971) 112.

83 Král, 'D'un imaginaire réaliste' 9.

84 5.

85 Owen 11.

86 It must be said, moreover, that tracing such historical influence is the primary objective of Owen's book. He does not make any definitive claims as to the surrealist status of the films he examines (v. Owen 15).

87 Owen 2, 31, 35.

88 Owen 3, 42.

89 Král, 'D'un Imaginaire réaliste' 8–9.

90 Qtd. in Škvorecký 91.

91 Král, *Le Surréalisme* 19–20. While fascinated by psychoanalysis, the Czech surrealists preferred, as mentioned, to emphasise the material nature of reality and let objects speak for themselves (Král, 'D'un Imaginaire réaliste' 4).

92 Buchar 9.

93 Buchar 146.

94 Hames, *New Wave* 106.

95 Hames, *New Wave* 107.

96 Buchar 146.

97 Král, 'D'un imaginaire réaliste' 9.

98 *Les Vases communicants* 131–33.

99 Although live animals cannot be defined as objects, the fact that here and in other Czech New Wave films they also make appearances as inanimate food items justifies consideration of the resonance that the animals take on when they are alive.

100 Hames, *New Wave* 200.

101 Hames, *New Wave* 200.

102 Hames, *New Wave* 158–59.

103 Owen comes closer to the Czech surrealist sensibility, and to my own sense of the nature of objects in *Closely Observed Trains*, when he locates 'visual affinities with Surrealism [...] in the film's taste for surface and texture, for the sensual appeal and multivalent significance of objects' (76). While Owen does mention that the film 'exploit[s] the identification between subjective and objective worlds that cinema can foster', the main focus of his chapter on *Closely Observed Trains* is the film's generalised 'Bataillean' emphasis on the 'base', the 'material' and the erotic (79).

104 Owen points out that the inspector associates the stamps with another official use: when he illustrates Nazi military manoeuvres on the map, the stamps stand for German armies (82).

105 Němec interviewed in Hames, *New Wave* 166.

106 Němec interviewed in Hames, *New Wave* 166.

107 Němec interviewed in Hames, *New Wave* 166–67.

108 Peter Hames in 'An Appreciation by Peter Hames', on Second Run DVD release of *The Party and the Guests*, 2007.

109 'An Appreciation by Peter Hames'.

110 Hames, 'An Appreciation by Peter Hames'.

111 Hames, *New Wave* 182.

112 Hames, 'An Appreciation by Peter Hames'.

113 Hames, in fact, labels the novel as 'Poetist' (*New Wave* 201).

114 Král, *Le Surréalisme* 13.

115 Hames, 'The Film Experiment' 26–27.

116 Hames, *New Wave* 78.

117 Hames, 'After the Spring' 124.

118 Hames, 'After the Spring' 129.

119 Hames, *New Wave* 189.

120 Hames, *New Wave* 78.

121 Hames, *New Wave* 200.

122 Hames, *New Wave* 188–89.

123 Hames, *New Wave* 191. In Russian the term '*babushka*' or 'little granny' also gives butterflies a feminine association: in Freud's 'Wolfman' case, the Russian patient's phobia of butterflies is in part based on the movement of their wings, which he associates with 'a woman

opening her legs' (Sigmund Freud, *The 'Wolfman' and Other Cases*, trans. Louise Adey Huish [London: Penguin, 2002] 288–89).

124 Hames, *New Wave* 183–84.

125 Hames, *New Wave* 191.

126 Hames, *New Wave* 188.

127 Hames, *New Wave* 196.

128 Hames, *New Wave* 188.

129 Hames, *New Wave* 212.

130 Hames, 'After the Spring' 132.

131 Paul Hammond, interviewed in 'The Cabinet of Jan Švankmajer' (dir. Keith Griffiths, Channel Four, 1984), on BFI DVD release of *Jan Švankmajer: The Complete Short Films*, 2007.

132 Hames, *New Wave* 211.

133 Švankmajer in Hames, 'Interview with Jan Švankmajer' 109.

134 In Hames, 'Interview with Jan Švankmajer' 120.

135 Dawn Ades interviewed in 'The Cabinet of Jan Švankmajer'.

136 Hames, 'The Film Experiment' 33.

137 Peter Hames, 'The Core of Reality: Puppets in the Feature Films of Jan Švankmajer', *The Cinema of Jan Švankmajer: Dark Alchemy*, 2nd edn, ed. Peter Hames (London: Wallflower, 2008) 100.

138 Michael O'Pray, 'In the Capital of Magic: The Black Theatre of Jan Švankmajer', *Monthly Film Bulletin* no. 630 (July 1986), reprinted in notes to BFI DVD release of *Jan Švankmajer: The Complete Short Films* (2007) 3.

139 Michael Brooke, 'A Game with Stones', in notes to BFI DVD release of *Jan Švankmajer: The Complete Short Films* (2007) 9.

140 Švankmajer in *Les Chimères des Švankmajer* (dir. Bertrand Schmitt and Michel Leclerc, 2001) on BFI DVD release of *Jan Švankmajer: The Complete Short Films*, 2007.

141 Švankmajer in *Les Chimères*.

142 Roger Cardinal similarly observes that Švankmajer's films turn attention strongly (at least initially) to the material rather than to the interpretative: he notes that the films often have a 'tactile, perhaps even a visceral, impact which inhibits conceptual reference' (in 'Thinking Through Things: The Presence of Objects in the Early Films of Jan Švankmajer', *The Cinema of Jan Švankmajer: Dark Alchemy*, 2nd edn, ed. Peter Hames [London: Wallflower, 2008] 76–78).

143 In his introduction to *Surovost života a cynismus fantasie*, qtd. in Hames, 'The Film Experiment' 34.

Chapter 4

Genre and the Hybrid Object in Late Buñuel

Introduction

This chapter returns to western Europe to examine its approach to cinematic modernism in the 1960s and 70s. However, it is not just any modernist director whose work will be studied: Luis Buñuel is a special case in the cinema of this period. The challenge his films made to established cinematic conventions was not primarily on a stylistic level, as was the case with the French New Wave directors. Buñuel's late work posed a challenge to mainstream cinema's very definition of reality, and in this sense was similar in spirit to his earliest work with the surrealists; however, coming at the end of a long career as a director of mainstream narrative sound cinema, these late films were the work of a director much more familiar with both the conventions of the medium and how most effectively to break them.

During the middle part of his career in the 1940s and 50s, Buñuel left Europe for Mexico where he made more popular narrative films: these have been commonly characterised as '*películas alimenticias*' ('bread-and-butter films') through which the director earned his living but did not express his artistic vision. Linda Williams considers these Mexican films as a mere stepping stone to the authorial freedom of Buñuel's later career back in France: it was only then that he was able to return to 'Surrealism proper', or in other words, the more ambitious sort of films he had made as a novice director.[1] It is tempting, then, to read Buñuel's career as following the arc of cinema's own historic development, from the short experimental films that could still be made at the end of the silent period, to the popular narratives governed by established conventions of the 1940s and 50s, and finally a return to more challenging films that questioned those established conventions in the 1960s and 70s. The distinction is not so simple, however. Williams' view of Buñuel's Mexican films has been subject to more recent revision by authors such as Charles Tesson and Peter William Evans, who believe that Buñuel was still able to express his personal vision and sense of connection to surrealism even in popular films.[2] Moreover, I will argue that Buñuel's late work in fact benefited from his experience with popular film-making. His late films give an initial impression of corresponding to familiar genres such as romance, society drama or psychological thriller, formats that he had mastered during the middle part of his career. It was less necessary in the 1960s and 70s than in other periods of film history to use popular genres in order to lure audiences into seeing more challenging films, but Buñuel's strategy was nonetheless a canny one. Familiar genre formats did more than create the initial appeal for a broader audience; later in the film, when Buñuel introduced elements that broke with the genre's conventions, all audience members were more likely to question what they were being shown rather than simply accepting or dismissing it as the director's artistic flourish.

As explained in the introductory chapter, according to Linda Williams, the surrealists, and more specifically Buñuel, used film to reproduce the figures of the unconscious rather than its content; this resulted in an imitation of the effect of unconscious intervention through 'the disruption of one level of discourse by another'.[3] Williams locates this disruption of diegetic reality in the figures of metaphor and metonymy; she explains the relevance of metaphor and metonymy to the unconscious through Lacan's psychoanalysis of language acquisition in early life, which he based on a reinterpretation of Freud.[4] I propose to take Williams' notion of the disruption of one level of discourse by another, but locate this disruption within the film's diegesis in the form of the hybrid object.

Marcel Oms has remarked upon the number of genres that Buñuel's films incorporate: 'comédie de moeurs'/'comedy of manners', 'drame mondain'/'society drama', 'mélodrame réligieux'/'religious melodrama', 'pamphlet politique'/'political pamphlet', 'vaudeville militaire'/'military vaudeville' and 'thriller' all feature in *Le Charme discret de la bourgeoisie/ The Discreet Charm of the Bourgeoisie*, for example.[5] Williams noted a proliferation of familiar genres in Buñuel's work as early as *L'Âge d'or*, and explained these genres as creating a semblance of reality that was then disrupted, allowing the surrealist effect to emerge from the gaps in the discourse; the familiar genres that initially served to lure the audience into engaging with the film ultimately involved them in assimilating the components of the previous reality into a new one when the initial genre was destabilised by the introduction of another.[6] I believe that objects are crucial in establishing the diegetic reality of a genre film. Conversely, objects' role in the narrative is both justified and closely defined by genre. As a result, if genre switches during the course of a film, objects are likely to be one of the first places where the change will manifest itself. Alterations in genre of the type practiced by Buñuel in his late work will thus create hybrid objects. The significance of the hybrid object, as it participates in a continual reorientation of the film's genre-based definition of reality, is that it reveals that the idea of a logical meaning and rational motivation for an object's presence in a film is as arbitrary as any genre's definition of realism.

All three of the films that will be studied in this chapter problematise popular narrative cinema's claims to realism. They do so by initially appearing to conform to a given genre's definition of realism, only to reveal the arbitrariness of this definition by switching to another genre with a quite different version of realism. However, not all of the films will contain as many genres as Oms discovered in *Le Charme discret de la bourgeoisie*. Williams made what she acknowledged to be a rough yet useful division of Buñuel's work into the 'psychological' and the 'anthropological'.[7] *Un Chien andalou* is the original example of the first category of film: Williams also sees *Belle de Jour* and *Cet obscur objet du désir/That Obscure Object of Desire* as falling into this category of 'psychological' films.[8] *Le Charme discret de la bourgeoisie* corresponds to the 'anthropological' tendency that originated with *L'Âge d'or*.[9] I have found that while both types of film involve hybrid objects as a source of instability, the latter group tends to create hybridity through switches in genre while the former does so by gradually leading the audience to accept the idea that the film's objective reality is being infiltrated by a character's subjectivity. While genre switching thus creates hybridity by pointing to new object meanings derived from surroundings, films that introduce subjectivity force the audience to switch between objective/narrative and subjective/symbolic understandings of the object in order to continue to make sense of the film's reality. In this way, the hybrid object again shows the audience the potential flexibility in a film's definition of what is real: when objects are introduced that violate that definition of reality, in order to assimilate those objects within an understandable structure, the audience is willing to radically expand their definition of what constitutes realism in film.

Past studies of Buñuel, most notably those by Evans, have tended to attempt an exhaustive interpretation of objects in his work by means of psychoanalysis. Williams also takes a psychoanalytic approach, but because her work is informed by Lacan, the ultimate resistance of the object to interpretation becomes a psychoanalytic principle in itself, reflecting the fact that it is impossible for the subject to attain the fulfilment of his or her desires.[10] Buñuel was drawn to Freudian psychoanalysis because it invited one to engage with objects in a thoughtful way, asking such relevant questions as why one object was present instead of another.[11] At the same time, he mistrusted psychoanalysis for the same reason that he was suspicious of the Church: because each claimed to have all the answers.[12] Tesson says that Buñuel's own refusal to explain his films locates responsibility for the film's meaning neither totally with the director nor totally with the audience.[13] Buñuel himself does not have one correct interpretation of his films in mind, an interpretation that he smugly hides from the audience, making the objects more or less impossible to interpret; nor, however, are objects in his films 'open symbols' that can be interpreted in any way the individual audience member may choose.[14] The real meaning of objects in Buñuel's films lies somewhere in between: both Tesson and Williams stress the importance of understanding objects in Buñuel in relation to every appearance that they make in the film.[15] This is so because, according to Tesson, meaning may be 'déplacé par rapport à son objet'/'separated from its object' and equally, an object in the context of one appearance may contain additional meanings that go beyond that immediate context, leaving what Tesson calls a 'remainder' of meaning that will only become clear in light of the object's collective appearances throughout the film.[16]

The later films of Buñuel's career that will be the subject of this chapter are *Belle de Jour* (1967), *Le Charme discret de la bourgeoisie* (1972) and *Cet obscur objet du désir* (1977).[17] *Le Charme discret* will be discussed first, in terms of the way in which objects function in a generically hybrid film. The chapter will then move on to a discussion of *Belle de Jour* and *Cet obscur objet* to examine the role of objects in the intrusion of the irrational in films which, like *Le Charme discret*, also initially appear to conform to classical narrative genres and their conventions. *Belle de Jour* and *Cet obscur objet* deserve to be grouped together not only for their relative generic uniformity in comparison with *Le Charme discret*. In addition to their focus on psychology, the feminine is a particularly crucial dimension to both of these films, and will be of special interest insofar as it may represent another disruptive force that will multiply the possible meaning of objects in these two films. The analysis of objects will not attempt a total explanation in the manner of psychoanalysis; although it will take other scholars' psychoanalytic readings into account, this will be in an overall spirit of exploration of possible meanings rather than to identify the most correct interpretation. The basis of this exploration will always remain the object and its role in the context of the film's own shifting diegetic reality.

Generic hybridity and subjectivity in the 1930s and 60s

The previous two chapters involved some consideration of the way in which a film's genre (or genres, in the case of hybrid films) influenced objects' meaning, which it is useful to recall here. In the early 1930s, Buñuel was of course a contemporary of René Clair. When he made *À Nous la liberté*, Clair was working at a privileged moment in film history, as explained in the earlier chapter. The psychologically motivated narrative that would become the standard model of classical film-making had not yet solidified into an institution, and so early sound film-makers still had a large degree of freedom to experiment. *À Nous la liberté* was hybrid as a result of these historical circumstances and Clair's own approach to the medium: the sets were theatrical, expressive and imposing, while the acting style, in keeping with its recent heritage of theatre and silent film, tended to be performative and cartoon-like; at the same time, the director was aware of his medium, and exploited the close-up as well as the extreme long shot for effect. The film moved from romance to chase film to political commentary, and shuttled between light comedy and ominous satire. The hybrid space within which objects operated translated itself into the way in which they signified, giving them a wide range of narrative, thematic and comic roles.

Shortly before Clair made *À Nous la liberté*, Buñuel also made a film with a hybrid generic identity: *L'Âge d'or*.[18] *Un Chien andalou* had been received, to the director's frustration, as an avant-garde film that one need not attempt to understand.[19] Buñuel therefore created his next film based on diverse yet related segments that each embodied one or more familiar genres (documentary, gangster film, historical film, romance, literary adaptation): his aim was to lure the audience into engaging with his revolutionary film as they would with any other film, at least initially.[20] Of the films to be discussed in this chapter, only *Le Charme discret* is comparable to *L'Âge d'or* in terms of the variety of genres it includes. There is a further, more unusual similarity between the two films, however: the characters in *Le Charme discret* are similar to those in *L'Âge d'or* as well as to those in Clair's *À Nous la liberté* in that they have only limited psychological motivation, and very rarely reflect on the consequences of their actions. The generic hybridity and limited characterisation of *Le Charme discret* may be interpreted in the context of modernist cinema's resistance to the rules of psychological narrative that had been firmly established since the 1940s and 50s; however, as Buñuel's career stretched back to the silent era, these characteristics in his late work should also be considered in terms of their connection to his earliest films.

The Czech New Wave directors' approach to objects is varied by virtue of the number of directors in the group, but in the last chapter three general categories of approach were discerned, all of which highlighted at least the possibility of multiple meaning held in a single object. There was what may be termed the realist tendency, adopted by the directors most influenced by documentary and, to a lesser degree, the conventions of classical narrative cinema. Miloš Forman, Ivan Passer and Jiří Menzel would occasionally allow objects in their films to speak for themselves before the prosaic meaning or diegetic metaphor represented by the object was explained; their films also tend to emphasise the way in which a single object may be interpreted in different ways by different people. A second tendency was to allow slightly more fantastic or unrealistic elements to intervene in the film, so that objects might take on a duality or even a mystery in their meaning. The meaning of objects within the diegesis was only partially explained in the case of a fantastic film, or suggested a social significance which was very real but which the characters might deny. The two examples of this approach were *Valerie* and *The Party*. Finally, the films of Jan Švankmajer and Věra Chytilová exemplified the tendency to exclude any relevant verbal explanation of the objects present, emphasising either the mysterious power of the object or opening it up to broader possibilities of interpretation.

Buñuel's own approach exemplifies, at times, all three of these different approaches to the object. Buñuel may be regarded as participating in a similar era of cinematic experiment to the Czech New Wave, but unlike the work of Švankmajer and Chytilová, his films give the disingenuous impression of not being specially experimental or innovative: self-conscious stylistic touches are either rare or subtly incorporated, their visual slickness once again drawing the viewer into the film unawares.[21] His films thus have the popular and accessible touch that initially seems more comparable to Menzel than to Chytilová; it is nonetheless absurd to compare Buñuel to the first group of Czech directors because their documentary leanings are clearly foreign to the polished artificiality of the mise-en-scène of Buñuel's late work.[22] As Buñuel's late films set the audience up to focus on narrative, they cannot be compared to the second group of Czech films in which social commentary or fantasy are foregrounded from the beginning; while Buñuel's films may be read as commenting on bourgeois existence, such interpretation does not lead to particularly meaningful conclusions. Although the illogical regularly appears, it comes as an intrusion rather than a dimension the audience is prepared to accept from the beginning. Buñuel thus does not simply escape narrative conventions, but highlights them in the course of his film by conforming to the rules some of the time only to flout them later on; moreover, by making such boundary breaking part of his film, Buñuel may lead viewers to realise, as they attempt to distinguish between what may be accepted as reality and what may not, that even familiar classical narrative and its genres represent an unrealistic fantasy.[23]

Objects in Buñuel's films thus appear at first to take their place in what the audience has been conditioned to think of as a conventionally realistic diegesis, realism covering the ridiculously broad spectrum of Menzel, Forman and Passer's documentary-influenced film-making on the one hand and the artificiality of classical narration and genres on the other.

Buñuel then introduces elements (objects, but also characters, events and dialogue) that break the bounds of what is likely or possible in classical narration; these elements never completely colonise the film, however. Ultimately, the meaning of objects in Buñuel is at least as broad and mysterious as that of objects in Švankmajer or Chytilová, yet Buñuel's films always maintain the audience's safety net of familiar narrative. A familiar narrative framework allows the audience to engage with the film and attempt to understand it, even if there are elements in the film that cannot be explained within classical narrative conventions of logic and verisimilitude. In order to assimilate such objects, audiences will ultimately be forced to confront the possibility of dream, subjectivity or the impossible intruding into what initially seemed a familiar and rational diegesis. In this way Buñuel continues to exploit a method that he developed as early as *L'Âge d'or*.

Finally, it is useful to return to Buñuel's first film in order to shed further light on the way in which objects work in some of his final films. As mentioned, *L'Âge d'or* has been interpreted as a pseudo return to conventions in order to lead audiences to engage differently with his films than they did with *Un Chien andalou*.[24] Although Buñuel did not continue to allow impossible events to dominate in his films, the aesthetic methods that he used in his first film to portray the functioning of the unconscious are still relevant to his later work; this is especially the case for *Belle de Jour* and *Cet obscur objet* as films that are arguably more similar to *Un Chien andalou* than *L'Âge d'or*, in that they too explore the individual unconscious, albeit within a narrative framework that is easier for the audience to assimilate.[25] In *Un Chien andalou*, objects were co-opted to the overriding surrealist objective of demonstrating the functioning of the unconscious: Williams has noted that associations were made between objects both within and outside the diegesis based on the repetition of round shapes.[26] Although Buñuel stopped making such extra-diegetic associations in his later work, he continued to make use of repetition: rather than a shape-based repetition, however, it tends instead to be a type of object that is repeated. Various types of containers make multiple appearances in both *Belle de Jour* and *Cet obscur objet*: the former features a number of different kinds of box, while in the latter film it is bags that recur. These containers constitute particularly intriguing objects, both physically and semiotically. They take on importance because they are stylistically emphasised; however, the reason why they are so important may never be made clear, either by preventing the audience from seeing inside the container, or by revealing the contents to be just as mysterious as the container itself.

Le Charme discret de la bourgeoisie

A film is not a dream, and cannot be effectively interpreted as such. For this reason, a purely symbolic reading of any of Buñuel's films will not take one very far. In the director's later films, attempts at interpreting objects and situations symbolically lead to ridiculously simplistic conclusions, and this is the case in *Le Charme discret* as much as in either of the other two films examined here. While scenes such as the one where the main characters walk along a country road (a scene that occurs three times at roughly symmetrical points in the narrative, moreover), or actual dream sequences seem to encourage moving beyond a denotative reading, it is important not to fall into the trap of pursuing narrow interpretations.

This is not to say that *Le Charme discret* as a whole should be taken only as a narrative; on the contrary, Buñuel does much more than simply tell a story in this film. The film's underlying message is not about class politics, however, as one might think; rather, it consists of a much broader surrealist questioning of the definition of reality in cinema, which may cause the audience to examine the criteria by which they judge the realism of the situations presented in a film. In *Le Charme discret*, Buñuel does this by mixing genres. Because each type of film has its own set of conventional elements (characters, props, scenarios, etc.), a film that makes sudden switches from one genre to another or combines genres will tend to defamiliarise the conventions that are normally accepted so readily as defining realism in the context of any single genre. Such defamiliarisation of genres also alters the role that familiar objects might normally play within that genre, often resulting in comedy. The following three examples will demonstrate the way in which two or more genres combine in individual sequences in *Le Charme discret* such that the artificiality of these genres' conventions of realism is highlighted. The way in which the characters interact with objects will be of particular interest, as objects' meaning will noticeably shift in relation to genre.

Audience expectations of a dignified society drama are destabilised from the very first sequence: guests, all but the youngest seeming entirely affable and genteel, arrive at the Sénéchals' large secluded house in anticipation of a dinner party, only to find that nothing is prepared for them. Alice Sénéchal conforms perfectly to polite behaviour, greeting them calmly and graciously as though she has not immediately realised that they have come for dinner on the wrong day: their conventional interaction begins to appear ridiculous in the context of a disruption to the habitual smoothness with which their leisured lives must typically run. As the genre begins to slide away from drama towards comedy by means of a simple yet unusual misunderstanding, Florence, the guest who from the beginning did not quite conform, subtly localises the shift in an object. While the other guests and Alice are still struggling to understand how the misunderstanding occurred and what should be done, a servant attempts to take the bouquet of flowers that had been brought as a hostess gift. Florence contributes to the switch from drama to comedy as she indignantly snatches the flowers back from the servant, a gesture that crudely highlights their symbolism as a material exchange of favours between friends, and shatters their façade as a thoughtful gift.

A later scene in a tea room once again upsets the expectation that life, in its minor but important details, should run smoothly for the bourgeoisie, especially in a film. Although the waiter takes the women's orders in detail, he keeps coming back to tell them that the establishment has run out of the requested items. This time the characters have an appropriate reaction of disbelief and outrage, as although it may be understandable for a tea room to run out of one or two items, it is absurd for it to run out of everything except water. The waiter's explanation that there has been an 'affluence extraordinaire'/'unusually high number of customers' ceases to be acceptable, and there is a sense that everyday expectations (specifically, that if one has money to spend, there will be something to buy) are undermined by taking the premise of a believable situation and pushing it to extreme. Buñuel leads the audience to examine the question, at what point does a situation turn from believable to (as Alice puts it) 'invraisemblable'/'incredible'? This question is significantly localised in the absent drinks as verbal objects.

Moreover, in the tea room scene the society drama is undermined not only by humorous obstacles to bourgeois pastimes: the scene also involves a more radical switch in genre through the insertion of a ghost story told by a lieutenant. Although his story is entirely acceptable according to the conventions of gothic horror film, these conventions are denaturalised by introducing the story in the middle of a scene that is not of that genre. The real shift in genre in this scene, then, is between the society drama and the horror film, and the tea room's absent drinks serve to frame the shift from one genre to the other and back again: just before the lieutenant introduces himself, the waiter comes to tell the women that there is no tea, and as the story ends, the waiter returns to announce that there is no coffee, milk or even herbal tea left. In contrast with their reaction to the waiter's words, the women respond graciously when the lieutenant introduces himself and asks to sit with them. When he requests permission to tell them about his childhood, Alice reacts with some surprise, but he is allowed to continue. The women's reactions again lead the audience to consider the distinction between believable and unbelievable events in the context of a film's genre, as does the lieutenant's story that follows.

Taken on its own, the lieutenant's story is, as mentioned, conventional in the gothic horror genre, even ostentatiously so: the sombre old mansion, the stern father figure, the austere childhood, ghosts with white and expressionless faces, tales of romantic intrigue and murder, and a storm to accompany the story's final climax. The story is denaturalised, however, when the genre shifts back to the society drama/comedy again. The outrageousness of the events of the ghost story itself, as well as the fact that the lieutenant feels compelled to tell it to strangers, lead the audience to expect it to be a decisive episode in his life. His mother's ghost appears to him and instructs him to poison his father to avenge the murder of his real father and mother; the boy does so, and his adoptive father dies. When the film shifts back to the tea room, however, the lieutenant ends his story simply by saying that after this event he immediately went on to military school 'où une vie passionnante [l]'attendait'/'where a life of excitement awaited [him]'. This is a statement in conflict with his melancholy demeanour (on which Alice and Simone had commented earlier in the scene before he joined them). His words imply, moreover, that the extraordinary episode had no real effect on his life. This is at odds not only with expectations in everyday life, where psychology has led us to believe that the events of one's childhood have a formative effect; in cinema, too, conventional narrative films never include gratuitous stories that both depart from generic expectations and do nothing to advance the plot.

There is another unusual aspect to the lieutenant's story: although his concluding words suggest that the events he recounted had no repercussions in his life, in the film as a whole his story has some significance, as it is one that returns twice in metamorphosed form. Through shifts in genre, the film foregrounds cinema's conventional insistence on the importance of such stories. Their repetition again results in intrusive shifts in genre, which draw attention to the artificiality of all genre conventions. First, there is the example of the gardener who murdered the bishop's parents. Before the murders, this gardener had acted as a supplementary father figure to the bishop, instilling in him a love of gardening and teaching him the necessary skills. When an unbelievable coincidence leads the adult bishop to meet the gardener and to discover that he was the murderer, like the lieutenant the bishop does not hesitate to take violent revenge on his parents' killer.[27] The second allusion to the lieutenant's story comes in the form of another soldier who feels compelled to share personal experiences with others. At the Sénéchals' dinner party, a young member of the cavalry recounts a dream to a rapt audience of fellow guests. Although no murders take place in the dream, it is revealed that all of its characters are in the land of the dead. The dream's events also highlight the Oedipal dimension present in the other two stories (which, moreover, frame this story in the film's sequence) by blurring the boundaries between romantic and filial relationships. After meeting two men close to his own age (both of whom are never seen again after they enter a shop), the soldier meets a woman, again of similar age to himself, and their conversation suggests that she was his girlfriend. When she too disappears however, he calls for her disconsolately as 'Mère!'/'Mother!', and as the soldier finishes verbally recounting his dream to the guests at the dinner party, he says that he continued to look for his mother but could not find her.

All three of these Oedipal episodes in the film result in shifts in genre, and two of them clearly hinge on objects. I explained above that the lieutenant's original story was framed by references to the drinks that the women were unable to obtain in the tea room. There is an additional shift in genre within the space of the story, again localised in a drink: the glass of milk that is used to poison the lieutenant's father evokes the Hitchcock thriller *Suspicion* (1941), and thus may even cast doubt on the truth of the lieutenant's story, implying that it may have been a boyhood fantasy. This conflicts with the gothic horror, in which supernatural events are accepted as realistic within the genre. The example of the bishop's chance discovery of his parents' killer highlights the unbelievable coincidences characteristic of popular films; the greater surprise, however, comes with the shift in genre, for which an object is responsible. The gardener confesses his sin of murder, but it is the photograph at his bedside that confirms beyond a doubt that it was the bishop's parents that he killed. The photograph of a happier time, the bishop in a family portrait that includes the gardener, determines a shift in the bishop's own role from confessor/gardener to executioner/murderer, and the shift from what Oms would term 'religious melodrama' to 'thriller'.

The drinks in which genre shifts were localised in the tea room scene and the original lieutenant's story are part of a larger trend in this film in which the fetishisation of items of food and drink and their consumption is the hallmark of bourgeois sophistication. More than one scholar has interpreted the fact that the characters in the film are never able to enjoy a meal together as a metaphor for the way in which an excessively codified lifestyle actually threatens the ability to fulfil basic human requirements such as eating, drinking and even sex.[28] More intriguing than this interpretation, however, is the film's act of pointing to the multiple meanings attached to a single food item or beverage, and using this destabilisation of meaning to foreshadow and introduce the film's final elaborate shifts in genre.

Early in the film, Thévenot demonstrates the correct way to prepare a martini and has Rafael's chauffeur summoned to unwittingly demonstrate the incorrect way of consuming the drink. This is more than just an illustration of a lack of sophistication among the working classes and a dissimulating cruelty in bourgeois circles, however. Thévenot is certainly shown to be pompous and unkind, and the chauffeur in fact appears more polite than coarse in his manners. The frivolousness of knowing the correct way to prepare and drink a martini had, moreover, been suggested by Thévenot's unselfconscious admission that he learnt this skill from a women's magazine. Another surprise is that while Alice comes to the defence of the chauffeur's manners, Rafael, who initially seemed reluctant to allow Thévenot's demonstration, seems to agree with Thévenot's contempt for the chauffeur's simplicity; in the same breath, Rafael paradoxically professes himself to be 'aucun réactionnaire'/'no reactionary'. Rafael and Thévenot's calm superiority disappears, however, when the genre shifts to that of a political thriller. Incorrectly suspecting that their hosts are absent because a police raid is about to take place, the guests scurry outside to the car where they will rely on the chauffeur to make their escape.

The proletariat take their revenge in Rafael's dream near the end of the film. Once again, the friends have gathered for a dinner party, and the conversation revolves even more than usual around food. Alice talks almost exclusively of her 'gigot'/'leg of lamb' and her 'potage aux herbes du jardin'/'soup with garden herbs'. The camera reinforces the obsession by following the servant as she brings out the tureen, and following Alice to the kitchen where she ensures that the leg of lamb is properly cooked and presented. It is notable, too, that despite having two servants, Alice is personally involved more than usual with the meal: as well as presiding over the preparation of the lamb, she has told her guests that she made the soup herself. Moreover, when the leg of lamb is served, Sénéchal pedantically demonstrates the correct way to carve it, and even asks for Thévenot's corroboration, all of which recalls the earlier episode of the martini. Florence's attempt at a high-flown astrological analysis of Rafael's character is interrupted by the hosts' offers of food to the guests and by observations on its preparation, by Thévenot's promise to have them taste his special caviar next time they visit him, and by Simone confessing her pedestrian taste for tinned beans. The anodyne, inconsequential nature of these food items is placed in even starker perspective by a change in genre from society drama to action movie, as gangsters break into the house and summarily shoot down all the friends, except for Rafael who has slipped under the table. Ironically, given the care taken over the cooking and serving of the lamb, Rafael gives away his hiding place because he cannot resist reaching up to take a slice of meat (figure 4.1), which he eats with his hands. This object in turn localises the sequence's final shift in genre; as the scene changes and shows Rafael waking up in bed, the genre of the earlier sequence shifts retroactively from society drama and action film to dream narrative. However, Rafael's next

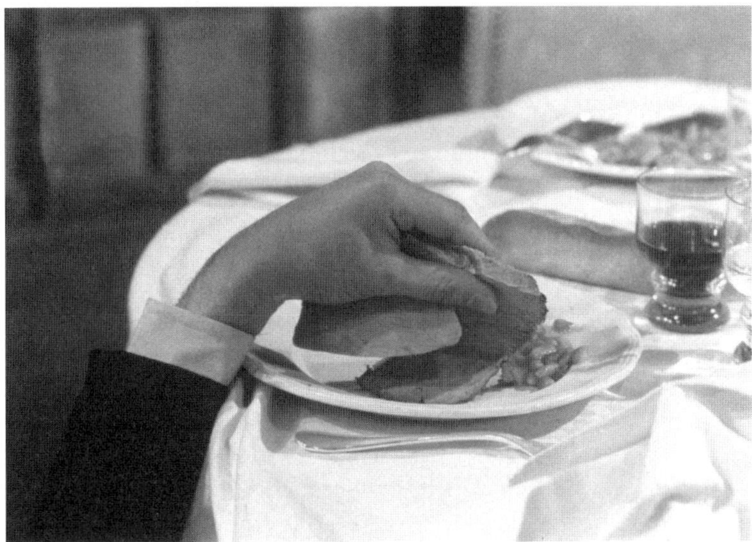

Figure 4.1: Rafael reaches up for a slice of lamb while hiding from gangsters in *Le Charme discret de la bourgeoisie.*

action disrupts any attempts that the audience might make, in retrospect, at interpreting the food items in the dream symbolically: Rafael's reaction to his dream is not distress but hunger, and he goes to the kitchen where he avidly resumes the solitary meal that was interrupted by the violent conclusion of his dream.

The film's final sequence thus undermines the audience's assumptions about the distinction between dreams and reality in film. Focusing as it did on the familiar group of friends and their perpetual attempts to share a meal together, much of the dream corresponded broadly to what the film had so far set up as reality; it was only when the gangsters broke in and shot the main characters that the audience might have begun to suspect that the events were not real. At the same time, the film had also prepared the audience to accept such sudden shifts in genre, and as the film was nearing its end, it was possible that the group of friends might meet such a demise. Indeed, given that their previous lunch party had been interrupted by a police raid (most likely related to the men's drug trafficking), it was not implausible that outlaws might also pay a visit.

In *Le Charme Discret*, as in *L'Âge d'or*, the viewer is encouraged, in the first instance, to engage with the film's illusion of reality: this is achieved by initially establishing the film within the conventions of a familiar genre. The objects that appear are understood in the context of that genre: the flowers as a hostess gift, for example, or the rituals of food preparation as a sign of bourgeois sophistication. When the genre shifts, however, the audience realises that an object has no one 'natural' meaning, but that its significance is determined by one's perspective on reality. *Le Charme Discret* does more than pass moral judgement on the emptiness of bourgeois pretension surrounding objects: it draws attention to the very process by which object meaning is determined. Through changes in genre, the same objects switch from outwardly signalling gentility to revealing the selfishness and cruelty that lie just below the surface. Again, the fact that façades exist is not as significant as the way in which shifts in conventions of meaning can allow the same objects to signal entirely different things.

Belle de Jour

As in *Le Charme discret*, Buñuel uses familiar genres to lead viewers to engage with *Belle de Jour* as they would with any narrative film, at least initially. The genres used in this film are chiefly limited to three, however. Within the space of its first sequence, what at first appears to be another society drama or sophisticated romance reveals itself to be a misleadingly tame introduction to an erotic film, which, at the sequence's end, is shown to be taking place entirely in the mind of the film's protagonist, Séverine. These three genres (society drama, erotic film and fantasy/dream) may not seem to be a particularly revolutionary combination: that a respectable character should have taboo sexual fantasies, and perhaps even act on them, only serves to increase a film's degree of titillation, in a manner comparable to the cliché of erotic film, in which there is an actualisation of the sexual potential in situations that bring together people of different backgrounds, such as servant and master, or leisured lady and repairman. Indeed, *Belle de Jour* itself brings up this very scenario, its first scene showing Séverine's coldness towards her husband being punished by sexual attention from her servants. Later, the film even includes a shot cast as a flashback from Séverine's childhood, in which she is caressed by a labourer in her home. This image in particular has served as a strong source of motivation to psychoanalyse Séverine, leading to the believable yet disappointingly simplistic conclusion that because of this episode of childhood abuse, the character suffers from frigidity towards men of her own class and, based on the precedent of the repairman, is perversely driven to seek out men who are different from her, an urge that may or may not ultimately 'cure' her.[29] Much more interesting than taking *Belle de Jour* as a psychoanalytic case study is to take it as a film and examine the manner in which Buñuel leads the audience into a familiar engagement with the film, only to introduce questions that become increasingly difficult to answer as to the status of any one scene: society drama, erotic film or dream?

This last question is one to which a number of scholars have given thoughtful consideration, and cinematically it is a much more worthwhile question to ask, as it leads to an examination of the manner in which genres are signalled. The audience quickly learns to become suspicious of cues that seem to indicate sophisticated romance, as they see how quickly a sequence can become frankly erotic and how either of these scenarios may in retrospect be cast as a dream. Ultimately, the realism of all of these genres is brought into question, as the audience witnesses how easily both the society drama and erotic sequence may turn out to be either dream or reality: they are realistic in terms of their conformity to generic expectations, but the artificiality of these genres also allows them to readily fit the description of a dream. Of course, when the final dream cue is given in the first sequence (the intrusion of an unexpected question into the dream space and a new image of Séverine deep in thought as she sits in bed), the supposedly real space of Séverine's waking life into which the film then moves is just as artificial as the film's opening shots in terms of the relationship between Séverine and her husband, and the perfection of their appearance and surroundings.[30]

The viewer's experience of a film, then, is similar to that of a dream, in that the tendency is to initially accept whatever is shown as reality, in spite of so many indications to the contrary. In a very short space of time, Buñuel succeeds in pointing to the artificiality of all three types of narrative film featured in *Belle de Jour*, while still allowing the viewer to use these genres as orientation points in the (at times) disorienting space of the film. Ultimately, the film will include scenes where the boundary between Séverine's fantasy and reality is never made clear.[31] Indeed, several scholars have suggested that it is possible to consider almost the entire film as Séverine's fantasy,[32] just as all but the last scene of *Le Charme discret* may be understood as the dream of Rafael, the ambassador of an imaginary republic.[33] However, because it is usually possible to assume that certain parts of the film are Séverine's reality and certain parts are her fantasy, the audience will maintain their engagement with the film, and be subtly led into questioning the boundary between the two only when it becomes absolutely necessary: namely, at the very end of the film when a sequence that appears to be part of Séverine's reality involves an impossible point-of-view shot through the window onto the Paris street, and sounds from her fantasies invade what appears to be the space of her waking reality.

Because the most enigmatic part of *Belle de Jour* seems to be the distinction between fantasy and reality, the temptation is to move away from the three main genres enumerated at the beginning. In terms of objects, however, Buñuel's use of genres is of great interest, because it helps to describe the shifts in meaning that objects in this film undergo. To return to the film's opening sequence, for example, the significance of the items surrounding Séverine and Pierre is modulated by switches in genre. When the sequence seems to correspond to a classic romantic drama, items included in the shot take on a clear signifying role: the carriage is a charming, old-fashioned means of conveyance that passes through the sombre yet picturesque autumn landscape with which it is in harmony; the whips held by the coachmen are neutral means of spurring on the horses, and the coachmen's old-fashioned costumes indicative of the luxury enjoyed by the carriage's occupants; Séverine's own stylish yet conservative clothes are signs of her privileged lifestyle. With the couple's disagreement, however, the tone of the scene changes, and in the ensuing shots the same objects correspondingly alter their significance: as Séverine resists leaving the coach, it becomes a space of safety set against the unknown torments that her husband and servants have planned for her in the surrounding forest; as they drag her through the forest and fields, her clothing now signals her degradation, as a stocking falls down, or her husband rips her blouse to expose her back; similarly, as the coachmen begin the torture and sexual assault, their whips become sadistic accessories and their costumes indicators of perverse role play rather than servility. Finally, when the scene ends with Pierre's question ('À quoi penses-tu?'/'What are you thinking about?') and Séverine describes only the anodyne beginning of the dream, the fact that Pierre is familiar with the dream as being of 'le landau'/'the coach' points to the provocative double-meaning of objects within the preceding scene: his indulgent reaction implies that he is only aware of the romantic meaning of the coach, but the audience is familiar with it as the turning point in the dream, where the situation moves from romance and gentility to perversion and violence.

As discussed in the introduction to this chapter, the way in which objects signify in Buñuel may be compared to the three different varieties of objects distinguished in the films of the Czech New Wave film-makers. Here, it is useful to take one of the most famous examples of objects in Buñuel, the mysterious box in *Belle de Jour*, to show even more clearly how an object may shuttle from one meaning to another within not just a single sequence but a single shot.

The audience never sees what is inside the box that the Asian client brings to the brothel, and the only clues as to what it contains are the high-pitched buzzing noise that issues from the box when it is opened, and the girls' reactions to whatever is making that noise. When the man displays the contents of the box to Mathilde, one of Séverine's colleagues, she stares for moment before declaring, almost angrily, 'Non merci, Monsieur! Pas moi!'/'No, thank you Sir! Not me!'. Similarly, when Séverine first looks inside the box, her expression turns from alarm to discontent (figure 4.2): she is evidently not convinced by the man's hurried attempts to reassure her with, 'Non, pas peur!'/'No, no fear!', the only French words he seems to know. When the maid enters the room after the Asian man has left, she discovers a bloodstained towel, the lamp overturned and Séverine lying prostrate. These signs of violence, and the maid's words of sympathy suggest that there was indeed something to be feared in the box, yet Séverine raises her head and dismisses the maid's understanding of the situation.

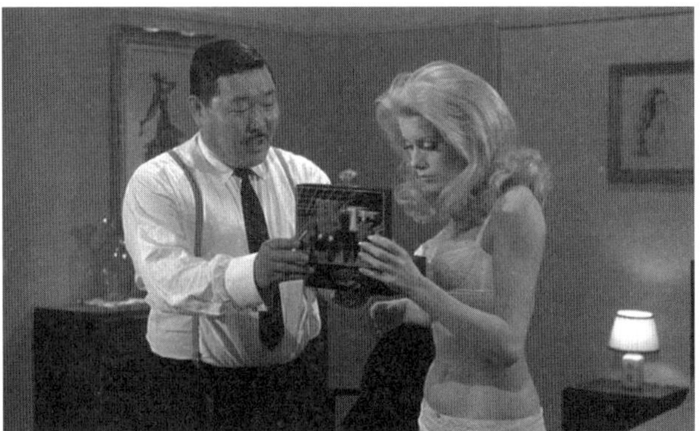

Figure 4.2: Séverine looks inside her client's mysterious box in *Belle de Jour.*

Séverine's expression of 'drowsy content' makes this 'one of her most erotic sequences',[34] and shows that the dominant effect of the man and his box was intense pleasure.

Before examining some reactions that audiences and scholars have had to the box, it is of interest to consider the object as a possible catalyst for a shift in the film. In the sequence following the one just described, Séverine is approached by an older aristocratic gentleman while she is sitting at a café; he invites her to come to his house to participate in what he refers to mysteriously as a 'ceremony'. It is interesting to compare the ensuing sequence with the lieutenant's story in *Le Charme discret*, as the same actor who played the father in that scene plays the aristocratic necrophile here; moreover, both sequences take place in gloomy manor houses, and both have conventionally gothic tendencies in their use of stormy weather alongside their evocation of death. The presence, in the *Belle de Jour* sequence, of the carriage from Séverine's first fantasy has rightly made scholars suspect that this sequence is also a fantasy. Alberto Farassino says that 'all the other elements [of the sequence] nonetheless signal it as being "real"' except that it stands 'outside of time and space' in the film.[35] Farassino seems to overlook the fact that this scene is introduced by the image of Séverine resting after her encounter with the Asian client. Although her previous fantasies have typically taken place while she is in bed at home, there is no reason why they should not also occur at work. Moreover, her fantasy of the necrophilic ceremony may be seen as responding to the experience she has just had with the Asian client and his strange rituals: in addition to the box and whatever it contains, the client rings a pair of small bells and insists that Séverine leave her brassiere on.[36]

Although the client's box may thus be seen as announcing a switch from erotic reality to gothic fantasy sequence, more interesting is the change that takes place in Séverine herself within the same sequence. As mentioned in the introduction, *Belle de Jour* and *Cet obscur objet* are much more orientated towards psychology than *Le Charme discret*. Although my intention is not to discover a single correct interpretation of the box by means of a psychoanalytic assessment of the film's main character, it is of interest to understand the box in relation to the changes that take place in her; the film's ambiguous shifts between reality and fantasy may be described less as shifts in genre than shifts from the film's more objective account of reality to Séverine's subjective experience of it.

A noticeable change in Séverine takes place when she meets the Asian client, and this occurs even before the box is opened. Until this point, Séverine's habitual facial expression has tended to be serious, melancholy or distant. In a sexual context, whether with her patient husband, fending off the flirtatious Husson, or in reaction to clients at the brothel, she has been timid, uneasy and cold. If she has shown any strong emotion, it has been panic or hostility. Yet suddenly, when she meets the Asian man, she glows with the warmth and confidence of an adult woman, rather than the child she has been until this point.[37] Smiling broadly and completely at ease, she never lowers her gaze. She puts her arm around her client's neck, and takes pleasure in giving and receiving kisses. It seems unlikely that the man himself should be responsible for this change: plain-looking and overweight, he is as unattractive as any of her other clients. Furthermore, just before she meets the Asian man,

Séverine has been forced to watch the sadomasochistic role play of the professor with one of the other prostitutes, something that she finds shocking and (in her words to Madame Anaïs) 'repugnant'. It is the only time that Séverine expresses her disgust towards a sexual act in such a direct manner, and equally the moment at which she appears most obviously troubled by what occurs in the brothel. Yet immediately after this experience she appears relaxed, beaming with pleasure, and accepts the Asian man's peculiar sexual requirements with relative equanimity. After her encounter with him, we see her appear sexually satisfied for the first time in the film (apart from those scenes clearly marked as fantasies).

Séverine's fantasies up to this point in the film have been clearly sadomasochistic, with Séverine herself taking the submissive role of the one being tortured or humiliated. When Anaïs sends her to the professor, who is a masochist, Séverine therefore has difficulty playing the dominant role of 'Madame la Marquise'. When Séverine goes into an adjoining room to observe, through a peephole, the professor being dominated correctly by another prostitute, she is 'confront[ed] [...] with a mirror image of herself' in him.[38] Evans believes that Séverine's 'detachment is temporary': she is driven to watch not only because she is 'curio[us]', but also because the professor is of her own class and yet shares those masochistic desires that bourgeois gentility would seem to forbid.[39] While it is true that Séverine first moves away from the peephole, but is then driven by curiosity to keep watching, she also expresses disgust to Anaïs, as already mentioned, when she has finished watching.

It is certainly possible that Séverine suddenly appears more relaxed when she meets the Asian man because she has come to accept her own sexuality, having seen that her masochistic desires are not foreign to her social status. In this case, looking inside the Asian man's box could duplicate her action in the previous scene when she looked into the adjoining room through a peephole. Andrea Sabbadini has referred to the Asian man's box as a 'fetishistic object'[40] (in a similar category, then, to the professor's sadomasochistic fetish). He notes, however, that a box evokes the female genitals, whereas a fetish normally stands in for the phallus (though it does not necessarily imitate its form).[41] Although it may be going too far to suggest, as Sabbadini does, that the box symbolises a womb and that its contents could then be a baby,[42] the box certainly seems more significant in relation to Séverine than to the Asian man. Although she is initially scared of the contents, just as she was scared of her own sexuality (which she saw acted out before her by the professor), by accepting the box (and accepting herself) she is relieved of her neurosis and able to experience physical pleasure.[43] Séverine's initial mistrust of the box and the pleasure that she ultimately seems to derive from it corresponds, moreover, to the combination of emotions of 'hostility' and 'affection' inherent in the fetish,[44] which Freud highlighted in the example of the Chinese practice of disfiguring women's feet through binding, then 'revering' them as erotic objects.[45] It is interesting, in light of this, that towards the end of the film when Séverine has given up her job at the brothel, she is seen at home in her living room opening a box with shoes inside (figure 4.3). In case the audience misses this detail the first time, the shoebox is emphasised again later in the sequence when a servant comes to take it away; this happens just before a series of shootings in which Séverine's husband nearly dies and her

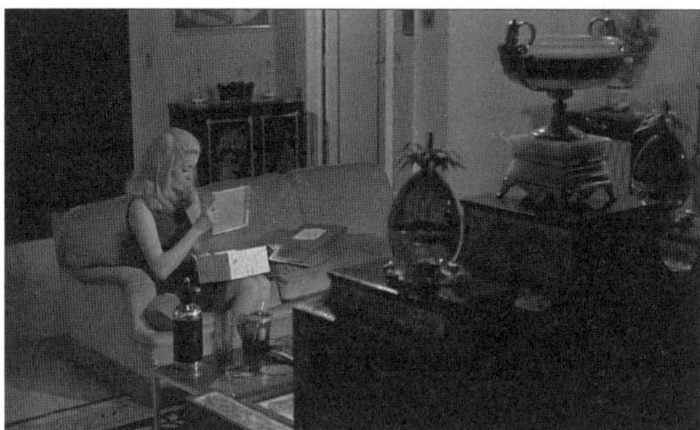

Figure 4.3: Séverine opens a shoebox in *Belle de Jour*.

lover, Marcel, is killed. It is possible that the box is thus again used, this time indirectly, in connection with combined emotions of love and hate at this point in the narrative as Marcel attempts to win Séverine for himself through an act of aggression against the man she loves. Earlier, in the brothel, Marcel took his anger out on a framed image of an odalisque on the wall because Séverine forbid him to hit her; now, having seen a photo of Pierre in Séverine's home, Marcel is able to identify him in the street in order to attack his person.

Although Evans characterises Séverine's reaction to the masochist professor as one of conflicted identification, there is evidence in the film that Séverine is perhaps not being hypocritical when she asks Anaïs, regarding the professor, 'Comment peut-on descendre aussi bas?'/'How can anyone stoop so low?'. Séverine's enjoyment of receiving violent treatment is consistently limited to her fantasies; it is possible that she would not in fact enjoy it in real life, and that witnessing it acted out by others has convinced her of this. When Marcel attempts to punish her for her absence by hitting her with his belt, she is, of course, concerned that he should not mark her face, and one assumes that it is out of pride in her appearance, or because it would be difficult to explain to Pierre how it happened. Yet she gives no sign of wanting to be struck on any other part of her body, and although Marcel can be brusque in his speech, the relationship that she enjoys with him is primarily one of tenderness, differing from that which she shares with her husband mainly in the degree of passion involved. Furthermore, after watching the professor, Séverine's fantasies are markedly less violent. Before, she dreamt of being whipped or of being pelted with mud. After witnessing sadomasochism in real life, the violence in her fantasies immediately becomes more understated: she is thrown out of the duke's house into the rain; she is accidentally wounded by a bullet while she is tied to a tree (but it is not clear whether it is a life-threatening wound, and as she is still conscious, Pierre begins passionately kissing her); in another fantasy she and Husson, smiling in a very natural manner, hide under a table to play a game that involves a broken bottle (though it is not clear how it will be used). Even more significant than the moderation of violence, however, is the change in the language used in Séverine's dreams: her earlier fantasies all involved her being insulted, but after hearing the professor verbally humiliated by another prostitute, the abusive language in Séverine's own fantasies quickly disappears. In this respect, there is a significant contrast between the scene with the professor and the one with the Asian man. The professor's sexual pleasure was dependent to a large degree on language, and he rejected Séverine because she was unable to reprimand and insult him. Her interaction with the Asian man, on the other hand, necessarily excludes virtually all verbal communication, as they do not share a common language. In spite of this, he keeps up a ceaseless flow of words, incomprehensible apart from his insistence that Séverine should have 'no fear' of the object inside the box. The failure of language to explain the box in the context of Séverine's interaction with the Asian man may be representative of an ability that she herself needs to develop, to navigate effectively between the verbal tendencies of the class to which she belongs, and more physical forms of expression that may explain in part her attraction to the lower classes. The lack of a common language that forces Séverine and the Asian man to communicate physically is, in this sense, crucial to their successful sexual encounter.

Of course, a psychoanalytic interpretation of the box is by no means the only possible way of interpreting it; it may be approached on a purely denotative level, can be used to explore one's own imagination and fantasies, or its very resistance to interpretation may be taken as a meaning in itself. The Asian man's box may be read rationally on the plane of realism (a sex toy or fetishistic accessory), on the plane of fantasy (some imaginable or unimaginable device) or on the plane of open symbolism (an object that may stand for many different things, tangible and intangible, both Séverine's specific fantasies and hidden parts of herself). In this way, an object from one scene in Buñuel is able to function simultaneously in ways I discerned in the Czech New Wave's three different approaches to objects. This is because, as explained, *Belle de Jour* may usually be read as occupying three different types of film at once: it is a film that, like the work of Švankmajer and Chytilová, may be understood in many different ways and involves a crucial element of mystery; like *Valerie and her Week of Wonders* and *The Party and the Guests*, it slips into the realm of fantasy; yet most of the time, it also provides the familiar signals of generic narrative cinema's brand of realism, which encourages viewers to engage with the film on all of these levels by first engaging with it as they would with a mainstream film in which objects and events tend to find their rational motivation within the diegesis.

In a sense, scholars have been correct to hesitate in speculating on the contents of the box: uncertainty is inherent in the object and, most importantly, crucial to its function. Thus the box seems not only to defy but forbid any restriction to one correct symbolic interpretation. Laura Martins has suggested that the box and other mystery objects in Buñuel's films are part of the director's strategy through which he targets institutions of power, both political and aesthetic; objects that do not come with a complete explanation alter the way in which viewers engage with the film, leading them to think independently about what they see, rather than accepting the meaning handed down to them by an omnipotent figure of authority (be that a despot or a director).[46] As Tesson points out, however, the Asian man's box in particular 'est devenu le paragon de cet objet dont l'auteur, supposé tout savoir, garde l'entière maîtrise, tel un Dieu rieur se moquant de l'insatiable appétit d'interprétation de ses fidèles sujets'/'has become the paragon of an object which the auteur, who is assumed to know everything, controls completely, like a laughing God mocking his loyal subjects' insatiable appetite for interpretation'.[47] As noted in the introduction to this chapter, Tesson himself does not subscribe to the notion, however popular it may have become, that Buñuel deliberately withholds meaning from his audience. Indeed, when asked what was inside the box, Buñuel said "'I myself have no idea'".[48] He considered it a "'senseless'" question, but as people continued to ask him what was inside, he would usually say, "'Whatever you want there to be'".[49] For this reason, Sabbadini is correct to say that we will 'never know' what is inside the box, yet Martins is also right in saying that Buñuel 'provi[des] the necessary conditions for spectators [...] to search for their own answers, to discover the secrets hidden in the box'.[50] Although there is no one correct answer, then, as to what the box contains, the way in which Buñuel presents this and other mystery objects encourages the audience to explore the many possible meanings that an object may hold. That a film could include such a mystery and yet be so popular[51] proves that audiences have a certain degree of tolerance for objects that are never fully explained.

The Asian man's box, the shoe box and the box room with the peephole are far from the only examples of boxes in this film. Box-like containers of various kinds recur throughout the film, and although they will not reveal the mysterious contents of the first box, they certainly offer some provocative examples of the surprises that a box may contain, and the resonance that these contents may have beyond their purely physical status as objects. There are a number of different containers related to other clients at the brothel, containers that also exist without verbal explanation; indeed, their owners may keep a deliberate degree of silence regarding these containers and their contents. The containers most similar to the Asian man's box are the professor's case and the present that Monsieur Adolphe brings for Mathilde. The professional tools with which the gynaecologist exercises control over his female clients are tangled up in the case with the accessories by which he becomes submissive to women;[52] when he takes on his submissive role, he assumes that his partner will not need an explanation of what he wants. Like Séverine, the professor with his placid exterior would not lead one to guess what he carries inside him (or his case).[53] Monsieur Adolphe's *boîte*[54] is a trick present, and also depends on a lack of verbal clues; when Mathilde asks what is inside, he of course does not tell her, and covers his mouth to hide his smile as she opens it (figure 4.4). Having just expressed a wish that her client would give her a gift such as Séverine's designer dress, Mathilde is instead surprised by the snake-like (or even phallic) springs that pop out of the can, and that need no verbal treatment, only laughter. Séverine's inability to enjoy this type of humour with the same gusto as the other people in the brothel underlines her separation from them, both socio-economic (in her elegant clothes) and sexual (in her repression).

Séverine's other two clients are also associated with containers, but at a remove from her interactions with them. One of the objects that characterises Marcel is his cane, an unusual

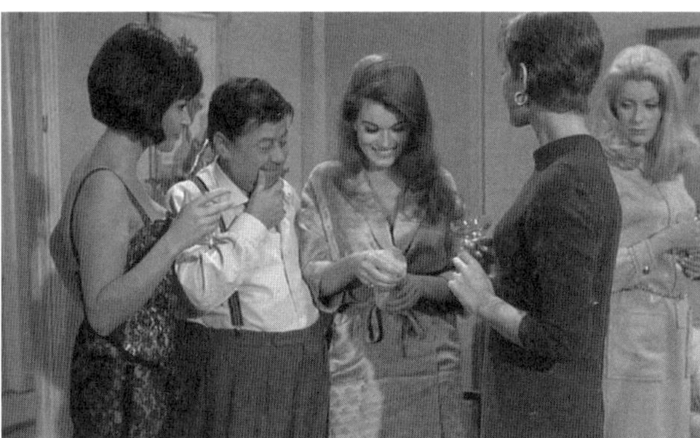

Figure 4.4: Mathilde opens a present from Monsieur Adolphe in *Belle de Jour.*

accessory for an able-bodied man; the cane in fact contains a knife, another hidden object of phallic shape. Although Séverine never sees this knife, as Marcel only unsheathes it in response to an insult from another man, she is fully aware of the violence in Marcel, hiding just below the surface, both on his body (in the metal teeth that his lips conceal, and the long scar hidden under his shirt) and in his dangerous bravado and quick temper. The physicality of Marcel and the connection Séverine feels with him find their opposite in Husson, who has no sexual interest in Séverine once he has discovered that she is a prostitute. In contrast with Marcel, who once attempts physical violence towards Séverine, Husson attacks her much more effectively with words. It is significant, then, that the container associated with Husson also exists only verbally: before he leaves, he gives Séverine money, but specifies that it is for her to buy Pierre some chocolates (which typically come in a box).

Most notably, the film's central sequence is one in which Séverine herself is placed inside a box, an open coffin, to fulfil the sexual fantasy of the aristocratic older man. The sequence also involves a self-reflexive element, as Buñuel has a cameo in the café scene that opens the sequence; in addition, before the man begins his strange ritual with Séverine at the mansion, like a film director he sets up a camera to record everything. This scene also evokes (or in Séverine's mind is perhaps inspired by) the sequence that came only shortly before it, in which she was the spectator to the professor's sadomasochistic ritual: there, the box room with its single peephole may also be compared to a camera.

Belle de Jour thus emphasises objects through the subtle repetition of one type of object (the container) and modulates the meaning of these objects through the different contexts in which they appear as they continually resurface in the film. More than switches in genre, the changes in the film's levels of reality may be interpreted as switching between a more conventional (if still obviously artificial) reality and the subjectivity of Séverine's fantasies. Given the fact that the film is focused on a central female character, it is worthwhile considering the effect of the feminine on object meaning: does it tend to limit or to open up meaning? The answer to this question depends on whether the film is conservative in its portrayal of women.

Stephen Forcer offers an interesting new reading of the film, suggesting that Séverine's liberation is located not in her decision to become a prostitute, but in her move from masochist to sadist.[55] Séverine finds no more satisfaction at the brothel than at home, he says, because both places are 'organized by the same sorts of alienating power structures' that are 'constructed and perpetuated by a dominant male order'.[56] It is only when she embraces her sadistic side that Séverine is able to 'recover an active, libidinal self':[57] according to Forcer, Séverine becomes a sadist by failing to prevent the death of her lover or the debilitating attack on her husband, and through the dominant role that she subsequently takes on as her husband's carer.[58] Forcer emphasises, however, that there is much further study to be done with regard to the film's portrayal of women, particularly in light of the 'contradictions [...] in the fact that Belle's active/sadistic position is not physical but causal',[59] a serious limitation to his argument in my view. Forcer's analysis also fails to recognise that the more confident Séverine emerges precisely at the moment when she first encounters the Asian customer, not after she allows the attacks on Pierre and Marcel.

The genre of the erotic film as well as any film based on the notion of the feminine as a mystery to be solved does not have a strong record of providing a truly progressive or empowering image of women. Séverine is portrayed as frigid and neurotic, and is frequently compared to a child. She first embodies the cliché of the virgin, in her beautiful blonde innocence and purity, and her aristocratic façade only adds to the titillation when she becomes a whore. Although the switch from virgin to whore may be interpreted as Séverine's assertion of her freedom, she takes the step timidly, seemingly as a result of Husson's power of suggestion (he gives her the address of the brothel). She is perpetually on the point of changing her mind, even when she is actually in the room with her first client – indeed, if Madame Anaïs did not force her to stay, one has the impression that Séverine would have abandoned the idea altogether. Although Séverine becomes more self-assured as she continues in her career, and her new-found confidence seeps through to her private life where it is noticed by her husband, it is nonetheless true that she lacks the power to select her clients; Anaïs must insist to make Séverine stay in the room with Husson on her last day at the brothel just as she forced her to stay with Adolphe on the first day. While Séverine may appear to become more confident, none of her decisions are entirely her own. She first visits the brothel because of Husson and leaves it after he discovers her there. Moreover, when she does make the decision to end her double life, Marcel attempts to prevent her from doing so. Although Séverine tries, for a time, to be both virgin and whore, occupying a middle ground, she is always being controlled or taken care of by others, whether it is her husband at home or Anaïs at the brothel.[60] If everything that happens to Séverine is, in fact, a fantasy, she is a woman who lives in her head rather than in reality. If, on the other hand, she really does go to the brothel to find her freedom, it is a freedom defined by her sexuality, and one that ultimately ends with her punishment in the form of looking after her disabled husband, to whom her double life is sadistically revealed, after the fact, by the very man who led her to adopt it.

Ultimately, then, Séverine's role is one defined by stereotypes, and does not disturb the status quo. If it is unusual for a woman to decide to become a prostitute for her own satisfaction, this is because it is a role that seems to correspond more to male fantasies than to real female desire. In *Belle de Jour*, then, it is only Séverine's alternation between virginal bourgeois wife and woman with erotic fantasies and pastimes that destabilises the meaning of objects in the film. Object meaning is not multiplied by means of any fundamental questioning of conventional female roles.

Cet obscur objet du désir

Buñuel's last film seems to reinforce the virgin-whore dichotomy just as *Belle de Jour* did: in *Cet obscur objet*, the main female character is played by two different actresses, one a cool Frenchwoman, the other a sultry Spaniard.[61] Yet the very fact of using two actresses to incarnate one character seems to mock the way in which one woman can be categorised by both extremes, virgin and whore, in the way that Séverine was in *Belle de Jour*. Moreover, the supposedly virginal version of Conchita is the one who promises to be Mathieu's mistress if he takes her to his country house, while it is her seemingly more sexual incarnation who rebuffs his advances and tells him that she is '*mozita*' (a virgin). Conchita certainly has a more rebellious and assertive spirit than Séverine, who was perhaps limited by her bourgeois status. Conchita's mother, in an expression of quasi-aristocratic pretension, does not want her daughter to work, but this means that the *petite bourgeoise* Conchita has, like Séverine, ample opportunity for mischief in her spare time; unlike the respectable middle-class wife, though, Conchita is not afraid of what others might think of her behaviour. Furthermore, the poverty in which Conchita and her mother live makes her all the more vulnerable to wealthy older men, predators like Mathieu who represent her only real escape from such a lifestyle.[62] It is to Conchita's credit, then, that she refuses to be bought and sold like a piece of furniture, and succeeds in taking as much as possible from Mathieu while giving as little as possible in return. Although such behaviour may seem opportunistic, it also shows that she recognises the probability that she will lose all of her privileges if she allows Mathieu the one privilege he desires most of all, to have sex with her:[63] it is important for her to maintain her mystery in this respect, however ridiculous such 'obscurity' may seem when defined so narrowly.

Fernando Rey said that 'Buñuel thought of him in some respects as a dark alter-ego [...] the younger, wish-fulfilment version of a self'.[64] There are in fact marked similarities between Rafael in *Le Charme discret* and Mathieu in *Cet obscur objet*, both characters played by Rey. Rafael and Mathieu are similar, most of all, in their relationship to the opposite sex: theirs is an old-fashioned masculinity, and while they know how to be charming and gallant towards women, they also see them as the weaker sex, who need to be humoured and protected, and whose role and identity are closely defined.[65] When women attempt to escape from that definition, men such as Rafael and Mathieu may become more brutal; there are examples of this in Rafael's sexual assault and sexist remarks towards the young female terrorist who comes to assassinate him in his apartment, and in Mathieu's beating of Conchita when she appears to have sex with another man right in front of him, then comes to his house to observe his reaction. While the terrorist in *Le Charme discret* is easily dealt with, Conchita acts as the nemesis of such old-fashioned attitudes towards the sexes.[66] Evans has described the relationship between Conchita and Mathieu as one in which each is inexorably drawn to the other,[67] but Conchita is clearly in control in the relationship, and is arguably able to live without Mathieu much more easily than he can live without her. At the same time, while Conchita may appear selfish and heartless, or 'a nightmarish apparition of female empowerment',[68] she is not ultimately cast as an evil enchantress who enslaves an innocent man against his will. Rather, it is Mathieu who pursues Conchita because she is beautiful, and he does so in inappropriate circumstances and using dubious means. He engages in what Evans refers to as 'outmoded victimising strategies toward women':[69] he abuses his position of power by trying to seduce Conchita when she is employed as a maid in his house, and later offers her mother money in exchange for persuading her to live with him, although he is not prepared to marry her. The reason that Mathieu appears pitiable is that he is obsessed with attaining something that forever eludes him; as the film never shows how he would behave after reaching his goal, the audience can only infer that he might disappear from Conchita's life as quickly as she glides in and out of his.

Cet obscur objet was Buñuel's adaptation of the Pierre Louÿs novel *La Femme et le pantin/ The Woman and the Puppet* (1898). Williams has noted that Buñuel's film is markedly less misogynistic than previous adaptations (von Sternberg's 1935 film *The Devil is a Woman*, for example).[70] Evans believes that Buñuel, like Rey's character, may have been 'compromised by all sorts of prejudices against women' but that he was also interested in the way in which the oppression of women led them to react against men, taking their revenge.[71] Evans also suggests that it may have been Buñuel's persisting surrealist spirit that made him define desire in part through a 'yearning for release from [...] ideologically-determined notions of role and gender'.[72] Conchita's own changing identity may be interpreted in many ways: as making ironically literal Mathieu's conflicting expectations of her (that she be mysterious and virginal and yet tell him everything about herself and be sexually available to him); the changes may also reflect Mathieu's inability to see Conchita for who she is because he is projecting two different images of the feminine onto an individual who may correspond to neither of these.[73] The switching of actresses might also literally indicate that Mathieu's story should not be trusted, as it is based on fantasy. Oms suggests that Conchita 'n'a peut-être pas d'autre identité que celle conférée par l'imagination de l'homme'/'may have no identity other than that which man's imagination bestows on her',[74] and Michael Richardson too wonders whether she 'in fact does not exist but is solely a projection of Mathieu's desire'.[75] Evans points out that the film's structure of the flashback also serves to 'place in question the premises and events of the frame-text'.[76]

Although *Cet obscur objet* alternates between actresses, it does not mix genres in the same way as *Le Charme discret* or *Belle de Jour*, or at least not as obviously. The beginning and end of *Cet obscur objet* portray events in the present, as they happen. The central portion of the film is devoted mainly to a retelling of events from the past, interspersed with short segments in the present showing Mathieu and his audience of fellow passengers in a train compartment. Although the device of the flashback will be familiar to the audience, the use of two different actresses to portray one person, without any diegetic acknowledgement of this radical change, is surprising and a disruption to the narrative's illusion of reality. The audience may nonetheless be astonished to discover that they do not immediately notice the striking difference between the two women. Oms says that the spectator thus finds him or herself, like Mathieu, 'piégé par sa propre participation au phénomène de projection/identification'/'caught in the trap of their own participation in the phenomenon of projection/identification'.[77] In the context of this chapter's discussion of the filmic definition of reality, it is less the mechanism of audience identification that is of interest, but more the degree to which the audience will automatically assimilate even the most implausible aspects of a film in the interest of maintaining the intelligibility of the diegesis. Notably, when they realise that there are two actresses playing one character, the audience will nonetheless continue to assimilate this discrepancy consciously; the physical impossibility is justified as possible in the space of Mathieu's mental recollection, while the semiotic puzzle as to why he would remember one woman in this way is understood as symbolic of either her nature or his understanding of her. However, at the end of the film, Buñuel abruptly pulls this carpet of rational explanation out from beneath the audience's feet. Like Mathieu as he is doused with a bucket of cold water, the audience will be shocked as they realise that this film, which they had rationalised into a more or less logical system of representational conventions, albeit unusual ones, is in fact a film in which the fantastic may have been occurring all along. Any unusual events and objects in the previous scenes, objects and events that were accepted as logical within the film's system of representation, demand to be revisited and other explanations more fully considered.

As in Buñuel's other films, it is not only objects that stand out as bizarre or seemingly inexplicable; characters' behaviour and speech may also seem anomalous, and events difficult to explain rationally. There is an inexorable presence to an object, however, as it cannot be overlooked or passed off as easily as a gesture or phrase, particularly when similar objects keep cropping up throughout the film. Just as the viewer may have considered the notion of subjectivity as a means of explaining the changes in Conchita's appearance, so other elements of Mathieu's story may be more easily accepted as his unconscious influencing his recollection of the past. Although it pushes the bounds of narrative conventions in the genres with which audiences are familiar, it is even possible to understand unexplained objects as symbols, like those that appear in dreams. If the audience accepts such an idea, however, Buñuel has succeeded in radically broadening the possible meanings that objects may take on in his film; no longer limited to an instrumental role, objects are allowed to take on unconscious meaning as they would in dreams, and yet the audience remains actively engaged in following the story because of the presence of familiar mainstream cinematic devices such as storytelling and flashbacks.

While box-like containers of various kinds were the most notable type of object in *Belle de Jour*, in *Cet obscur objet* it is a burlap sack that stands out the most. Williams engages in a nuanced analysis of the sack, noting the relevance of Mathieu's valet's verbal reference to women as 'sacs d'excrément'/'bags of excrement' and the parallel between the burlap of the sacks that continually reappear and the sackcloth chastity pants with which Conchita confronts Mathieu.[78] As it thus embodies 'preconceived notions about the supposed filth or purity of women', the sack is seen by Williams as representing both extremes of the virgin-whore dichotomy; in the film, this dichotomy becomes, literally as well as figuratively, a 'cumbersome burden' as it is carried by Mathieu or other characters.[79]

Conchita is never entirely investigated and understood by the film; Williams herself says that it is to Buñuel's credit that unlike Loüys or von Sternberg, he does not engage in a 'striptease' of her true nature, and even the question of whether or not she is really a virgin is never conclusively answered.[80] I suggest that it is appropriate, then, that the object should maintain a similar mystery. For this reason, I believe it is necessary to consider the *way* in which the sack may take on meaning in the film, rather than limiting it, as Williams does, to one interpretation, however compelling. The remainder of this section on *Cet obscur objet* will consider each appearance that the sack makes in the film and examine the possible meanings that arise, both in the space of one appearance, and as the effect of a series of meanings accumulated by the object as it keeps resurfacing.

When the sack makes its first appearance, it is being carried through Mathieu's garden by a labourer (figure 4.5). Here, one of Buñuel's own favourite explanations for an object's presence may be given: that it is 'natural' in the given context.[81] The sack may contain manure, for example, foreshadowing Mathieu's valet's metaphorical reference to 'sacs d'excrément' later on. The camera follows the gardener who is carrying the sack, and as this character has no other significant role in the film, Buñuel's stylistic choice implies that the object is more than a natural part of the décor, making it, as Tesson would put it, 'sursignifiant'/'over-determined'.[82] It is possible to interpret this camera movement as symbolising the way in which Mathieu is compelled to chase after Conchita, another servant from his household. The sack may thus exist as an object that is realistic in the context, and at the same time contain possible symbolic importance.

The sack's next appearance coincides with the moment when Conchita agrees to be Mathieu's mistress if he takes her to his country house. Rather than continuing to pursue Mathieu and Conchita as they walk through a Paris park together, the camera veers off to follow a labourer with a burlap sack over his shoulder, and this switch from main characters to another insignificant character makes the camera movement even more noticeable than in the earlier scene. Here, a symbolic reading of the sack is even more likely, although the fact that the setting is once again a garden still allows for the possibility of interpreting the sack as having only a literal role.

The next two times that the sack appears, it is directly connected with Mathieu. In the first instance, he and Conchita are walking along the Allée des Cygnes. When they begin (as in the earlier scene) to walk away from the camera together, Mathieu (now seemingly resigned

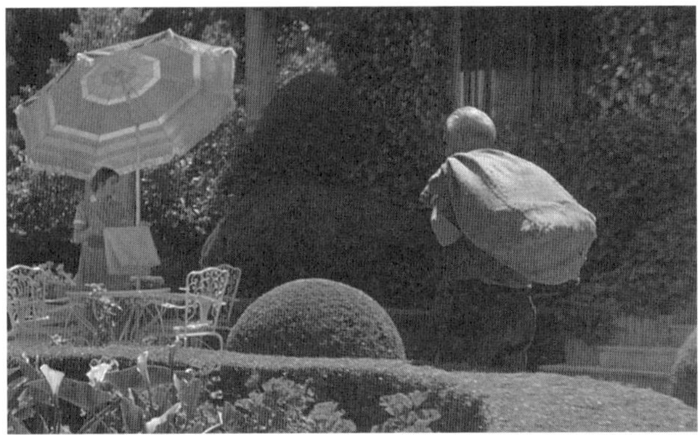

Figure 4.5: A labourer carries a sack in *Cet obscur objet du désir*.

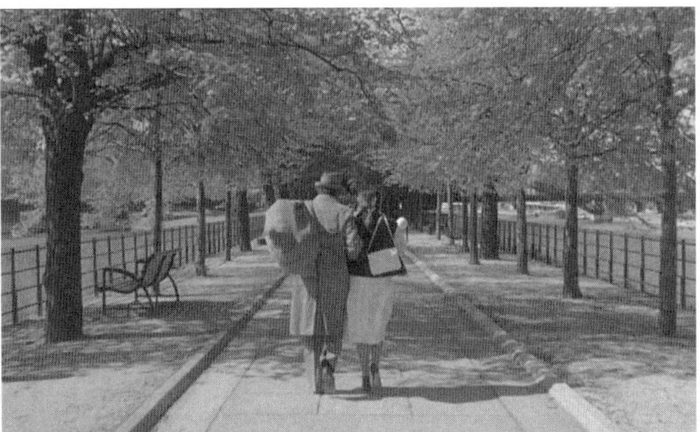

Figure 4.6: Mathieu carries a sack in *Cet obscur objet du désir*.

to never getting what he wants from Conchita) picks up a burlap sack that he carries over his shoulder (figure 4.6). The object here appears clearly out of place: it is difficult to imagine what could be inside the sack or why Mathieu is carrying it (and, moreover, in the manner of the labourers seen earlier). If one interprets the sack as a symbol of his enslavement to Conchita, does the sack then represent her person, the financial burden of the things she is asking him to buy her, or the great compromise he has had to make in order simply to keep her in his life? None of these symbolic interpretations seems compelling enough to accept, and the audience is left more than ever hovering between literal and figurative readings of the object.

In the second instance, Mathieu is living in Seville and is about to go on the walk where he will unexpectedly rediscover Conchita. His servant calls out to him that he has forgotten 'the bag', another large, rough sack similar to previous ones. Mathieu is on the point of taking it with him, but changes his mind and says that he will take it later. Here, once again, the realistic explanation is possible but seems unlikely: why would Mathieu take such a bag with him on an evening walk? It is strange for a film that generally corresponds to narrative conventions to include an item that is never explained and that seems to serve no purpose in the narrative. The symbolic readings suggested earlier are complicated by the fact that Conchita is not in his life at this point. Is he trying to leave her behind, while unconsciously knowing that he will ultimately fail to do so? Does it symbolise Mathieu's positive attitude to Conchita, in contrast with his valet's recently expressed disdain for all women? Or does the fact that he says he will come back for the sack suggest that he will finally take on the valet's view of women after he witnesses Conchita dancing naked at a tourist spot and having sex with another man in the house that he has bought for her? Even if this last symbolic interpretation is correct, it conflicts with previous symbolic readings, as Mathieu's attitude to Conchita was indulgent when he was carrying the sack on the Allée des Cygnes. Once again, neither a literal nor a figurative understanding of the object is entirely satisfactory.

The sack makes two more appearances towards the end of the film. In the first, a large pile of sacks are seen being transported on a luggage cart at the train station where Conchita and Mathieu are reconciled; the shot is separate from Mathieu and Conchita, however, and easily lost among the other shots of passengers and luggage at the station. For those viewers who do notice it, perhaps they have been led by Buñuel to experience the way in which the unconscious, as a means of making its desires known, leads one to notice certain objects more than others. Here, of course, the audience's attention is being influenced by significance that the film has associated with the sack so far, through its repetition and its privileging within the image; thus the audience may be led to take note of the sack's appearance even in apparently anodyne and believable circumstances, and attempt to attach significance where, perhaps, none at all lies. The film's use of repetition draws the audience's attention to this very process whereby films may create significance in relation to objects.

The most important appearance of the sack is its final one, however, and one that no viewer can ignore: a sack is placed in a shop window where, crucially, it is opened (figure 4.7). As a fascinated Mathieu watches, a white nightgown with a bloodstain is taken out of the sack, and a woman begins repairing a tear in the garment. This event, far from solving the mystery of the sack, only serves to create more equivocal symbolism. Does this sack solve any of the mysteries that came before it? The nightgown with its bloodied hole has been interpreted by Williams as a fetish standing for castration, which it asserts (with the bloodied hole) through its very attempt to deny it (sewing up the hole, or hiding the garment in a sack).[83] Other scholars interpret the item more literally, seeing it as a bridal nightgown that signifies the end of virginity, but also embodies an attempt to repair it;[84] such symbolism is obviously relevant to Conchita and her debatable sexual purity. Both literal and figurative explanations may thus account for Mathieu's absorption as he watches the mystery of the sack being revealed and the delicate process of attempting to repair that which seems to have been definitively destroyed.

Buñuel gives *Cet obscur objet* many of the characteristics of a mainstream film: a love story, a goal-oriented narrative and a flashback structure, for example. For this reason, viewers will

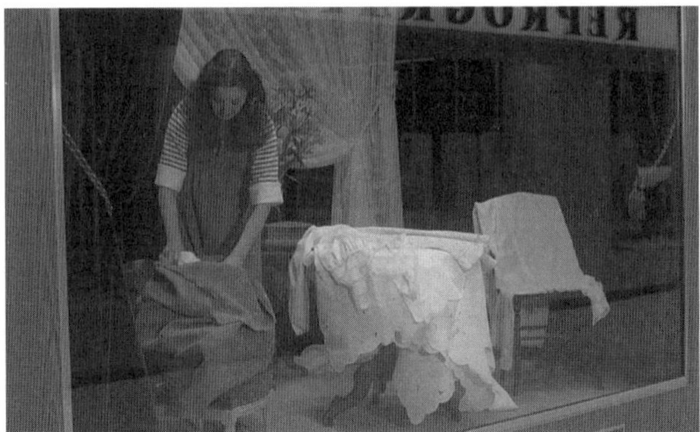

Figure 4.7: A sack is opened in a shop window in *Cet obscur objet du désir.*

first attempt to understand objects within the film according to the conventions of classical narration: in other words, they will look for a motivation based on context (location) and narrative progression (story) or, as a last resort, a symbolic significance related to the film's theme. The idea of a woman as a mystery, either a sacred or a horrifying one, seems to be one of the overriding ideas governing the narrative. The fact that the viewer can never be sure of whether Conchita is a virgin, a whore, or something in between, destabilises object meaning. A foregrounded object (a sack, in the case of this study) may be interpreted in multiple ways as a result of the ambiguous status of the feminine and the associated lack of finality in any pronouncement made about women or the objects associated with them.

Conclusion

The common element linking these narratively quite disparate films is their misleading surface appearance of conforming to familiar genres: *Le Charme discret* features many different genres, *Belle de Jour* a more limited number, and *Cet obscur objet* imitates just one type of film (the love story/confession mainly told in flashback). Ultimately, however, the films' stories are merely a guise for a pursuit that motivated Buñuel his entire career: to explore what lurks beneath the surface of the everyday, making the familiar unfamiliar, and the unfamiliar more accessible. Buñuel's smallest achievement is to lead viewers to accept diversions from the practice of rational motivation in film; his greatest achievement is to send up the very idea of rational motivation. His use of familiar genres is more than simply a trick to lure in the unsuspecting viewer: through the course of the film, the familiar genres on which it appears to be based are subverted in a way that implicitly questions the generic conventions by which the verisimilitude of a film is judged. The ways in which Buñuel creates this subversion of the genres featured (or, better, alluded to) in his films are diverse.

Although objects are a major source of subversion, this chapter also took into consideration other means that the director employs, a necessary consideration since objects do not function in isolation but in concert with other dimensions of mise-en-scène.

Humour may not seem a dominant feature in all of the films examined here. It was discussed in relation to *Le Charme discret* as there are more clearly ridiculous situations portrayed in this film, which makes fun of bourgeois mores by juxtaposing them with unusual types of disruption, from simple misunderstandings and minor inconveniences, to major threats. Of the three films, *Cet obscur objet* is the next most comic, even if much of the audience's enjoyment stems from schadenfreude at the outrageous ways in which Mathieu is perpetually dismayed, thwarted and humiliated by Conchita. *Belle de Jour*'s element of comedy is much more unexpected when it appears: Séverine's psychological plight is truly a tormented one, and her solution more astonishing than comic. Although one may not be able to feel truly sorry for a woman who has everything except the correct libido, Séverine's neurosis is not in itself entertaining, as it allows her few moments of truly relaxed pleasure, and produces unease and awkwardness rather than amusing situations. There is perhaps an element of black humour in the film, in its presentation of a life that appears perfect but is in fact sterile, the contrast between Séverine's frigid, virginal appearance and her racy fantasies, or the initial juxtaposition of her reserved nature with the spirited atmosphere of the brothel. There are more frankly comic moments too, but these are related to men's surprising sexual practices rather than Séverine's own: for example, the professor's strict rules about what should be said and when in his sadomasochistic game, or the onanistic ending to the necrophile's ritual that causes Séverine to sit up in the coffin and look down at her client in surprise.

In all three films, humour often derives from the way in which unbelievable situations are treated within the diegesis. Typically, the characters accept the most unbelievable occurrences without hesitation, or else behave as if they had not happened. Meanwhile unlikely events, closer to the type that routinely occur in many mainstream narrative films, are exaggerated so that they become ridiculous and/or are highlighted with extreme outrage by the characters.[85] In this way, Buñuel points to the fact that, through the establishment of generic clichés, the audience has been conditioned to accept some unbelievable events while rejecting others. In apparently seeking to redress the balance, the director asks the audience to re-examine the very criteria by which events are judged as believable or not.

Dialogue offers Buñuel another means of mocking the artificiality of most films. The audience's own credulity is highlighted when they are lulled by the genre into accepting stilted conversations, even those sprinkled with non sequiturs, as part of waking reality, only for a sequence to be revealed as a dream in which no rational criteria apply. Ultimately, devices such as dream sequences (whether or not they are introduced as such) and flashbacks broaden the possibilities for what may be plausibly said while in fact only straying marginally from the unnatural style of speech common to many popular films. Alternately, particularly in the case of *Le Charme discret*, characters' conversations are spectacularly banal, as if to send up the respect audiences typically feel toward dialogue in film simply because it comes from a script.

In the case of the last two films discussed in the chapter, there was an examination of the effect of feminine characters on object meaning. However conservative it may be overall in its portrayal of the female, *Belle de Jour* also arguably takes gender stereotypes ad absurdum by making its main character scarcely believable, as she exists so effectively at two extremes. By showing a character who is a prostitute for part of the day and a respectable middle-class wife the rest of the time, the film also shows how unlikely it is for anyone to correspond entirely to one extreme – yet mainstream films have frequently traced the demise of the fallen woman, or set up a contrast between an utterly virginal character and her dangerous opposite. At the beginning of *Belle de Jour*, Husson the dark, aging roué presents a striking contrast with the young, blonde, virginal Séverine. In light of his predatory flirtation with her, he comes across as hypocritical as well as sanctimonious in his reaction when he discovers her secret life towards the end of the film. Rejecting the opportunity to be her client at the brothel, he disdainfully sets himself apart from her, saying that he, unlike her, has 'principles'. Similarly, Séverine's path is much more complicated than a single downward descent, and the film's equivocal ending precludes any serious discussion of whether she is ultimately lost or redeemed – indeed, it suggests the possibility that the fundamental premise of her supposed demise, the prostitution, never occurred outside her head, and thus downplays the significance of a fact that has been so crucial to many mainstream films.

Finally, and most importantly, objects play a particularly important role in the subversion of the audience's uncomplicated acceptance of genre film conventions. This chapter explored the notion that objects in Buñuel's films are able simultaneously to occupy the status of all three types of object discerned earlier in the films of the Czech New Wave. Because Buñuel's films initially appear to have a familiar basis in classical narrative and its conventions of realism, audiences readily seek a narrative or at least a practical motivation for the presence of any object, and indeed, Buñuel initially provides one. However, as the films progress, this type of rationale may cease to exist. Of course, mainstream narrative cinema also includes the possibility of a symbolic reading for an object, though that object will conventionally also have a diegetic motivation. In Buñuel, however, there are so many possible ideas that an object may symbolise that any single meaning becomes unsatisfactory. Unaccustomed to accepting this multitude of possible symbolic readings, the audience will find that the director has undermined their conventional ability to passively rely on the film to provide all the answers. Such multiple possibilities of interpretation point to the notion of an open or undefined symbolism commonly associated with experimental film, to which Buñuel's late work, in its overall aspect, seems not to belong. In this sense, Buñuel's films frequently combine not only familiar genres, but also a broad spectrum of modes of film-making, juxtaposing avant-garde techniques with mainstream classical narrative. Through his use of objects, then, Buñuel emphasises the arbitrariness of that which is or is not included in mainstream narrative: when the object's clear practical or thematic motivation is taken away, the narrative's absent puppeteer is exposed, its tyranny ended. Buñuel's deployment of objects in his late films serves to point out that rational narrative motivation is a highly artificial means of defining realism.

Notes

1 *Figures of Desire* 151.
2 Tesson, *Luis Buñuel* (Paris: Étoile/Cahiers, 1995) 14; Evans, *The Films of Luis Buñuel: Subjectivity and Desire* (Oxford: Clarendon Press, 1995) 36.
3 *Figures of Desire* 28, 32–33.
4 *Figures of Desire* xvi–xvii.
5 *Don Luis Buñuel* (Paris: Cerf, 1985) 165–67.
6 *Figures of Desire* 110–11, 141.
7 *Figures of Desire* 153.
8 *Figures of Desire* 153–54.
9 Williams, *Figures of Desire* 153–54.
10 *Figures of Desire* 38.
11 Tesson 95–97.
12 Tesson 95–97.
13 *Luis Buñuel* 64–65.
14 Tesson 64–65.
15 Tesson 64; Williams 204.
16 *Luis Buñuel* 63–64, 87.
17 Given the length of the last two titles, subsequent references to these films will be abbreviated to the first three words of their titles only: hence, *Le Charme discret* and *Cet obscur objet*.
18 Williams, *Figures of Desire* 141.
19 Williams, *Figures of Desire* 110–11.
20 Williams, *Figures of Desire* 137–42.
21 Williams, *Figures of Desire* 48–49, 152–53.
22 Maurice Drouzy, *Luis Buñuel: Architecte du rêve* (Paris: Lherminier, 1978) 136.
23 Williams, *Figures of Desire* 100–02, 143.
24 Williams, *Figures of Desire* 110–11, 137–42.
25 Williams, *Figures of Desire* 153–54.
26 *Figures of Desire* 68–72.
27 It is notable that both bishop and lieutenant found their true calling in careers inspired by their adoptive fathers rather than their real ones.
28 Peter William Evans, 'An *Amour* Still *Fou*: Late Buñuel', *The Unsilvered Screen: Surrealism on Film*, eds. Graeme Harper and Rob Stone (London: Wallflower, 2007) 41; Richardson 36–37; Williams, *Figures of Desire* 185.
29 Evans, *The Films of Luis Buñuel* 163. In 'Trust Me, I'm a Director: Sex, Sado-Masochism and Institutionalization in Luis Buñuel's *Belle de Jour* (1967)' (*Studies in European Cinema* 1, no. 1 [April 2004]: 19–29), Stephen Forcer agrees that 'there is something slightly convenient about these scenes' from Séverine's childhood: it is 'as if they have been specifically designed to coax the spectator into an overly formulaic interpretation of Belle's character' (24).
30 Alberto Farassino, *Tutto il cinema di Luis Buñuel* (Milan: Baldini & Castoldi, 2000) 269.
31 Evans, *The Films of Luis Buñuel* 166–67; Farassino 269; J. H. Matthews, *Surrealism and Film* (Ann Arbor: University of Michigan Press, 1971) 172–73.

32 Drouzy 135; Oms 134; Andrea Sabbadini, 'Of Boxes, Peepholes and Other Perverse Objects: A Psychoanalytic Look at Luis Buñuel's *Belle de Jour*', *Luis Buñuel: New Readings,* eds. Peter William Evans and Isabel Santaolalla (London: BFI, 2004) 124. Forcer suggests that the final fantasy is in fact Pierre's and represents the 'masculine, able-bodied self' that he has lost (28).

33 Oms 168.

34 John Baxter, *Buñuel* (London: Fourth Estate, 1994) 284.

35 *Tutto il cinema di Luis Buñuel* 269, translation mine.

36 Forcer, too, discerns a ceremonial quality to the Asian man's sexual rituals, and connects it with Séverine's childhood flashback of Catholic communion where she refuses to open her mouth to receive the host: the mystery associated with the Asian man's box finds its parallel in the tabernacle and its 'idea of a hidden enigma held within a decorated vessel' (25).

37 On the childlike aspects of Séverine, see Evans, *The Films of Luis Buñuel* 160 and Farassino 273.

38 Evans, *The Films of Luis Buñuel* 161.

39 *The Films of Luis Buñuel* 161.

40 'Of Boxes, Peepholes and Other Perverse Objects' 119.

41 'Of Boxes, Peepholes and Other Perverse Objects' 118–19.

42 'Of Boxes, Peepholes and Other Perverse Objects' 119–20. Admittedly, Pierre says that he is looking forward to Séverine announcing to him that she is pregnant, so the association Sabbadini makes is not without support in the film. Also, there is an instance in Freud of a patient who dreams of her teenage daughter lying in a coffin: unable to accept this as a wish-fulfilment dream, she looks for other possible interpretations of the coffin, and makes a connection between the English word 'box' and the German word '*Büchse*' (tin can), which is also slang for the female genitals. Using these associations, Freud ultimately interprets the dream as a delayed wish-fulfilment, referring to the time when the woman was unhappy to be pregnant, and wished that the baby would die in her womb (*The Interpretation of Dreams* 121–22).

43 Forcer notes that Buñuel was interested in Freud, so the box with its buzzing contents may be connected to a dream of a box containing two may-beetles, described by a female patient in *The Interpretation of Dreams* (Forcer 25). Buñuel's fascination with entomology (Baxter 226) lends weight to the idea of the box containing one or more insects. Freud also notes that the may-beetle dream is 'about the relations of sexuality to cruelty' (*The Interpretation of Dreams* 233): this understanding supports the link with the ostensibly violent pleasures Séverine experiences with the Asian client and his box, as well as Séverine's sadomasochistic fantasies more generally.

44 Sabbadini 120.

45 Freud, 'Fetishism', *Standard Edition, Vol. 21* (London: Hogarth Press) p. 157 qtd. in Sabbadini 120. The allusion to fetishes related to the feet is, moreover, never entirely misplaced in relation to Buñuel's films as, a foot fetishist himself (Baxter 6), he regularly turned the camera towards his actors' feet and legs.

46 'Luis Buñuel, or Ways of Disturbing Spectatorship', *Luis Buñuel: New Readings* (London: BFI, 2004) 195.

47 *Luis Buñuel* 64.

48 Buñuel, *My Last Breath* (1994, p. 243) qtd. in Sabbadini 118.

49 Buñuel, *My Last Breath* (1994, p. 243) qtd. in Sabbadini 118.

50   Sabbadini 118; Martins 195.

51   Sabbadini 117–18.

52   Evans, *The Films of Luis Buñuel* 161–62.

53   Evans in fact compares the professor's case with Pandora's box (*The Films of Luis Buñuel* 160), and this reference to a box again suggests a connection between Séverine's experience with the professor and her experience with the Asian man immediately afterwards. Indeed, Pandora's box is a term which could be applied more fruitfully to the Asian man's box: the sadomasochistic paraphernalia in the professor's case is used in a highly coded game that is predictable by comparison with the mysterious contents of the box and the Asian man's arcane ritual which surrounds them. The professor's game, which he successfully limits to a set time and place, also seems innocuous when compared with the ultimate ramifications of Séverine's presence at the brothel.

54   Here the *boîte* (tin can) as a container for a phallic object could evoke the *Büchse*/female genitals association from *The Interpretation of Dreams*, mentioned earlier.

55   'Trust me, I'm a director' 25–27.

56   Forcer 25.

57   Forcer 25.

58   Forcer 26–27. Quoting Freud as well as Laplanche and Pontalis, Forcer explains that sadomasochism crucially involves a combination of both persuasions, in varying degrees, within one individual.

59   Forcer 28.

60   Farassino 273.

61   Oms 186; Williams 199.

62   Evans, 'An *Amour* Still *Fou*' 45.

63   Richardson 40.

64   Evans 'An *Amour* Still *Fou*' 45.

65   Evans, *The Films of Luis Buñuel* 127–28.

66   Evans, *The Films of Luis Buñuel* 132.

67   'An *Amour* Still *Fou*' 38.

68   Evans, 'An *Amour* Still *Fou*' 40.

69   *The Films of Luis Buñuel* 126.

70   *Figures of Desire* 186.

71   *The Films of Luis Buñuel* 128.

72   'An *Amour* Still *Fou*' 40.

73   Oms 185.

74   *Don Luis Buñuel* 185.

75   *Surrealism and Cinema* 40.

76   *The Films of Luis Buñuel* 124.

77   *Don Luis Buñuel* 185.

78   *Figures of Desire* 205.

79   Figures of Desire 200–01, 205.

80   Figures of Desire 199.

81   Tesson 27.

82　*Luis Buñuel* 27–28.

83　*Figures of Desire* 205, 208.

84　Oms 187; Tesson 274–77. Malt's *Obscure Objects of Desire* raises hopes of a discussion of *Cet obscur objet du désir*, but disappointingly Buñuel's film is never mentioned. Reading Malt with *Cet obscur objet* in mind, however, opens up interesting possibilities for reading this scene in the Parisian *passage* in light of Benjamin's, Breton's and Aragon's understanding of arcades and their shop windows. On the one hand, they are a locus of dream and fantasy, but on the other, they are a repository for consumer commodities that, being 'outmoded', reveal the empty capitalist ideology behind them (see Malt, Chapter 2).

85　Tesson (119, 122–23) observes that Buñuel's films highlight the fact that the same gesture may be acceptable or unacceptable depending on the context and the beneficiary of the gesture. He also notes (139) that the characters' lack of reaction to surprising events may constitute a political commentary on Buñuel's part: it expresses the idea that many situations that are accepted as normal in fact clearly demand a reaction.

Chapter 5

Media Objects in *Le Fabuleux destin d'Amélie Poulain*

Introduction

It has been said that postmodernism is 'haunted by the spectre of Surrealism'.[1] This chapter will situate Jean-Pierre Jeunet's work in the context of the postmodernity of the *cinéma du look*. It will also explore the way in which objects in *Le Fabuleux destin d'Amélie Poulain* (2001) display the characteristics of surrealist objects and will examine whether this impression of surrealist objects is related to the presence of hybrid objects. However, it will do so with the awareness of the terms 'haunt' and 'spectre', which imply that it is a surrealism without substance that manifests itself in postmodern art and culture. As the effect of hybrid objects is as important as their form, this chapter will engage in a particularly extensive analysis of objects in *Amélie* in order to discover not only whether objects become hybrid in the film, but whether that hybridity is implicated in the film's overall effect.

Jean-Pierre Jeunet is like the other directors whose work has been examined in this book in that his films blend popular appeal with artistic vision. *Amélie* has been subject to marked critical neglect in France, as if it were being punished for being too popular. More recent studies have re-evaluated Jeunet's work,[2] and *Amélie* in particular, and discovered that it is not just of interest as a virtuoso stylistic performance and a sign of its times: the film explores its themes on the level of form as well as content, which points to the director's having invested great thought in the elaboration of his film, and to its stylistic effects representing more than simple visual flourishes.

Jeunet's attention to the relationship between form and content will become clear in the analysis that I will undertake in this chapter. *Amélie* was chosen to form part of the corpus of this book because the way in which it foregrounded objects suggested that they could be understood on a deeper level if they were examined more closely and in relation to each other. The film draws attention, specifically, to media of communication and artistic expression; in fact, the director seems deliberately to have included as many different media as possible in the diegesis of his film. These media are successfully incorporated as a believable part of the diegesis; what makes them stand out is not only their number, but more particularly the way in which they are used. Almost all of the media of communication that appear in the film are used in an unconventional way. As a result, their usual status as *means* is disrupted, and attention is drawn to the medium itself. A self-reflexive dimension also highlights Jeunet's own process of mediating reality for his audience. It is for these reasons that I will refer to media of communication in this film as 'media objects'.

The idea of placing emphasis on familiar means of communication and using them in a creative manner immediately suggests surrealist processes of defamiliarisation and subversion. While in this and many other ways Jeunet's film appears to be more surrealist than any of the films studied so far, the question that must be asked is whether this is merely a façade, the 'spectre of Surrealism' passing across the surface of this postmodern film. This chapter will engage in an analysis of the way in which media objects are highlighted through stylistic means, the way in which their usual use is disrupted within the film's diegesis, and the implications that this has for the object's meaning. By studying the object in the context of the film and in relation to its themes, it should be possible to answer with more certainty whether not only a hybridity of meaning but a deeper instability lies beneath the surface impression of surrealism in *Amélie*'s media objects.

Before engaging in a close analysis of media objects in the film, however, I will begin by situating Jeunet in relation to Clair, with whose work Jeunet's is readily compared. I will also contextualise Jeunet's work within more recent trends in French cinema, moving the study forward from modernism to postmodernism.

Jean-Pierre Jeunet and René Clair

Jean-Pierre Jeunet can be compared to René Clair in a number of respects. In terms of popularity, both directors gained prestigious reputations and became known throughout the world,[3] with the difference that Clair's prestige was built on a succession of films whereas Jeunet may find his entire career overshadowed by the success of *Amélie*. Nonetheless, Jeunet will continue to benefit from his association with the most popular French film of 2001: with audience figures of 8.85 million in France and about 30 million globally,[4] *Amélie* is considered to have played an important role in renewing confidence in the country's cinematic talent, both in France and internationally.[5]

Clair and Jeunet are also similar in that their work evokes cartoon. Jeunet's only formal film training was in animation, and he met his collaborator Marc Caro at the Annecy International Animated Film Festival.[6] The pair began co-directing short animated puppet films: *L'Évasion/The Escape* (1978) and *Le Manège/The Merry-go-round* (1980).[7] They also wrote essays together on animators such as Tex Avery, Jacques Rouxel and the Fleischer brothers.[8] Although Jeunet continued to incorporate animation in his live-action films, including *Amélie*, he also makes stylistic references to cartoon that draw him closer to Clair's approach. My study of *À Nous la liberté* in Chapter 1 highlighted a number of characteristics reminiscent of animated comedy: its playful use of sound effects, the physical orientation of its humour and the pristine minimalism of its purpose-designed sets. Jeunet's film, too, features 'cartoon-like mimetic sounds' and a preference for physical humour, often in combination with 'complex mechanical devices and chain reactions'.[9] In both films, the characters who take part in the action are cartoon-like in that their distinctive personalities are nudged towards comical extremes, and their facial expressions may be exaggerated in a cartoon-like way (though in Clair this is achieved solely through acting, whereas Jeunet may film his actors with wide-angle lenses to emphasise certain facial features[10]). The (at times) unnaturally precise synchronisation[11] and fast pacing of the action in which characters take part also serves to link both Clair's and Jeunet's films with animated comedy. However, the eclectic detail of *Amélie's* sets seems far removed from Clair's minimalist aesthetic, even if both approaches are possible in cartoon. Moreover, while *À Nous la liberté* was entirely studio bound, Jeunet filmed his exteriors on location for the first time when he made *Amélie*. Like Clair, though, Jeunet 'want[ed] to control everything',[12] and so took full advantage of digital post-production. Thus not only was he able to add computer-generated special effects to his film, making it more like animation but less like Clair's films; as an animator would delineate his ideal space, Jeunet was able to erase any elements of the real Paris that did not fit with his vision, from bystanders and supermarkets to graffiti and dog excrement.[13]

One final point of comparison between Clair and Jeunet is their subject matter and the associated criticism that their films have sometimes attracted. 'The first master of poetic realism', Clair reflects the tendency not only in his ambitious and pristine sets, but especially (in *Sous les toits de Paris/Under the Roofs of Paris* [1930], *Le Million* [1931] and *Quatorze juillet/Bastille Day* [1933]) his focus on Paris and its 'little people'.[14] Although *Amélie* has been compared to *Sous les toits de Paris*,[15] Jeunet's favourite poetic realist director is Marcel Carné:[16] Jeunet told his crew to watch *Le Quai des brumes/Port of Shadows* (1938), *Hôtel du Nord* (1938) and *Le Jour se lève/Daybreak* (1939) to understand the type of look and atmosphere he wanted in *Amélie*.[17] Jeunet's film thus reflects the general poetic realist orientation towards the daily life of the common people of Paris and their sense of community. One way in which he suggests this sense of community is precisely in the poetic realist style, with an emphasis on the windows, staircases and landings that connect the main character to her neighbours.[18] While a focus on the working class constituted the realist dimension of the 1930s films, it was a reality that was stylised through its recreation in studio sets.[19] Jeunet's film achieves a similarly stylised effect through post-production techniques.[20] In spite of the stylistic similarities, *Amélie* nonetheless differs from poetic realist films not only in the fact that it adopts their approach to reality sixty years after the original movement ended; Jeunet's film also features a happy ending, conspicuously lacking in most poetic realist films.[21]

A major characteristic uniting *À Nous la liberté* and *Amélie* and distinguishing them from the majority of poetic realist films is the breadth of their comic element; that said, neither fits uncomplicatedly into the genre of comedy. Clair's film features the slightly darker comedy of satire alongside its lighter element of slapstick; this point was not understood by some viewers and thus, although Clair had intended to criticise the dehumanising effect of modern technology and lampoon the utopia that it purported to offer, some took this utopia at face value.[22] *Amélie*, too, criticises the isolation and lack of spontaneity in modern urban life,[23] and aims to overcome them through (unconventional use of) media of expression and communication which, when used normally, often exacerbate these problems. Rather than satirising the most recent developments in modern communication (mobile phones, computers and the Internet)[24] in a manner similar to Clair, Jeunet excludes them from his film, choosing instead to subvert only those tools of communication that already existed in his own 1950s childhood (with the exception of photocopy and video, somewhat more recent technology in relation to the film's 1997 setting). Jeunet's retro-aesthetic may thus be understood not just as an unthinking nostalgia, but as an argument for a return to past ways of living;[25] if he idealises the past, it is chiefly insofar as he sees it as a time when it still seemed possible to work against the isolating effect of the city and its mediated communication, and enjoy the pleasure of the direct experience of life and a personal connection with one's community.

While many think of *Amélie* as an optimistic comedy,[26] its function as a memento mori should not be overlooked. Two of the most important characters in the film, Amélie and Raymond Dufayel, are concerned with making people happy, but the importance of their success is based on a sombre alternative. *Amélie* is a film that is acutely aware of mortality, from Amélie's childhood loss of her mother, and fantasy of her own television eulogy-biopic, to Dufayel's old age: its motto is not simply to seize the day, but to do so before it is too late. In the minor key of the accordion music on the soundtrack and through Amélie's own faraway expression even as she presses her cheek against Nino's back like a comforted child, the film's happy ending maintains the melancholy associated with a sense of life's brevity. At the same time, the film is not motivated by a simple fear of death, but of a life not fully lived. The film places an emphasis on the appreciation of sensual pleasures, and Dufayel exhorts Amélie, in order that her heart not become as brittle as his bones, to take action to connect with Nino. The sensual encounter between Amélie and Nino in the ghost train is more impressive than any of the traditionally spooky elements found there; the contrast implies that death is less daunting than a life lived in loneliness.

As a film aimed at mainstream audiences, *Amélie* lightens what could otherwise become a film with an excessive emphasis on contemporary problems of loneliness and neurosis; it injects a strong element of humour and concludes with what is generally interpreted as an upbeat resolution, conforming to the genre of romantic comedy.[27] One scholar has noted that 'comedy allows issues often ignored by "serious" genres to be aired but recuperates them through conservative narrative resolutions',[28] a statement that applies in the case of *Amélie*, its positive ending glossing over the fact that some characters achieve no final escape from their isolation. The same scholar has suggested two reasons why *Amélie* has received more scrutiny than other comedies. The first is its 'ambivalence and absence of clear ideological discourse', seeming to echo the implicit accusation made of Clair's film, given the radically differing interpretations of it.[29] The second reason, however, is *Amélie's* nostalgia: the film replicates the codes of poetic realism (among other past styles) long after the original movement disappeared, and thus represents not only a stylised world but a world that does not actually exist, even though the film was shot on location.[30] Thus it is that Serge Kaganski, editor of the magazine *Les Inrockuptibles*, was able to shock *Amélie's* adoring public[31] by accusing a film that seemed so optimistic and generous of representing 'une vision de Paris, de la France et du monde (sans même parler du cinéma) particulièrement réactionnaire et droitière, pour rester poli'/'a vision of Paris, France and the world (not to mention cinema) which is particularly reactionary and rightwing, to put it nicely'. More specifically, he complained that Jeunet's Paris had been 'soigneusement "nettoyé" de toute sa polysémie ethnique, sociale, sexuelle et culturelle'/'carefully "cleansed" of all its ethnic, social, sexual and cultural polysemy'.[32]

It is certainly difficult to justify the fact that a film set in the multi-ethnic community of northern Paris has managed to exclude or assimilate[33] that diversity almost entirely. Ethnic uniformity may have characterised Jeunet's own childhood in 1950s Roanne, and thereby informed his choice of actors and names in this film, which looks to the past for its models of community. It nonetheless seems strange that having moved to Paris in the 1970s, Jeunet did not attempt to reconcile the ethnic makeup of the city he knew as an adult with the community he knew as a child, given that he easily achieved this synthesis of older and newer technologies of communication (featuring both handwritten letters and photocopies in his film, for example). It is incorrect to consider *Amélie* to be completely out of touch with its modern context, however. On the contrary, Jeunet shows his awareness of the conditions of contemporary existence in his portrayal of urban loneliness and desire to undermine the monolithic and stultifying tendencies of mediated communication. Furthermore, his style and focus not only reflect past modes of poetic realism, but also exemplify much more recent trends in film and culture, namely *cinéma du look* and postmodernism.[34]

Cinéma du look

Those features of *Amélie* that I have so far connected with Clair and the poetic realist tendency find their deeper motivation and context in *cinéma du look* and the larger, overarching trend of postmodernism. In the intervening years that separated Jeunet's career from poetic realism, the French New Wave had come into being and dismissed the '*tradition de qualité*' that developed after the end of World War II.[35] They believed in a cinema that was youth-oriented, personal or militant, and experimental; in support of these three goals, they advocated less concern for the technical perfection of the film, allowing an escape from the physical restrictions and economic demands of studio film-making.[36] While this practice had the benefit of making it easier for new film-makers to get started, it could also result in films set in drab and ugly interiors, and films that were depressing, naively self-absorbed and verbally rather than visually oriented.[37] Strong low-budget, personal films aimed at a more specialised audience continue to be made in France to this day; however, in the 1980s film-makers such as Jean-Jacques Beineix, Luc Besson and Léos Carax challenged the hegemony of the French New Wave's approach to cinema.[38] They began making films that appealed to mainstream and youth audiences: films that were inspired by Hollywood, and of a technical quality that could compete with Hollywood.[39] Jeunet's digitally-corrected fantasy version of Montmartre not only refers to the stylised Paris of the poetic realist sets, then, but to the 'théâtralisation de l'espace urbain'/'theatricalisation of urban space' characteristic of the films of Beineix, Besson and Carax.[40] Jeunet's success may be associated with Clair's insofar as *Amélie* takes part in a trend of films that balance artistic vision with popular appeal,[41] a trend that may signal a wider revival of the old studio approach to French film-making which privileged the audience as much as the auteur.[42] Moreover, this return to a type of film-making that expressed an artistic vision yet also aimed to please was not limited to the 1980s and 90s, but was also noticeable in 2001, the year that *Amélie* was released along with a series of other successful films from French directors such as Christophe Gans (*Le Pacte des loups/Brotherhood of the Wolf*), Jean-Paul Salomé (*Belphégor – Le fantôme du Louvre/Belphegor, Phantom of the Louvre*) and Olivier Dahan (*Le Petit Poucet/Tom Thumb*).[43]

The 1980s cinematic challenge to the New Wave was called the *cinéma du look*, a term that refers to the aesthetic perfection of its images, but also to the belief held by some critics that appearance is the only salient feature of this type of cinema.[44] It is true that the films of Besson, Beineix and Carax are distinguished by their tendency to turn reality into spectacle, making use of 'exaggerated sounds, a saturated colour scheme, abrupt changes of scale, [and] huge close-ups of objects or faces [which are] balanced by long takes that use intricate camera movements'.[45] The high-tech visual fantasy that these techniques created showed the influence of comic book or 'BD' (*bande dessinée*) aesthetics,[46] one of the many genres and cultural products, both high and low, that these films adopted as modes of expression or one-off quotations.[47] However, it was the influence of the 'advertising aesthetic' that was immediately apparent in the exaggeration and slick perfection of the *cinéma du look* images;[48] this similarity, combined with the movement's appetite for borrowing images from other sources, turned cinema into a form of 'image consumption', both for the director and for audiences.[49] Jeunet's film corresponds to the *cinéma du look* in all of these respects. Like the movement's directors, he too developed an early taste for television[50] and *bandes dessinées*;[51] like many of them he worked in advertising for a time.[52] All of these influences are reflected in his cinema. Jeunet's earlier films such as *Delicatessen* (1991) and *La Cité des enfants perdus/The City of Lost Children* (1995) were made when the original *cinéma du look* movement was still alive.[53] *Amélie* can thus be seen as a continuation of the tendency towards high-tech visual appeal and eclectic sources of reference[54] (such as cartoon and poetic realism, in *Amélie*'s case) that Jeunet and other directors cultivated during this period.

As explained with respect to the term *cinéma du look*, the critical establishment regarded these films with distrust, as they felt that there was no real substance behind them. To these critics, the *cinéma du look* made use of a glossy aesthetic for its own sake; they believed that the *look* directors borrowed unthinkingly, from high and low culture alike, anything that would contribute to the creation of a pleasing image.[55] However, the films of Besson, Beineix and Carax quickly became renowned internationally, and the *cinéma du look* was vindicated when it was later acknowledged to have revitalised mainstream cinema in France.[56] Nonetheless, some scholars feel that it is Jeunet's association with the *look* aesthetic that has led to the dismissal of his work by serious critics and even its scholarly neglect.[57]

Postmodernism

While many characteristics of the *cinéma du look* are also part of general tendencies in postmodernism, any discussion of the relevance of Jeunet's film as something more than visually appealing entertainment is more likely to come from its contextualisation within the larger cultural landscape.[58] In *Cinema Studies: The Key Concepts*, Susan Hayward discusses the origins and preoccupations of postmodernism and highlights some examples in cinema, noting differences between mainstream and counter-cultural approaches. She compares the era of postmodernism (the end of the twentieth century) to the last *fin de siècle*, linking the two periods through their crisis of ideology.[59] The nineteenth-century response to an ideological absence was to focus on 'art for art's sake';[60] a manifestation of the same response in the postmodern era can be found in Jeunet's own concern with surface appearances in *Amélie*, leading some commentators to criticise him, as they had the *cinéma du look* directors, for 'overusing technology for its own sake, and for creating expensive empty visual effects'.[61] The director seems to feel no regret at this lack of ideology, however, declaring that 'we live at a time when there are no longer big political (or otherwise) ideals [sic] and to be able to focus on small pleasures, I think that's great'.[62]

Postmodern cinema tends to borrow from a wide range of past and present imagery; more thoughtful and innovative strands will engage in a dialogue with the sources they adopt, in order to create something new. The mainstream, on the other hand, is more reactionary and simply imitates the past.[63] Mainstream postmodern cinema tends to please people of all political affiliations, and its ability to be subject to 'contradictory readings' makes it 'potentially dangerous'.[64] This sounds very much like the danger that Kaganski discerned as inherent in *Amélie*, making him one of a very small number of dissenting voices at a time when the public and, significantly, the full spectrum of France's political parties were expressing their admiration for the film and its relevance to contemporary life.[65] As an example of postmodern cinema that engages intelligently with the material it quotes, Hayward highlights Quentin Tarantino's films, with their self-conscious and parodic references.[66] She also praises the way in which Tarantino has been able to draw mainstream audiences 'without reducing his film [...] to a mere series of good images',[67] thus reconciling art and popular appeal in a way that Kaganski (and others) feel Jeunet failed to do in *Amélie*.[68] Although it is true that his film in many ways simply reflects poetic realism, Jeunet has also updated it in other ways and thus arguably made it his own, through the inclusion of new character types,[69] and a focus on media of communication and expression that featured less prominently if at all in the original poetic realist films. Moreover, scholars have consistently acknowledged at the very least an attempt on Jeunet's part to engage more thoughtfully with this plethora of media that form one of the distinguishing features of *Amélie*'s diegesis; in particular, they have discerned a self-reflexive engagement with the filmic medium[70] and described certain examples of media as 'metaphor',[71] 'mimesis', 'echo',[72] '*reflet*'/'reflection', '*embl[ème]*'/'emblem', '*représent[ation]*'/'representation'[73], 'thematis[ation]'[74] or 'mise-en-abyme'[75] of Jeunet's own film-making process. Objects that can thus be read on more than one level offer further evidence that, more than a popular crowd-pleaser, *Amélie* is a complex film that treats diverse themes concurrently.

Once more evoking a comparison of the nineteenth and twentieth-century experience, Hayward points out the differing ways in which machines marked individual consciousness. Taking over from physical labour, the industrial machine 'alienat[ed]' the individual from his or her work; later, the post-industrial machine, with its capacity to make endless copies, undermined the concept of the original and left the individual with a feeling of 'fragmentation'.[76] Baudrillard explains that the dominance of the 'electronic mass media', and the postmodern tendency to copy and 'recycle' that which has already been created, results in a society that becomes in many ways distanced from reality.[77] Further, he points out that postmodernism aims for 'perfect simulation', in which there is no longer any difference perceived between reality and its imitation.[78] The tendency of mainstream postmodern films to 'manipulat[e] and elevat[e] virtual reality and computer graphics to the status of real',[79] a practice that perpetuates this erasure of the boundary between reality and imitation, can also be found in *Amélie*, where certain digital special effects added in post-production are indistinguishable from elements of the real world captured at the moment of filming. Within the diegesis, there is an implicit respect for simulation insofar as the positive changes that Amélie brings about in people's lives are achieved by means of tricks and illusions. Nonetheless, even if dubious means are used to achieve them, immediacy and authenticity are ultimately valued the most in the film's diegesis, with its theme of enjoying life's small pleasures and unexpected opportunities. Stylistically, the film balances its special effects that are indistinguishable from reality by constantly pointing to its own artificiality. Few will be gullible enough to believe that Jeunet's polished images of Paris reflect the city's reality, and for those who do, discernable special effects such as animated monsters and cloud shapes in the sky clearly point to the director's ability to create a misleading digital blend of fantasy and reality.[80]

One final characteristic of the postmodern that will be of particular relevance to this study is its relationship with technology. Here, Hayward discerns two possible attitudes. In its 'positive mode', postmodernism is 'far more accepting of late capitalism', 'delights in and is fascinated by technology', and 'celebrates the fact that mass communication and electronics have revolutionized the world'.[81] This corresponds with Baudrillard's description of postmodern society as 'liv[ing] in the ecstasy of communication'.[82] However, postmodernism may also, conversely, be ambivalent about the value of science and technology:[83] a culture that lives on scientific and technological invention, then, but with an underlying sense of unease about the implications of such a lifestyle. This is yet another characteristic of postmodernism that finds its illustration in both Jeunet's work and earlier manifestations of the *cinéma du look*: these films aim for commercial success, and new technology is to a large degree responsible for the appealing visual quality that helps to ensure this success. At the same time, within the diegesis of these films, the benefits of capitalism and of science and technology are rejected or act as a destabilising force. *Cinéma du look* narratives that move towards more simple, instinctual or immediate modes of living include *Le Grand bleu/The Big*

Blue (1988), in which protagonists dive to great depths without any equipment; *Diva* (1981), with its title character who does not want her voice to be recorded; and *Les Amants du Pont-Neuf/The Lovers on the Bridge* (1991), where a couple united in misfortune is threatened by a new eye operation allowing one of them to return to her previous life of comfort.

In Jeunet's film, the seamless way in which media and communication technology have been assimilated into modern life is undermined by a refusal to engage with them according to conventional practices of use and reception. Because interacting with these media in unconventional ways brings pleasurable creativity and spontaneity to life, and facilitates communication between people, it implicitly questions the capacity of these media to do so when used (or consumed) as they were originally intended to be. In addition, this subversion of media and communications involves little or no expense—it is most frequently childlike in its resourcefulness. Indeed, the unconventional use often hinges on found objects that are inherently anti-capitalist because, though they may have great personal value to characters in the film, they have no monetary exchange value. Jeunet's avowed determination to focus on small pleasures points to a belief in immediacy, which his film promotes not only by attempting to reawaken the audience's sensitivity to the diverse sensual dimensions of everyday life, but in its advocacy of delivering characters from their monotonous and solitary existence, often perpetuated by media and technology, and instead allowing them to reconnect with life's diversity.

Media of expression and communication as objects

Despite many basic similarities to past and present cinematic and cultural models, *Amélie* demonstrates great originality in the number of media of expression and communication it includes and, most of all, in the way in which they are used. The way in which media become objects in the film and their use as objects suggest that Jeunet had taken the surrealist object—its form, at least—and transposed it directly to film. Media objects are engaged with actively and innovatively by the film's characters, resulting in defamiliarisation. Media objects are also used to reveal characters' conscious and unconscious preoccupations and demonstrate their influence on waking perceptions. Finally, many of the media can be interpreted as metaphors of Jeunet's own approach to film-making, offering the potential to complicate any straightforward reading of the film. The following six sections will name the majority of media objects featured in *Amélie* and explore how they become media objects and any new meanings that their unconventional use may allow them to take on.

Painting

Amélie's neighbour Raymond Dufayel, a man confined to his apartment by brittle bone disease, spends his days working on a copy of *Le Déjeuner des canotiers/Luncheon of the Boating Party*. A reasonable and believable pastime is made remarkable by the fact that he has been painting one copy of this painting every year for some time. Far from a postmodern one-off citation of high art, or a pretentious and unjustified allusion, Renoir's painting forms a pivotal object in *Amélie*, serving as an index of Dufayel's life, a metaphor for Amélie's, and a self-reflexive reference to numerous aspects of Jeunet's film as a work of art. Moreover, it is one of the film's many examples of a medium that has its conventional place and role undermined. The painting's traditional place is in an art collection or museum, and its traditional role is twofold: it is a unique object, which therefore takes on both monetary value and aesthetic value. Although a painting's aesthetic value may be subjective, it is more conventional to assess a painting based on objective artistic criteria or, at most, on individual taste; it is much less common to interpret a painting in terms of its direct relationship to one's personal life.

The making of copies has long been a common practice, whether hand-painted reproductions of masterpieces, made openly and legitimately for the mass market, or forgeries that deliberately blur the line between the copy and the original. While Dufayel's copy is different from these precedents in that it is not made for profit, the mere fact of making a copy may seem automatically to undermine one of the key qualities of a masterpiece, that of its being unique. The confrontation between the copy and the original is certainly a postmodern concern, and is necessarily present in the use of the Renoir in *Amélie*: as Dufayel is working at home and not in a museum, he cannot base his copy on the original Renoir painting but must work from a large photograph of the original. However, while there is a necessary physical distance between Dufayel's photographic model and Renoir's masterpiece, the film does not develop an ideological erasure of the difference between copy and original. On the contrary, it is admiration for Renoir and a respect for the art of painting that seem to be Dufayel's major motivations for making copies. When Amélie first enters Dufayel's apartment, he introduces her to the painting in tones that make his respect for the master clear, as he explains the subtleties and complexities that have allowed him to copy the same painting over and over.

Although the film portrays Dufayel's painstaking work with respect, there is at least a small element of the make-work project in his copying, and a sense that the characters on the canvas have served as the housebound man's chief source of company for some time. Amélie's visit introduces an outsider's (astonished) gaze, and acknowledges limits to the quest for perfection via repetition; in this light, Dufayel's copies point to his monotonous and mainly solitary existence. It is also Amélie who will help Dufayel to broaden his interests and the change, too, will be reflected in the painting. This role is underlined at the end of the film as Dufayel is shown working on a new interpretation of *Le Déjeuner des canotiers* as part of a montage of various characters in the film who have had their lives changed in some way by the film's heroine. After he has met Amélie, Dufayel's gaze is no longer confined to the inanimate community of characters on his canvas: his neighbour's activities provide an outside source of interest for him, as indicated by the dialogue (which reveals his surprising degree of knowledge of the events occurring in the lives of everyone in his building), as well as visually when he observes Amélie's actions through binoculars.

The most important function of the Renoir painting is as a means for Dufayel and Amélie to discuss her *vie sentimentale*. Although the elderly man is wise and unafraid to speak plainly, his wisdom also makes him tactful; having only just met his shy neighbour, he knows that he must win her confidence, and cannot immediately force her to discuss her private life. For this reason, the Renoir painting serves an important role as a metaphor for Amélie, her life and her relationships with those around her; it allows for a comfortable degree of distance when she and Dufayel want to discuss such sensitive topics. While Dufayel's obsessive devotion to the painting serves as an index of his lonely life, it is the image itself that reflects Amélie's own isolation. Dufayel identifies his neighbour with 'la fille au verre d'eau'/'the girl with the glass of water', the figure that he finds the most elusive and a continual challenge to paint (figure 5.1). Although the image remains principally unchanged throughout the film, Dufayel and Amélie are able to continue using it to discuss new developments in her life, as she moves from detachment from her community, to attempts to influence other people's lives, to finally taking positive steps to end her own loneliness. The film thus demonstrates the way in which one's own frame of mind intervenes to determine the way in which one relates to a work of art: everything from its general appeal to its interpretation may be determined by its relevance to the individual. The notion that the unconscious influences our perception in waking life as much as in dreams is, of course, one that was fundamental to the surrealists' beliefs. Although it is Dufayel who loves the painting, and the greatest insights into Amélie's character actually seem to come from him, Dufayel's and Amélie's changing interpretations of the painting may constitute an example of a phenomenon that will be encountered in the following section of this chapter ('Television and video') in which Dufayel's wisdom allows him to perceive and draw Amélie's attention to the unconscious preoccupations that inform her choice of clips in the collage videos that she sends to him.

Through the painting, Dufayel expresses insights into his neighbour's character from the moment they meet, leading the audience to suspect a supernatural ability in the old man; as the film progresses, however, the audience learns that Dufayel is able to keep abreast

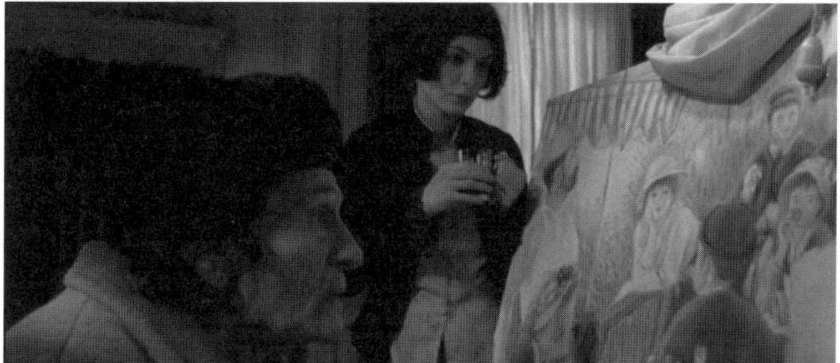

Figure 5.1: Dufayel implicitly compares Amélie to 'la fille au verre d'eau' in Renoir's painting in *Amélie*.

of events in his building without leaving his flat, by means of conversation with Lucien and by watching his neighbours through binoculars. Moreover, the friendship that develops between Amélie and Dufayel, as well as their shared reclusive tendencies, suggests that the two neighbours have some character traits in common. Therefore it may also be the old man's personal experience that allows him to alert the young woman to inhibitions that she must overcome in order to avoid a lonely old age.

Other more prominent examples of seemingly magical phenomena in the film can always be explained as visual representations of characters' subjectivity: their feelings, imagination or dreams. Thus when Amélie appears to melt away after she fails to respond appropriately to Nino when he talks to her, it reflects the emotions that overwhelm her; similarly, the monster she plays with as a child is obviously a product of her imagination. Although there are no scenes in the film that are indisputably framed as dreams, on two occasions a photo or painting comes to life when Nino or Amélie is asleep, and thus may be logically explained as a dream. The example concerning Nino will be discussed in the subsequent 'Photography' section of this chapter. The scene involving Amélie, if taken as a dream rather than an independent magical event, offers even more compelling evidence of the medium of painting being used to reflect a character's personal preoccupations: while she is asleep, her unconscious uses the animals in the paintings in her room to express something of which she may or may not be consciously aware, that she is falling in love with Nino.

The Renoir painting has, finally, non-diegetic relevance as a metaphor for Jeunet's process of film-making. The director admits that the obsessive nature of many of the characters is a reflection of his own neurotic tendencies.[84] Dufayel's perfectionism, leading him to spend years working on the same painting, is among the film's most representative models of Jeunet's meticulous attention to detail in his film-making. The art of painting itself is also relevant in terms of the director's conception of the filmic image, as Jeunet has been quoted as having said that 'every shot should be like a painting', a statement that helps to explain his attention not only to detail, but also to aesthetics and careful composition.[85] Dudley Andrew sees a further similarity between Jeunet's art and that of a painter in the way in which he digitally cleans up the images of the real world captured by his camera.[86] Choosing a Renoir painting in particular as a focus of the film also reflects the director's own cinematic tastes. Although Jeunet first explains that the image of *Le Déjeuner des canotiers* was free (whereas other paintings may have required him to pay for the rights to use their image in his film), he then adds his perennial justification for the inclusion of any element in his film: a personal love for it.[87] In this sense, Jeunet is again similar to Dufayel who copies a painting simply because he likes it so much; Dufayel's admiration for Renoir père may also be compared to Jeunet's respect for and imitation of the masters of poetic realism, which include Renoir fils. The painting itself and its reproducibility can also be said to represent Jeunet's film as a whole; one other reason that the director gives for choosing *Le Déjeuner des canotiers* is that the different gazes connecting the figures in the painting can be compared to the network of relationships connecting the characters in his film.

Television and video

A New Wave director might have indicated that characters in his or her film belonged to the middle class by having them ostentatiously reading books, perhaps ones with thematic relevance to the film, which the well-read viewer would be expected to understand. Jeunet acknowledges that his audiences may have more television than literature in their daily lives; indeed, TV images are used several times in the film as part of his practice of characterisation by likes and dislikes (Amélie's mother, for instance, likes the costumes of figure skaters that she sees on the television station TF1). While television is included in the film as a realistic part of the modern environment, watching it is never a passive pursuit. By controlling the transmission (what and how much she watches), using a standard broadcast as a basis for personal fantasy, and collecting images on video, Amélie makes television active, purposeful, and relevant to the individual. Dufayel also adopts some of his neighbour's creativity, and makes a video of his advice to Amélie. The interactive use of television and video spurs characters to action so that they are able to overcome the need for an interface of separation.

The possibility of controlling a broadcast by switching it on or off, or switching from one station to another, is the means of interaction with television with which most of us are familiar. In *Amélie*, there is always a surprising element to this interaction, however. As a child, Amélie is tricked by a neighbour into thinking that she causes accidents with her Instamatic camera. When she turns on the television that evening, she flips from one station to the next not, as one usually does, to find something enjoyable to watch; rather, Amélie becomes increasingly horrified by the cumulative effect of images from various evening news programmes, all showing accidents for which she believes she is responsible. When she later exacts revenge on the neighbour for his cruel joke, it is again through controlling the transmission of television, this time in an even more unusual way. Seated on the roof of her neighbour's house, listening to a radio broadcast of the football game, she unplugs his television aerial just before each goal and replaces it just afterwards; parallel montage shows the neighbour's predictably intense frustration as the television image inexplicably blurs at every key moment.

Later in the film, Amélie as an adult switches off her television during a news report on the death of the Princess of Wales. This is a surprising action because she is initially very much interested in the programme (as shown by her expression, the fact that she turns up the volume, and the way that the camera tracks in on the television screen as if to reflect her fascination and emotion); she is so shocked by the news that she drops the cap of her perfume bottle. Earlier in the film, when the narrator spoke of an event that would 'bouleverser la vie'/'completely change the life' of the film's heroine, the brief montage of shots of the famous car crash also makes it seem counter-intuitive for Amélie, on the day of this event, to switch the news report off as though it were annoying her. The most important part of this scene, however, is not that Amélie switches the television off, but that her initial interaction with it leads to an important event in her own life, which will ultimately bring about other important events in the lives of those around her.

By making her drop the perfume cap, the news report changes Amélie's life indirectly, leading her to find the little box of toys hidden behind her bathroom wall and thus starting her on her quest to help others. While Princess Diana's humanitarian projects may have been a partial inspiration for Amélie's good deeds, Amélie's sudden loss of interest in the television after she has found the treasure chest suggests that the shock of the princess's sudden death was most important, and that Amélie's attention has now shifted to an event that, while small on a global scale, will have more relevance to the reality of Amélie and her immediate community. Rather than listening to the television's endless repetition of another person's past, Amélie prefers to focus on her own future deeds.

The second way in which Amélie interacts with the television is to project herself or her concerns into a programme or televised film that she is watching. These projections tend to be influenced not only by what happens in her life, but by Dufayel's observations about her.[88] Filled with a combination of elation at having begun to help others and deflation as she recognises the truth in Dufayel's allusion to her loneliness, Amélie watches a television biography and sees it as her own, narrating a life tragically shortened, which she devoted to helping others while neglecting herself and her father. Significantly, the documentary stresses a modest humanitarianism rather than a glamorous one. Although, like the princess, Amélie is shown as a centre of attention, wearing pretty outfits and shyly courting the media, she also appears in a modest nurse's uniform (figure 5.2) or nun's habit performing humble deeds; this and the black-and-white 1930s-style setting of the documentary suggest an affinity for Mother Teresa, not just Princess Diana. The second time that Amélie's personal concerns are projected onto what she is watching on television, the subtitles of an old Soviet film are changed so that Stalin seems to be vigorously asserting Amélie's right to 'rater sa vie'/'make a mess of her life'; here again, the projection is the result of her preoccupation with Dufayel's criticism of her shyness combined with her own disappointment at having failed to take the opportunity to talk to Nino. In both cases, Amélie's interaction with the television does not remain on the level of fantasy, leaving her a passive 'spectatrice de sa propre vie'/'spectator of her own life'.[89] Following the first fantasy, she immediately takes action to prevent one of the two imagined tragedies, that of neglecting her own father's happiness. Wearing a black trench coat, she sneaks into her father's garden at night and steals his garden gnome, the first step of a stunt that will see her father receive photos from the gnome's holiday, and ultimately encourage him to take advantage of his retirement and travel a little himself. Although she does not take such practical action after she imagines Stalin defending her right to ruin her life, this fantasy does increase her anxiety to such a level that she must go out (again in her black trench coat) to skip stones on the canal in order to release her tension. Evidently, Amélie finds it easier to change other people's lives than her own; nonetheless, after the second fantasy she comes close to doing as Dufayel suggests, taking 'une vraie risque'/'a genuine risk' rather than maintaining a safe distance by means of her 'stratagèmes'/'schemes'. Pursuing her previous plan of setting Nino up to discover the identity of the mystery man from his album, she very nearly goes to talk to Nino herself; as

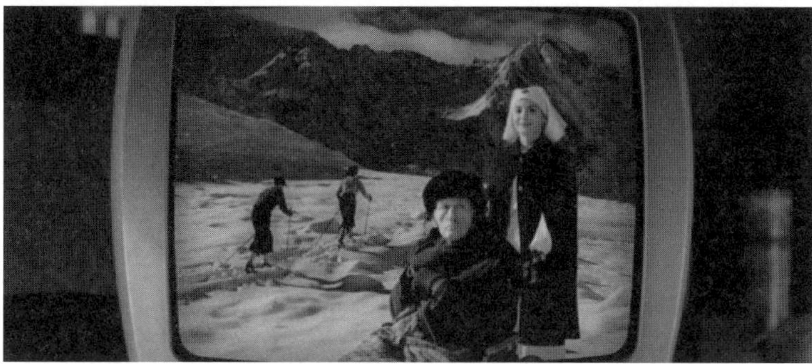

Figure 5.2: Amélie imagines herself as a famous humanitarian in a television documentary in *Amélie*.

she walks towards the photo booth, however, a luggage cart blocks her path, giving her time to think, hesitate and miss her opportunity.

Amélie clearly shows the influence of the attention-grabbing spectacular effects and glossy images of TV advertising; in this respect, any inclusion of television may automatically be considered to refer self-reflexively to a medium that has influenced Jeunet since childhood. The use of television most directly imitates the director's own style in this film when it is used in combination with video. Using her video recorder, Amélie collects a series of unusual television clips; this collage may be compared to Jeunet's eclectic approach to film-making, which itself brings together a variety of styles and allusions.[90]

Jeunet reveals that the source of inspiration for the film's collage videos was 'Zapping', a French television programme consisting of a series of interesting clips taken from other programmes.[91] The brevity and variety of the clips in that programme may evoke 'zapping', yet by presenting a series of images selected by somebody else, it misses the fundamental element of the actual practice of 'channel surfing' from which it takes its name: 'Zapping' does away with the spectator's active role by removing the need for switching from one station to another and thus its clips cannot reflect the spectator's personal tastes in the same way. Although the programme sets a precedent for subverting the usual status of the television image as something that is seen only once and in context, Amélie's video compilations of TV clips retain this subversion as well as restoring some of the interactivity of channel surfing that is lost in 'Zapping'. The audience only sees Amélie record one of the images, and it does not occur while she is flipping through channels on TV; having fallen asleep with the television left on, Amélie happens to wake up just in time to see an interesting image and, though barely awake, she presses the record button. In this sense, she may not be fully conscious of her choice of images (at least not when she selects this first clip); nonetheless, her video compilations reflect choices based on her personal taste, or a guess at what a specific person (Dufayel) would enjoy, whereas the creators of 'Zapping' never met the majority of their target audience, and could only make general guesses about the types of images that would please most people. When Dufayel watches the collage videos sent to him anonymously by his neighbour, his experience is different to watching 'Zapping', as he knows that the images have been assembled just for him and, like the viewer of *Amélie*, he may try to discern the common thread that links the apparently random selection of clips, constituting a hidden message from the sender. In both the making and the receiving of the videos, then, Amélie and Dufayel become more actively involved as television viewers, and the film's audience may also be led to become more active in their thinking about the film in order to unravel a perceived mystery.

As to the possible meaning behind the video images, Isabelle Vanderschelden, one of the scholars who has written most extensively on the film, considers the collage videos to be an example of 'recycled audio-visual material' used for a 'non-narrative end' in *Amélie*, and believes that they do no more than 'illustrat[e] the quaintness of the film'.[92] Apart from saying that he was inspired by 'Zapping', Jeunet himself provides no greater insight. He says that that the images in the collage videos were part of his personal collection of TV clips, and offers his characteristic explanation for having included them in *Amélie*: because he himself liked them.[93] Yet both the audience and Dufayel know that Amélie has begun devoting herself to good deeds, and so it is very likely that if she is sending videos to her neighbour, there is a specifically positive intention behind her action. The desire to understand the meaning of the videos is particularly great because their purpose is never clearly revealed to the audience, while all of her other interventions are either immediately understandable (describing local surroundings in detail to a blind man as she guides him to the metro, for example) or soon become clear (as in the effect of the booby traps that she sets up in Collignon's apartment). As Dufayel reacts with surprise or delight to the collage videos, it is possible to assume that Amélie intended them to inject a little variety and interest into her neighbour's life; she may have given them to him anonymously in order to add an element of mystery that would stimulate his imagination. Until he receives the videos from Amélie, Dufayel only uses his television and video camera as a timepiece: the camera is set up near the window and focused on the clock outside a watchmaker's shop, and the television connected to the video camera displays the image of that clock. By sending him recordings of television clips, Amélie may also intend to show her neighbour that there are interesting things to watch on TV, and other ways of using his video camera. The videos may thus be seen as a means of undermining Dufayel's dismissal of modern technology and his obsessive devotion to the traditional art form of painting; moreover, if this is Amélie's intention, she is more successful than she could have hoped. She does not turn Dufayel into a passive television or film addict; after watching the videos from his neighbour, Dufayel employs his video camera actively, making a video of his own for Amélie.

While the above may explain Amélie's purpose in sending the videos to Dufayel, if there is any message in the images themselves it is far from being as clear as the message in Dufayel's video to her, in which he directly urges her to live her life to the fullest degree. The metaphors that Dufayel uses in this video and in one of his conversations with Amélie constitute more or less direct references to images from the videos that she sent to him, and go some way towards explaining the meaning of her selection, a meaning that Amélie herself may not have consciously intended. Talking with Amélie about her life (using the intermediary of the girl in the painting) Dufayel tells her that she must 'sauter la barrière'/'jump over the fence', overcoming her doubts in order to approach Nino. This is a metaphor clearly inspired by an image from Amélie's first video, which showed a horse jumping over a fence, leaving its field to run alongside the Tour de France cyclists. Dufayel also alludes to the bicycle race, comparing opportunity to the Tour de France in that it takes a long time to arrive but passes very quickly. Through these references, Dufayel not only demonstrates that he is complicit in Amélie's good deed, but turns the good deed back on her, giving her advice that was subtly present in her own choice of image. Similarly, when Dufayel in his video tells Amélie that she doesn't have bones made of glass and that she can take any bumps that life deals out to her, he may not simply be referring to his own brittle bone disease in order to contrast his old age and frailty with the potential of Amélie's youth and strength. Amélie's second video featured performances that were surprising because of some physical limitation in the performers: babies, who are normally helpless or uncoordinated on land, swim gracefully underwater; an older man does a dance even though he has a wooden leg. Dufayel himself is unable to defy the fragility of his bones, but is once again able to articulate the message inherent in Amélie's video collage and send it back to her in his own video: as she does not have any physical impairment, she has all the more reason to take risks in life.

It seems, then, that the purpose of Amélie's video collages was to help Dufayel, but the meaning of the images that they contained was more relevant to Amélie's own situation. Like the director himself, Amélie may have selected images for the collage videos simply because she liked them. Although Jeunet regularly introduces characters based on their likes and dislikes, the film only engages on the most superficial level with the notion that personal preferences in trivial matters may be symptomatic of much deeper and more important preoccupations and psychological characteristics.[94] It is of particular relevance, from this perspective, that the only time Amélie is seen selecting an image for her collage video is when she is half-asleep, making it all the more plausible that her unconscious is guiding her in what the surrealists might have termed an automatic selection of the image. Although she may have been fully conscious when she selected the other images, the fact that all of them may be understood in terms of her own situation points to the role of personal preoccupations in determining her choices; her unconscious led her to select these images, making them symptomatic in the same way as the surrealist *objet trouvé*/found object. Amélie knew that there was no reason for her to live her life so cautiously, and by regulating her choice of image, her own desire to be freed of her inhibitions exteriorised itself and, with the help of Dufayel, made its message compellingly clear.

Newspapers and magazines

Shocked by the way in which the French media used the death of the Princess of Wales in order to sell newspapers, Jeunet dramatises opposing viewpoints about the relevance of the story by means of a conversation between Amélie and the proprietor of her local kiosk. The newsagent laments the death of Princess Diana because she was 'jeune et jolie'/'young and pretty' and, missing the irony of Amélie's question, confirms that the death of someone 'vieille et moche'/'old and ugly' is 'moins grave'/'less serious', offering the example of Mother Teresa without hesitation. If there is a self-reflexive dimension to this particular use of printed media in the film, Jeunet may, in spite of his disdain for journalists' opportunism, be subtly justifying a moderate degree of emphasis on appearance over substance (something of which his own film has been accused) because this is what the general public desires.[95] At the same time, the film not only includes but sides with Amélie's dissenting voice. Moreover, as if to compensate for the extensive correction of the film's images in post-production, the film's diegesis includes characters who are not conventionally attractive, or may even be considered 'old and ugly', and focuses on qualities that make these characters appear childish or eccentric rather than those that give the impression of well-adjusted adults.

As an additional counterpoint to the media's privileging of the biggest news of the day, the film gives equal attention to smaller news items; this again constitutes a reflection of Jeunet's own tendency as a director to focus on small things, but also demonstrates the way in which an individual's mindset determines his or her attitude to the news. For example, when they are in love, the normally morose Joseph and anxious Georgette react with delight to a sentimental *fait divers*/small news item about a little boy who takes to the highway in his toy car in order to admire the night sky. Similarly, when Amélie has turned her focus to helping others, a small report on the discovery of a mailbag lost almost 30 years previously in a plane crash in the Alps is more than an interesting anecdote; for her, it is the perfect excuse for her heartbroken neighbour to receive a final (forged) letter of apology from her philandering husband, who had died in the meantime.

There is one other example of the convergence of printed media, current events and individual preoccupations that cannot be left out, even though it only exists as a verbal reference in the film. Collignon entertains his customers by revealing that his assistant, Lucien, cut out pictures of Princess Diana's head from the news and used them to replace the heads of the lingerie models in a clothing catalogue. In addition to being a reflection of Jeunet's tendency to borrow from diverse sources and the way in which he uses technology to shape his film's reality in accordance with his wishes, Lucien's collage offers an excellent example of the way in which individual desire can work to subvert the intended use and reception of familiar media and the images they present.

Letters

When Amélie forges the letter for her neighbour Madeleine, it is a multi-step process: having stolen the woman's collection of love letters and read them in order to select useful phrases that she may extract, Amélie photocopies the letters, cuts out the selected phrases (figure 5.3), pastes them onto a new sheet of paper, photocopies this collage letter, and finally dips the photocopy in tea in order to age it. She then mails the forged letter to Madeleine with another forged letter from the post office apologising for the delayed delivery. Even more than in the earlier examples of video collages and Lucien's substitution of heads in the catalogue, Jeunet's own style of film-making is reflected in the way in which Amélie takes phrases out of context

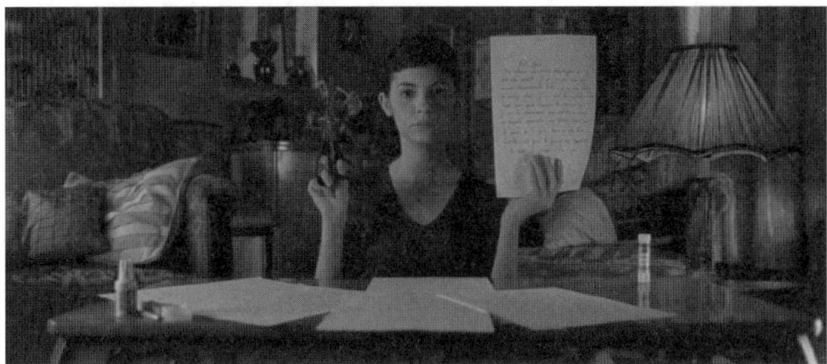

Figure 5.3: Amélie forges a love letter for her neighbour Madeleine in *Amélie.*

in order to create a forged letter that expresses an idea never contained in the original love letters (specifically, an apology for adultery). Jeunet, too, takes his filmed images of the real Paris and alters them in order to create an idealised city which pleases him and most audiences, but which has never actually existed.[96] Moreover, just as Amélie uses both modern and rudimentary means (photocopying as well as cut-and-paste) in order to create an illusion for her neighbour, Jeunet uses both high-tech computer imaging and artisanal mechanics to create the illusions in his film.[97]

Taking phrases used by Madeleine's husband in his letters and rearranging them to say something else, Amélie certainly uses the letters in a way other than they were intended, just as she turns the newspaper article about the lost mailbag into an unexpected opportunity for a good deed. When she steals her father's gnome, Amélie transgresses the conventions of letter writing in a different way: she has her flight-attendant friend take photos of the inanimate figurine against world-famous backdrops, and send them to Monsieur Poulain without the accompanying letter that is normally included to identify the sender and the purpose of the communication. The absence of the usual information leaves his most pressing questions unanswered: who stole his gnome and why he or she is sending him pictures of it. Raphael Poulain is too caught up in his own world to recall a conversation with his daughter in which she encouraged him to travel, and is unable to guess that she has a friend who is a flight attendant. To his mind, the most logical conclusion is that he is the victim of an elaborate but unmotivated stunt. However, this explanation is so unusual and irrational that the photos, which stand in place of letters, begin to suggest an even more irrational conclusion: the gnome has gone on holiday by himself and it is he who is sending the photos. The film suggests that such a wild possibility is indeed beginning to present itself to Amélie's father when, after receiving several envelopes, he receives another, containing two photos of the gnome (figure 5.4): Monsieur Poulain's face is shown in a wide-angled close-up as he looks over his shoulder with a haunted expression, his eyes moving cautiously from left to right, and the eerie chirp of a frog brings the scene playfully to a close.

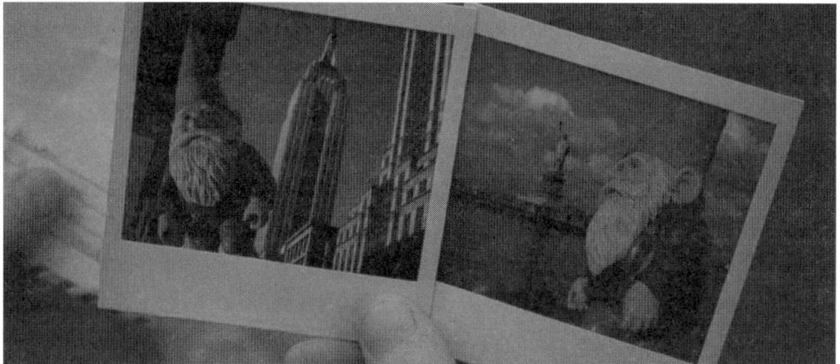

Figure 5.4: Raphael Poulain receives holiday snaps from his garden gnome in *Amélie*.

Although the mercilessly rational Raphael Poulain is initially exasperated rather than amused by the gratuitousness of the photo letters, and later frightened rather than intrigued by their suggestion of the irrational, they ultimately serve a specific and positive objective: encouraging him to get out and explore the world. Moreover, the element of the uncanny in the notion that it was the gnome that sent the photos points to the memento mori dimension of the film's theme, that it is important to take the opportunity to enjoy life before it is too late: if an inanimate figurine can travel the world, so can a living man.

Telephone

By disrupting expectations concerning telephone communication, Amélie creates uncanny and/or defamiliarising effects similar to those she created for her father through her play on the conventions of mail. It is in the guise of an avenging angel rather than a good fairy that Amélie plays on Collignon's expectations so that, when he picks up his phone and presses the button labelled 'Maman', instead of hearing his mother's reassuring voice he is connected to the 'urgence psychiatrique'/'psychiatric emergency' hotline. The wicked irony in Amélie's reprogramming of Collignon's speed dial is that it predicts the cumulative effect of her sabotage of his flat. Coming near the end of a series of engineered malfunctions and subtle alterations in objects' usual proportions or arrangement, Collignon's unintended call to the psychiatric hospital confirms what he is already beginning to believe: that he is going mad. Because he is so egotistical, Collignon cannot guess that his rudeness and cruel jokes have angered Amélie so much that she has broken into his apartment and created booby traps as punishment for him. Moreover, the genius of these booby traps is that devastating effects are created from tiny alterations to details to which Collignon would normally pay no attention: whether there is a handle or a doorknob on the outside of his bathroom door, for example, or the respective locations of his tubes of toothpaste and foot cream. As opening the bathroom door or putting toothpaste on his toothbrush are actions that have become automatic, Collignon has come to rely on not having to think consciously about them; he therefore becomes nervous when he cannot rely on his subconscious to take care of his interaction with familiar objects. Moreover, it is precisely because he does not normally need to pay attention to whether his bathroom door opens with a knob or a handle that he cannot be certain that there has been a change in the object rather than an alteration of his mind. When a more deliberate activity such as pressing a speed-dial button is also disrupted, Collignon becomes frightened as well as confused, as it seems that he can rely neither on his conscious nor subconscious mind to perform the correct actions. While Amélie's tricks may seem mean-spirited, as they lead a man much more frighteningly close to the irrational than the gnome letters did her father, Collignon needs to be shocked out of his habitual patterns of behaviour. Amélie's sabotage suggests a possible practical purpose of forcing Collignon to pay closer attention to all aspects of his behaviour, from his selfishness and rudeness, of which he may be unconscious, to his consciously elaborated cruel jokes.

Undermining standard expectations surrounding the use of telephones also plays a pivotal role in Amélie's first good deed. In order to return the treasure box to Dominique Bretodeau, its original owner, she places it in a telephone booth, waits for Bretodeau to pass by, and calls the phone so that its ringing will lead him to find the box. Ringing normally serves a subordinate function of making someone pick up the receiver so that the telephone may serve its primary function as a medium of conversation; Amélie subverts this order by using the phone's ringing to lure Bretodeau into the box, then hanging up without saying a word when he answers. When he discovers a long-lost personal treasure sitting on top of the phone, the enormity of the coincidence makes it impossible for Bretodeau to accept the usual assumption, that the call was a mistake. However, he is not quite able to make the next most logical assumption, that a creative person thought of making the phone ring in order to lead him to his treasure box. Rather like Raphael Poulain faced with the gnome letters, he cannot see how or why anyone would go to so much trouble. Shocked out of his rational thought patterns by both the discovery and the wave of memories and emotions that this discovery evokes, Bretodeau seems even more tempted than Raphael Poulain by the supernatural explanation. As he recounts his experience to a barman, Bretodeau says that it was as though the phone was 'calling' him. Immediately mocking him for implying that an inanimate object is capable of deliberate action, the barman says that he, too, is being 'called' by the microwave as its bell rings. Although made in jest, the distinction that the barman raises between animate and inanimate once again highlights the memento mori element in the film's carpe diem theme: rediscovering the box alerts Bretodeau to the passage of time, and makes him resolve to heal the rift between himself and his daughter, in order that he may get to know his grandson 'avant de finir à [son] tour dans une petite boîte'/'before ending up in a little box [him]self'. Although she could not predict the effect of her good deed, Amélie's unusual use of the telephone served a pivotal role in defamiliarising a familiar means of communication; leading Bretodeau to think about the telephone in a new way (suspecting it of having called him) played a contributing role in the creation of a larger shift in his usual way of thinking.

Photography

Amélie features three different brands of photographic equipment and/or the photographs produced by them: the Instamatic, the Polaroid and the Photomaton. As they were aimed at the general public, all of these photographic formats were designed with simplicity and a limited range of uses in mind. Jeunet's film demonstrates that creativity is not limited to professional photographers using expensive and complicated equipment, however; Amélie thinks of unconventional uses for all of these types of mass-market camera, and she and Nino both use the photographs produced by them in unusual ways.

When Amélie is given an Instamatic as a child, like many an inexperienced photographer she thinks that clouds constitute a good subject. The audience is unable to totally dismiss her optimistic delight, however. Placed behind the young Amélie's shoulder each time she takes a picture, Jeunet's camera shows that the clouds she is photographing are in the distinct shape of a rabbit (figure 5.5) and a teddy bear. The audience knows that the images have been digitally altered in order to allow them to take on Amélie's subjective point of view; the illusion is nonetheless particularly appealing and acceptable in that it reproduces an impression that many viewers will have had of being able to see an unbelievably distinct image of a object, animal or face in random cloud formations. This, then, is a use of special effects of which even the surrealists might have approved because the viewer is not tricked by the effect but complicit in it. In this case, Jeunet makes use of the medium in a way specifically prescribed by the surrealist group: to demonstrate the very real manner in which the unconscious shapes our experience of waking life. Because her imagination will continue to interpret the clouds in the same way, whether she is looking at the original clouds or a photo of them, Amélie will have succeeded in capturing the rabbit and teddy-shaped clouds for herself, even if other people will not see the animals in her photos as clearly as they appear in Jeunet's digitally-enhanced film image. Moreover, her use of the camera to capture an image with a uniquely subjective value subverts the emphasis conventionally (if incorrectly) placed on photography's objectivity. Amélie's attempt to use photography as a means to capture her imaginative vision of the world reflects aspirations that Jeunet, through advanced technology, is able to realise on film: he takes the images of reality recorded by his movie camera and alters them to reflect his imagination and desires.

The Polaroid photos in the film are like Amélie's cloud pictures in that they feature a subject equally unworthy, by conventional standards, of being recorded on film: a garden gnome. Neither a live human figure nor a work of sculptural excellence, this kitsch piece of mass-produced decoration mocks the practice of having one's photograph taken in front of a famous monument while on holiday. It is in part because it is so unusual to take photos of a gnome as though it were a human being that Raphael Poulain pays more attention to these photos than he would if they featured a real person. This is in turn due, more specifically, to the fact that the photo stands in place of a letter; moreover, because the gnome stands in for a human in the photo, there is the uncanny suggestion that the gnome is the sender. Through this photo, Jeunet seems to point to the fact that an image can sometimes express

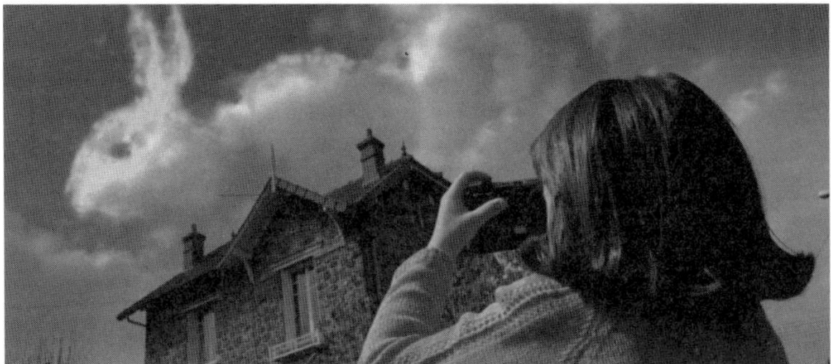

Figure 5.5: Young Amélie captures cloud shapes as she sees them in *Amélie*.

more than words, and also to the idea that a photo, by freezing a moment in time, in a sense serves to equalise animate and inanimate.

Both of these ideas resurface when Amélie uses another type of photograph in order to communicate with Nino after she has found his album. Perhaps to appeal to his taste for Photomaton images, she writes him a note on the back of a large photo consisting of four passport-style shots of the same man. This photo blurs the line between animate and inanimate much more radically than the gnome photo: rather than freezing its human subject, this photo allows all four copies of him to come to life, talking in unison and sometimes disagreeing with each other (figure 5.6) (perhaps to ironise the photograph's illusion of reproduction, or else as a humorous reflection of the co-existence of conflicting feelings in one individual). The animate-inanimate distinction is playfully highlighted, too, when the images comment on a privilege they have enjoyed because they are part of an object (the photograph): one of them snickers as it reveals that they have been in Amélie's pocket, next to her breast. It is perhaps because Nino is so imaginative, or because he is half asleep (it is the man in the photograph who wakes him up) that he is less fazed by an inanimate object coming to life than Raphael Poulain is by a gnome photographed as though it were a human being. It is also, perhaps, his eagerness to know more about the person who wrote the note that allows Nino to question the man in the photo as though an image were the same as a real person. Rather than the writing on the back of a photograph saying something about the image, here the image comes to life to say something about the writer, thus subverting the usual relationship between writing and photography. Although it reveals more than the silent photo of the gnome does, the speaking photo of a man does not explain everything, preserving an element of mystery and even a hint of the marvellous; when Nino hears its suggestion that the note's writer is in love with him, and he protests that he does not even know her, the photo responds by telling Nino that he knows her 'from his dreams'. Of course, the rational explanation for this exchange with the photo is that it is all Nino's dream: in this case, the photo's observations can be attributed to Nino's own desire, urging him to engage with the mystery woman in spite of any rational reservations he may have.

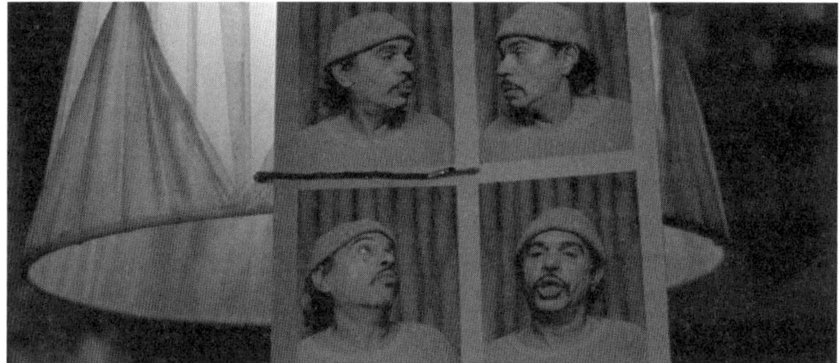

Figure 5.6: Four images of the same man come to life and have a debate in *Amélie*.

It is of interest to note that Photomatons began to appear in Paris from 1928 and were thus contemporary with the surrealist group, who did not hesitate to use them in a creative manner. There is an example of this in the December 1929 edition of *La Révolution surréaliste* (no. 12) where René Magritte's painting '*Je ne vois pas la [femme] cachée dans la forêt*'/ '*I do not see the [woman] hidden in the forest*' appears with a border of Photomaton images of members of the surrealist group with their eyes closed. While most Photomaton users would discard any images in which they appeared with their eyes shut, the surrealists took these kinds of photos deliberately and elevated them to the level of art. In *Amélie*, Nino's album similarly valorises unconventional Photomaton images; the difference here is that they are photographs that have actually been taken by accident, and that the subjects have thrown away because they consider them to have failed. In the production of *Amélie*, like the surrealists Jeunet had to create these seemingly mistaken photos deliberately, using a real Photomaton; in order to create the appearance of the accidental, he would trick the sitters into doing something that would spoil their photos (fixing their hair, etc.).[98] Some scholars have seen Nino's album as yet another self-reflexive element in the film: in particular, the collection of photographs evoking the series of still frames that make up the movie,[99] and the album's use of collage (bringing together a variety of photos which themselves have often had to be pieced back together) reflecting the process of montage in general as well as the eclectic sources of reference that specifically characterise Jeunet's own style.[100] Within the diegesis, Nino's collection is different from the example of surrealist art cited above, but nonetheless consistent with surrealist principles; seeing the value in that which is normally rejected as distasteful or ignored as irrelevant,[101] Nino reconstitutes torn up images of strangers into a most unconventional 'album de famille'/'family album' that inherently questions the tendency to privilege only those photographs in which one's own friends and relatives have adopted a standard pose.

In recent years, Photomatons have tended to be used for one of two purposes: the official passport photo or the personal photo that tends to be spontaneous and often silly. *Amélie* presents three types of variation on these uses: the ludic use of a Photomaton image for communication (which includes the handwritten note on the back of a photo, discussed earlier, as well as photos of Amélie in which some kind of written message for Nino is included within the image), Nino's collection of failed photos of other people (taken for either official or personal use), and the repairman's practical and serious test photos. For most of the film, this last example offers a source of mystery for Amélie, Nino and the audience.

Nino's album gives an impression of diversity, from the broad segment of society represented by the subjects (in terms of age, gender and ethnic origin), to the variety in the physical quality of their photographs (the degree of damage to the paper) and the types of infra-image errors that spoiled them. The album is nonetheless governed by one rule: any photo that is included must be one that was thrown away and that Nino then found, and as a result almost all of the photos are united by the fact that the image did not turn out as the sitter intended. Although it seems to be this very element of the unexpected that motivates Nino to collect these photos, he (like Amélie) is most intrigued by the exception to the album's rule: a photo that, according to conventional standards, has turned out perfectly, but which its subject has nonetheless thrown out. The mystery is augmented by the fact that this type of photo, always featuring the same man, appears in Nino's album more than once: whereas most people use Photomatons rarely, and therefore discard spoiled photos even more rarely, there is one person in Paris who habitually takes photos in the Photomaton and throws them away for no evident reason.

When Amélie picks up Nino's lost album, she is alerted to the mystery man's photos by Nino's handwritten notes ('Toujours lui!'/'Him again!'). She draws the anomaly to Dufayel's attention when she shows him the album (figure 5.7) and together they try to understand why someone would act contrary to standard rules of behaviour. Interestingly, rather than attempting to explain why the man would throw away perfect photos, they focus on the frequency with which they are taken. Dufayel considers the matter from a psychological perspective, suggesting that the man in the photo may have a particular fear of growing old, and thus takes photos 'pour se rassurer'/'to reassure himself'. Amélie, with her active imagination, requires only the smallest stimulus to depart from rational thought patterns; while it took her father some time to even begin to suspect that the gnome had come to life, and a huge coincidence for Bretodeau to think that the telephone itself had led him to make a discovery, Amélie quickly seizes upon a supernatural explanation for the mystery man's unconventional use of the Photomaton. She suggests that the man is in fact dead and that what he fears is being forgotten: he therefore uses the Photomaton as a means of 'faxing' his image from the world beyond to the world of the living. Once again, both Amélie and Dufayel's interpretations of the mysterious use of the Photomaton reflect the fact that Amélie's own situation is on their minds, as the fear of getting old and being forgotten forms part of the power of the memento mori. It is interesting that Nino's discovery of the mystery man's true identity once again points to the distinction between animate and inanimate, which keeps coming up in the film's unconventional uses of various media; having been alerted to the mystery man's presence by his characteristic red trainers visible in the lower part of the booth, Nino sees the inanimate image of him as it drops out of the machine, before the repairman himself emerges from the Photomaton.[102]

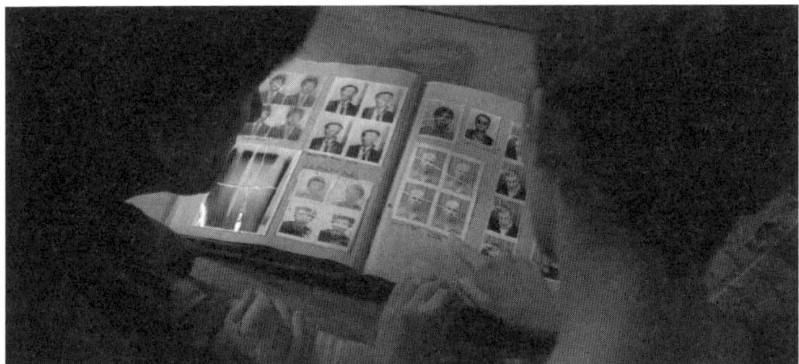

Figure 5.7: Amélie shows Dufayel the mystery man in Nino's album in *Amélie*.

Where previous examples of the uncanny and/or memento mori emerged from an unconventional use of media that shocked Amélie's father or Bretodeau out of their normal rational thought patterns, the example of the mystery man works in the opposite way. Faced with nothing more than a variation in the conventional use of Photomatons (i.e. without the added shock of a missing gnome or a returned treasure box), Amélie readily seizes on an irrational explanation that, moreover, is not really suggested by anything in the photos themselves; faced with much more disorienting situations, her father and Bretodeau, by contrast, tended towards the most obvious irrational conclusion. Also, unlike Raphael Poulain and Bretodeau who may never discover the explanation for their near-supernatural experiences, both Amélie and Nino ultimately learn the prosaic truth about the mystery man and his photos. Rather than demonstrating the way in which an unfamiliar (and uncanny) use of familiar media may lead people towards irrational thought patterns, the example of the mystery man's photos shows how a mind that already benefits from embracing the irrational perceives the marvellous even in the most mundane situations. Hence the film reflects Amélie's and Nino's delight at discovering the mystery man's identity (through the sound of a choir, a 360-degree camera roll, and a fade to white), as well as contrasting it humorously with the repairman's nervous incomprehension of Nino's ecstatic smile.

Conclusion

Variation in the conventional use of media objects is applied with astonishing consistency to all means of expression and communication in *Amélie*, so much so that it is in fact difficult to find any medium in the film being used in a wholly customary manner. These unusual and/or active means of employing media of expression and communication are not of interest simply because they are pleasantly surprising. As media that are encountered in everyday life, their most familiar use has become particularly well-established, almost to the point of preventing one from imagining a different way of using them. When a new use is suddenly discovered for them, the innovation is all the more powerful because of the sense that it had to overcome the inertia of established use. When a familiar object is made new, or defamiliarised, there is a sense that every familiar aspect of one's everyday surroundings may hold such potential, and the possibilities of the quotidian become subject to a sudden expansion. This is an impression that the film supplements through an emphasis on the power of chance.

For the surrealists, the unconscious was the foundation of the surrealist object, in the sense of both its cause and its effect. When an object was used in an unconventional way, it was the unconscious, by means of the imagination, that inspired it; likewise, the surrealist object that was created offered a concrete example of the influence of the unconscious in waking life, and an opportunity for this role to be more widely understood, accepted and thus broadened. In *Amélie*, there is only one example of an object put to a use that is genuinely new and which also clearly points to role of the unconscious in this use: the collage videos. It is notable that these are also the only objects, indeed the only part of the film, in which an element of genuine mystery is maintained.[103] The mystery pertains to Amélie's precise intention, normally revealed by the effect of her good/punitive deeds on the recipient. In the case of the collage videos, both the meaning behind the images and their positive effect on the recipient are unclear. The images on the collage videos cover five different subjects, and only one of these is unmistakeably used by Dufayel as a metaphor when he is giving advice to Amélie.[104] The audience is not, moreover, inevitably made to understand the videos as Amélie's unconscious message to herself. Indeed, Dufayel's use of the metaphor could be understood simply as proof of his perceptiveness: it demonstrates that he knows that Amélie is the anonymous sender, and that he pays attention to new stimuli and readily relates them to current situations, similar to the way in which he uses the Renoir painting as a medium for discussing Amélie's life. For the viewer watching the film for the first time, the meaning behind the other images will not be apparent; as mentioned in the analysis, even for some scholars the significance of the collage videos remains vague.[105] By contrast, when *Le Déjeuner des canotiers* is used as a means of exploring Amélie's psychological and emotional relationships with those around her, the metaphor is established subtly through visual parallel,[106] before being made unmistakably explicit through the dialogue.

When Amélie uses a media object in an unusual way, it is most often with the specific purpose of helping others rather than to explore her own unconscious: using the call box phone to lead Bretodeau to his treasure box, having photo-letters of the garden gnome sent to her father to encourage him to travel, forging a new love letter out of old ones to soothe Madeleine's broken heart, and reprogramming the telephone speed dial to punish Collignon on behalf of Lucien. Although the film does suggest that Amélie is trying to change other people's lives as a means to avoid making the necessary changes in her own, except in the case of the collage videos her own unconscious is not reflected in her unusual use of objects. Rather, the focus becomes the good deed to which the unusual use of the object contributes: specifically, bringing about a change in the thinking and, often, behaviour of the recipient of the good deed. Certainly, the variation on the media object's normal use often provokes the irrational side of the recipient's mind, playing on Madeleine's desire to believe in unlikely events, or leading to a blurring of the line between animate and inanimate for Raphael Poulain and Bretodeau, and between sanity and insanity for Collignon. This incursion into the irrational is treated as no more than a brief source of comedy, however. Collignon's terror and Madeleine's elation provide an entertaining contrast to their usual behaviour, and the fact that they have been so easily tricked is also amusing. Bretodeau is mocked by the barman for implying that the telephone itself summoned him, and Raphael Poulain is mocked by a stylistic parody of the horror genre when he momentarily suspects his gnome of independent action.

Sometimes it is Jeunet himself who uses a media object in an unusual way in his film in order to display a character's unconscious and/or its influence on perception. This is the case, in particular, when paintings or photos come to life in what may logically be interpreted as a dream, or when Amélie's subjectivity is projected into the programme or film she is watching on TV. The latter example is similar to the shots where special effects were used to show clouds in the shape of a rabbit or teddy bear; the audience understands and enjoys the way in which film can literally reflect the use of the intermediary of television to think and fantasise about one's own life. Jeunet even offers the audience pleasant surprises in his representation of dreams, usually one of film's most highly coded perspectives; here, the lack of the clichéd indicators might even lead one to suspect that the film is allowing the incursion of impossible events into reality rather than representing a dream. Instead of showing a shot of Amélie asleep and following it with shots of her dream, dream-like events are shown in the same shot as a sleeping Amélie; similarly, Nino is woken up *by* the dream-like event, rather than waking up after it. If they are interpreted as dreams, these scenes have the neat advantage of reproducing not only the impossible events of dreams but also their sense of confusion. Although one may not often see oneself asleep in one's dream, the shots of Amélie's dream accurately imitate for the audience the blending of unrealistic events and a convincingly realistic setting that are characteristic of dreams. Nino's dream does the same and, further, reproduces the experience of dreaming that one has woken up, as well as featuring illogical conversations. The one limitation of all of *Amélie*'s examples of media that reflect the characters' unconscious is that while the use of the medium may be surprising, the contents of the unconscious never are. Amélie as a child is concerned with cute animals; as an adult she is preoccupied with falling in love and finding a way to overcome her inhibitions; Nino, meanwhile, wants to know more about the mystery girl who is pursuing him.

The third and final notable use of media of expression and communication in *Amélie* is as a metaphor for the film itself. For the surrealists, self-reflexivity was a means of disrupting the usual relationship between the viewer and the work of art. Given *Amélie*'s systematic subversion of the conventional use of various media of expression and communication, one might be led to believe that Jeunet included these references as a means of disrupting the way in which the audience relates to his film. There is some degree of disruption in *Amélie*: characters sometimes look directly into the lens, virtuoso camera movements and occasional mechanical sound-effects (when Amélie is making the collage letter, for example) draw attention to the presence of the camera, while visible special effects remind the audience of the director's ability to modify the image, all of which break the illusion of film as unmediated observation of reality. However, in terms of the self-reflexivity in the film's diegetic use of media, it is only when Amélie actually engages in watching movies herself that the audience will be reminded that they too, by watching Jeunet's film, are interacting with a medium of expression. The majority of examples of self-reflexivity in *Amélie* pertain to Jeunet's own approach to the production process: the most common is the use of collage reflecting the way in which Jeunet adopts diverse styles and references that reflect his personal preferences (most notably, Amélie's collection of TV clips on video and Nino's photo album), sometimes in order to create an illusion that corresponds to desire but does not correspond to reality (as in the case of Madeleine's letter and Lucien's substitution of heads in the catalogue). Most audiences are unlikely to make a conscious link between the diegetic collages and Jeunet's style, and thus this third function of objects will simply add to a generalised sense of rich variety in the film's diverse media references.

Within the diegesis, objects are used in an innovative way and the characters' unconscious desires are to some degree revealed, but the result is not a greater exploration of the obscure parts of the mind and discovery of new modes of existence. Rather, the film suggests that the characters unconsciously desire nothing more than the contentment that can be achieved through the heterosexual couple (Amélie and Nino, or Madeleine and her deceased husband), the family (Bretodeau and his grandson), or familiar leisure pursuits (travel or painting for old men such as Raphael Poulain and Dufayel). The unusual use of objects and the exploration of the irrational thus serve two main purposes in the film: the first is to lead characters to the conventional sources of happiness mentioned. The second is to offer a pleasant source of temporary distraction that remains broadly within the bounds of convention: this is best demonstrated through Amélie's and Nino's playful use of media, and in particular the example of the mystery man of the Photomaton, where pleasure was to be found equally in imagining explanations for his behaviour (exploration of the irrational) and in discovering the man's prosaic identity (return to reason). Wherever mystery and the irrational are evoked in the film, they never represent any sustained challenge to life's reigning logic.

It was neither the purpose of this chapter nor of this book to find films containing surrealist objects that correspond exactly to the surrealists' original definition. For this reason, it is not in itself a problem that objects in *Amélie* which are surrealist in form do not reveal the unconscious in any meaningful sense; the hybrid objects examined in other films also had unconscious resonance only rarely, and again in arguably limited form. The interest of the hybrid object lies not in its unconscious relevance but in its relevance to the film's diegesis: the way in which the multiple roles and meanings that the object takes on serve to disrupt a simplistic understanding of that object in the film. The broader relevance of that disruption depended on the priorities of the individual director, whether he or she wanted to criticise the dominant regime or portray the complexity of everyday reality.

The initial interest of Jeunet's film was due only in part to the fact that its media objects appeared to be surrealist objects. *Amélie* was also of interest simply for emphasising such a diverse range of media and the associated impression that these objects might do more than serve an instrumental function in the film's diegesis. My initial impression that the objects had multiple roles in the film was correct: in addition to their use in advancing the narrative, objects also revealed important information about the characters' preoccupations. Beyond their diegetic function, the objects reflected the film's thematic preoccupations of isolation and the passage of time, and even pointed to the director's own process of physically creating a film that would respond to these themes.

Although objects in *Amélie* take on as many roles as objects in the films discussed in previous chapters, they do not take on the destabilising effect that forms the other essential component of the hybrid object's function. Just as media objects in the film are surrealist in form but not in content, as hybrid objects too they are missing the element of resistance against reality as it stands. Amélie overcomes her own isolation and seizes the day through entirely traditional means by forming a couple. Those characters in the film who fail to do so are left in their state of isolation. A film that was more resistant would show that reality can truly be other than what it appears. This was the case in the Czech New Wave's exploration of the everyday, Buñuel's challenges to the definition of realism, and Clair's critique of reality through exaggeration. Reality in *Amélie* is composed mainly of loneliness, disillusion and neurosis, and a change in that reality can only come from a wilful or accidental misconception of it: this is as true in the film's ostentatiously unrealistic form as in its content of child-like imagination and elaborate tricks. Objects in *Amélie* take on a form of resistance temporarily but, like the film's characters, their deeper motivation is largely based on traditional logic and simple and direct ways of understanding.

Notes

1 Michael O'Pray, 'Jan Švankmajer: A Mannerist Surrealist', *The Cinema of Jan Švankmajer: Dark Alchemy*, 2nd edn, ed. Peter Hames (London: Wallflower, 2008) 42 with ref. to Hal Foster, 'A Preface', *Postmodern Culture* (London: Pluto Press, 1985).

2 The most substantial are Isabelle Vanderschelden's *Amélie* (Champaign: University of Illinois Press, 2007) and Elizabeth Ezra's *Jean-Pierre Jeunet* (Urbana and Chicago: University of Illinois Press, 2008).

3 Billard, *Mystère* 7.

4 Vanderschelden 1.

5 Jean Cluzel refers to research carried out by *Télérama* which found that in 2001, 80 per cent of French audiences felt that domestic films had begun to have greater appeal to the general public: see *Propos impertinents sur le cinéma français* (Paris: PUF, 2003) 100. With respect to *Amélie*'s impact on France's contemporary cinematic reputation internationally,

see Dudley Andrew, 'Amélie, or Le Fabuleux Destin du Cinéma Français', *Film Quarterly* 57.3 (2004): 35.

6   Vanderschelden 5.

7   'Jean-Pierre Jeunet on *Delicatessen*', *Projections 9: French Film-makers on Film-making*, eds. Michel Ciment and Noël Herpe (London: Faber and Faber, 1999) 145.

8   Arnauld Visinet, 'Foutaises: Un film de Jean-Pierre Jeunet', *Six courts métrages*, ed. Térésa Faucon (BiFi: Lycéens au cinéma, 2000) 17–18; Vanderschelden 26.

9   Vanderschelden 64–65, 34.

10   Vanderschelden 23–24, 49.

11   Andrew, 'Amélie' 41, with reference to Marcia Butzel (doctoral dissertation) who, however, takes *Le Million* as her example.

12   Jeunet in 'Director's Commentary' on Momentum DVD release of *Amélie*, 2002. Pierre Billard notes the degree of control that Clair held over *À Nous la liberté*: he not only directed but also wrote and produced the film, and worked with René Le Hénaff on the editing. He even arranged to have his bedroom at the studio during production, so that he was literally living on the set (v. *L'Âge classique du cinéma français: Du cinéma parlant à la Nouvelle Vague* (Paris: Flammarion, 1995) 63–64).

13   Jeunet, 'Director's Commentary'; Ginette Vincendeau, 'Café Society', *Sight and Sound*, August 2001, 23.

14   Vincendeau 23.

15   Anna Gural-Migdal, 'Paris comme parc d'attractions à la Disney dans *Le Fabuleux destin d'Amélie Poulain*', *AUMLA* 108 (2007): 136. Andrew ('Amélie' 41) notes the similarly enormous success of Clair's film, which was 'the first sound film to outscore Hollywood in worldwide box-office receipts and critical reception'.

16   Ed Potton, 'Jean-Pierre Jeunet', *Times Online*, 9 April 2005.

17   Vanderschelden 37.

18   Vincendeau 23; Vanderschelden 68.

19   Vanderschelden 37.

20   Franck Garbarz, '*Le Fabuleux Destin d'Amélie Poulain*: La recolleuse de morceaux', *Positif*, no. 483, May 2001, 29; Gural-Migdal 136.

21   Vanderschelden 38.

22   Steven Kovács, *From Enchantment to Rage: The Story of Surrealist Cinema* (Cranbury, NJ: Associated University Presses, 1980) 39.

23   Vanderschelden 40–41, with ref. to Michelle Scatton-Tessier on the isolation of contemporary urban life ('Le Petisme: flirting with the sordid in *Le Fabuleux destin d'Amélie Poulain*', *Studies in French Cinema* 4.3 [2004]: 199).

24   Elizabeth Ezra, 'The Death of an Icon: *Le Fabuleux Destin d'Amélie Poulain*', *French Cultural Studies* 15.3 (2004): 302.

25   Ezra, 'Death of an Icon' 302.

26   Vanderschelden 2.

27   Vanderschelden 79.

28   Vincendeau 23.

29 Vanderschelden 25. For differing interpretations of *À Nous la liberté* at the time of its release, see Billard, *Mystère* 189–90.

30 Vincendeau 24.

31 Vanderschelden 83.

32 'Amélie pas jolie', *Libération*, 31 May 2001, qtd. in Ezra, 'Death of an Icon' 301.

33 Vincendeau 24–25 says that Jeunet does this by giving the only North African actor (Jamel Debbouze) a French name ('Lucien'). She overlooks Maurice Bénichou who plays Amélie's sought-after Dominique Bretodeau, but her observation holds true.

34 Dayna Oscherwitz and MaryEllen Higgins, *Historical Dictionary of French Cinema* (Lanham: Scarecrow, 2007) 217; Alison Smith, '*Nikita* as social fantasy', *France on Film: Reflections on Popular French Cinema*, ed. Lucy Mazdon (London: Wallflower, 2001) 27; Vincendeau 24. These authors have all made the comparison between Jeunet's work and *cinéma du look*. Vanderschelden (20) and Gural-Migdal (132, 136) have, in addition, evoked postmodernism as a means of understanding *Amélie*.

35 Vanderschelden 14.

36 Andrew, 'Amélie' 35.

37 Vanderschelden 14 and Andrew, 'Amélie' 37, quoting Jeunet's own opinion of the French New Wave.

38 Vanderschelden 14; Gilles Laprévotte, 'Les Années d'aujourd'hui (1980–2004)', *Une histoire du cinéma français*, ed. Claude Beylie (Paris: Larousse, 2005) 258–60.

39 Vanderschelden 14, 16.

40 Gural-Migdal 136.

41 Vanderschelden 11.

42 Cluzel 100; Vanderschelden 14.

43 Vanderschelden 10–11, 14.

44 Guy Austin, *Contemporary French Cinema* (Manchester: Manchester University Press, 1996) 119.

45 Vincendeau 24.

46 Vanderschelden 6.

47 Vanderschelden 40.

48 Marie-Thérèse Journot *'L'esthétique publicitaire' dans le cinéma français des années 80* (Paris: L'Harmattan, 2004) qtd. in Vanderschelden 16.

49 Vanderschelden 72.

50 Andrew, 'Amélie' 37.

51 Vanderschelden 5–6.

52 'Jean-Pierre Jeunet on *Delicatessen*' 145; Vanderschelden 16.

53 Vanderschelden 16; Vincendeau 24.

54 Vanderschelden 40, 72.

55 Austin 119.

56 Vanderschelden 16.

57 Vincendeau 24; Vanderschelden 15–16.

58 Vanderschelden 16, 40. French establishment critics writing at the time of the film's release seemed disinclined to evoke the term 'postmodern', and two major French film magazines

gave differing assessments of Jeunet's connection to contemporary culture. *Cahiers* critic Jérôme Larcher called the film 'ni passéiste ni moderne'/'neither old-fashioned nor modern', but nonetheless acknowledged that 'tout en s'inspirant du cinéma de papa'/'while taking inspiration from old-fashioned French cinema', the director 'fait un cinéma [...] d'aujourd'hui'/ 'is a creator of [...] contemporary cinema' (v. Larcher, 'Le Cabinet de curiosités', *Cahiers du cinéma*, no. 557, May 2001, 112). Franck Garbarz (writing for *Positif*), meanwhile, saw no connection between the director and his contemporary context, declaring that Jeunet 'n'appartient pas à son époque'/'does not belong to his era'. Because he 'n'hésite pas à se référer à des courants esthétiques tenus pour "dépassés" (réalisme poétique, expressionisme, dadaïsme...) par les chiens de garde de la modernité'/'doesn't hesitate to refer to aesthetic tendencies now classed as "old-fashioned" (poetic realism, expressionism, dadaism...) by modernity's watchdogs', Garbarz saw Jeunet as 'fuyant [...] les tendances actuelles du cinéma français'/'fleeing [...] current trends of French cinema' (v. Garbarz 29).

59 (London and New York: Routledge, 2000) 276.

60 Hayward 276.

61 Vanderschelden 20.

62 Vincendeau 25. She points out that everyday individuals obsessed with the pleasure of small things is also part of a contemporary cultural trend, as shown by the success of the French singer Bénabar's songs and the short stories of Philippe Delerm (in particular, *La Première gorgée de bière et autres plaisirs minuscules/The Small Pleasures of Life*) (v. Vincendeau 33).

63 Hayward 277.

64 Hayward 280 with ref. to John Orr, *Cinema and Modernity* (Cambridge: Polity Press, 1993) 12.

65 Vanderschelden 80–85; Vincendeau 22.

66 *Cinema Studies* 278–79.

67 *Cinema Studies* 279.

68 Vanderschelden 79.

69 Vincendeau 23.

70 Vincendeau 24.

71 Vanderschelden 59; Vincendeau 24.

72 Vanderschelden 59.

73 Gural-Migdal 142–43.

74 Ezra, 'Death of an Icon' 301.

75 Gural-Migdal 142; Vincendeau 24.

76 281 with ref. to Giuliana Bruno, 'Ramble City: Postmodernism and *Blade Runner*', *October* 41 (1987) 69.

77 Hayward 281.

78 Hayward 281.

79 Hayward 280.

80 Vanderschelden 59.

81 Hayward 283, with ref. to Jeremy Hawthorn, *A Concise Glossary of Contemporary Literary Theory* (London: Edward Arnold, 1992) 111.

82 Hayward 281.

83 Hayward 275.

84 'Director's Commentary'.

85 In interview, *New York Times* 28 October 2001, qtd. in Andrew ('Amélie' 38), who contrasts Jeunet's use of painting as a model for film-making with the dismissive attitude of a New Wave director such as Truffaut with regard to painting. Vanderschelden comments specifically on the similarity between Jeunet's composition and the painted image (v. 48).

86 'Amélie' 38.

87 'Director's Commentary'.

88 Significantly, while other people from her daily life appear in the first fantasy (the blind man and Philomène the flight attendant), it is only Dufayel who features in both, with an appearance in the documentary and a mention in the film subtitles.

89 Gural-Migdal 144.

90 Vincendeau 24, Garbarz 29–30.

91 'Director's Commentary'.

92 *Amélie* 33.

93 'Director's Commentary'.

94 For example, there is only the most simple correlation made between Amélie's parents' neurotic personalities and their taste for methodical activities that maintain order and cleanliness; it is the same for the relationship between Joseph's destructive sexual insecurity and his sole enjoyment of bursting the air bubbles on sheets of bubble wrap.

95 Perhaps this is one of the reasons that his own film glosses over the details of her death and, by casting it as bringing about a coincidental turning point in Amélie's life and inspiring her subsequent conduct, merely exaggerates the way in which one may take a media icon as a role model or fantasy alter-ego, and make a connection between global and local by remembering where one was or what mundane occupation one was involved with when an event of international interest took place.

96 Gural-Migdal 142–43. Vincendeau specifically notes, in addition, that both Jeunet and the heroine of his film employed 'fake ageing' (24): Amélie dipped her forged letter in tea, while Jeunet used various means to create a slightly old-fashioned image of Paris (in the mise-en-scène, through certain sets, costumes and props which evoke the past, and in post-production, giving the images a golden-yellow tint).

97 See Vanderschelden's table (56–58) which takes a selection of the film's special effects and divides them according to whether they were created by computers or manually.

98 'Director's Commentary'.

99 Vincendeau 24.

100 Garbarz 29–30.

101 Ezra, 'Death of an Icon' 305–06.

102 Jean-Pierre Jeunet, Guillaume Laurant and Phil Casoar, *Le Fabuleux album d'Amélie Poulain* (Paris: Arènes, 2001) [n.p.].

103 Andrew ('Amélie', 38) comments on this being the only element of mystery in the film.

104 I suggested that Dufayel's allusion to his own disability in his video message to Amélie may also evoke the theme of her second video to him. However, the audience only sees the images of the second video once (unlike the Tour de France image from the first video) and

may not perceive a theme: the audience will therefore be less sensitive to Dufayel's allusion which, moreover, is less obvious in this case.

105 Andrew ('Amélie' 38) suggests that these 'germs of gritty video' may have been 'introduce[d] [...] to contaminate the self-satisfaction of his [Jeunet's] carefully made-up celluloid images'.

106 Andrew ('Amélie' 38) notes that when Dufayel first starts talking about the 'fille au verre d'eau' in the painting, Amélie is seen in the background holding a glass: 'Somehow Jeunet restrained what must have been his impulse to zoom in on her hand'. Although Andrew's comment is misled, as this kind of intrusive camerawork is excluded from more contemplative scenes, it is true that Jeunet's tendency is to make everything extremely clear, whether visually or, more so in this case, through dialogue.

Conclusion

Surrealism's fascination with cinema resulted in many plans but few realised projects. Of the three official projects that were realised, two satisfied the surrealists, who were nonetheless aware that *Un Chien andalou* and *L'Âge d'or*, however strong, were only two short films, and could not stand in for a larger and ever more ambitious and revolutionary surrealist film output.

My aim in this book has been to explore a clearly defined, cinematically specific means by which a form of surrealism can exist in narrative feature films. I did this by taking the surrealists' notion of the surrealist object and adapting it for cinema, thus developing a theory of the hybrid object. Although the first chapter acknowledged that *Un Chien andalou* offers examples of surrealist objects as defined by the surrealists themselves, I argued that such objects are intrusive and uncinematic. As a demonstrative account of unconscious processes, *Un Chien andalou*'s surrealist objects are unsatisfactory because their meaning is either too simple (in terms of revealing character psychology) or excessively complex (insofar as it represents the wordplay encoded by Buñuel and Dalí). As a call for active engagement from the audience, asking them to discover their own connections and meaning, again these surrealist objects fall short, because the average viewer is prepared for a passive role, absorbing transparent meaning that relates directly to the film's storyline. It would be difficult to incorporate such surrealist objects into a more conventionally narrative feature-length film. The surrealist object in cinema would have to develop in a way that avoided the problem of attempting to portray the unconscious, which had historically been a stumbling block to the surrealists' practical attempts at film-making. Of course, *Un Chien andalou* remains fascinating insofar as it successfully uses film form to imitate unconscious processes such as condensation, displacement, the disruption of one level of discourse by another and even the word-image interaction of dreamwork, as highlighted by Williams and Liebman. However, the surrealists' ultimate abandonment of film attests to the fact that they were not able to effect their intended general revolution of public consciousness in this way. Where Buñuel continued to carry the surrealist torch in his later work, further exploring film form as a means of portraying unconscious processes, this activity was adapted to a largely conventional narrative feature film format; any aspirations to transform the audience's perceptions became subordinate to the necessity of creating a film with which the audience would know how to engage.

I argued that the hybrid object was the way of the future for the surrealist object in cinema and defined it as a physical object characterised by the multiple narrative, visual, semiotic and often comic roles that it takes on as it circulates through the space of the film. In this way, the surrealist object adapted to cinema would preserve the surrealist emphasis on the object's hybridity: as the first chapter explained, hybridity was a key notion for surrealism, and by bringing together a variety of sometimes contradictory meanings and functions in one place, that object exemplified the breaking down of boundaries between everyday life and the activity of the unconscious, one of the surrealists' most important objectives.

This study has traced a historical arc, from early sound film-making, to the modernist experimentation of the 1960s, to the technological accomplishment of the 2000s. It has also traced varying degrees of connection with French and Czech surrealist traditions, from Clair's past work for the dadaists, Buñuel's membership in the Paris surrealist group and Švankmajer's in the Prague group, to Jeunet's and the Czech New Wave's adoption of surrealism as a style. The major difference that emerged was this: where Jeunet takes up surrealism playfully but without its radical spirit of resistance against established structures, all the other directors successfully maintained something of the original surrealist impulse. Clair was against utilitarianism and Taylorisation; the Czech New Wave against Socialist Realism's prescriptions and proscriptions; and Buñuel against dull and false bourgeois façades of gentility.

However, it was the precise way in which objects became hybrid through their narrative, visual, semiotic and comic roles that was the principal concern of this study. In the last four chapters, I examined the different ways in which objects functioned in *À Nous la liberté*, 1960s Czech cinema, three of Buñuel's late films, and *Amélie*. All of the directors had reason to foreground objects: Clair did so in part as a habit from his silent film-making days, but also to demonstrate that objects were becoming more important than humans in industrial society. For the Czech New Wave directors, objects were a part of their revolutionary desire to portray everyday life. Buñuel's motivations are rarely so clear, but he may have retained an awareness of the power of objects from his days as a member of the surrealist group; alternately, he may have seen the abundance of material accessories defining the bourgeoisie as the very means by which their apparent mastery of the world could be challenged. Despite Jeunet's fetishisation of objects which crowd the frame in *Amélie*, I argued that he too may have considered using an object in a new way as a type of small resistance against impersonal and unimaginative consumerist ideology.

The way in which objects became hybrid also varied from one chapter to the next. In *À Nous la liberté*, objects accumulated meanings as they circulated through the film; although these meanings were invariably clichéd, a subtle ambiguity was created when contradictory meanings were associated with the same object. Objects also took on a destabilising effect in the diegesis of the film as they served as a catalyst to its chaotic slapstick comedy.

The Czech New Wave featured a different type of physical humour revolving around objects: through the films' connection with the natural world, objects often came to embody an erotic humour. This comic role constituted a major source of objects' hybridity in Czech New Wave films. However, multiple meanings were also developed through other means: for example, by suggesting through dialogue the way in which personal preoccupations might lead a character to consider an object in a different light, by creating mystery surrounding an object's significance and powers, or by leading the audience to move independently beyond thinking about objects in clichéd terms.

In Buñuel, objects could be comic but this was never their primary function; instead, the main role of objects was to serve as a locus of instability in the film. They existed as the boundary points marking out the film's reality, as defined by its genre: when a shift in genre occurred, objects were most noticeably affected by the change, as their meaning was dependent on genre and altered along with it. In this way, Buñuel used objects to point to the arbitrariness of generic definitions of reality and to the arbitrariness of object meaning. At the same time, he highlighted for the audience their own willingness to accept clearly implausible scenarios in the interest of maintaining the illusion of a logical and comprehensible reality.

Coming immediately after the chapter that focused on Buñuel's films, which clearly fulfil in cinematic terms the surrealist goal of fundamentally questioning the definition of reality, Jeunet's playful adoption of surrealist ideas seemed all the more superficial by contrast. The way in which Amélie made unconventional use of media of communication in order to bring people together constituted a brief rebellion against the isolation of urban capitalism. However, she offered no serious challenge to established social structures as she ultimately found fulfilment in the conventional union of the heterosexual couple. Objects did not become hybrid, even though they took part in the film's comedy and were put to an unconventional use. In spite of Amélie's imaginative tendencies, the notion of an object having a single, solid, rational explanation was virtually unchallenged by the film.

This study has found that hybrid objects exist not just in films with a more or less direct relationship to surrealism, but more particularly in films made during times of widespread experimentation: either at a moment when broad conventions of film-making are just beginning to be established (as was the case with *À Nous la liberté*), or when established conventions are being radically challenged (as was the case with the Czech New Wave and Buñuel's late work). Although comedy has been shown to produce hybrid objects (as well as resulting from them), the case of *Amélie* showed that comedy can also be, as Susan Hayward has observed, 'the most conservative of all genres'.[1] Future research on hybrid objects is therefore most likely to discover interesting examples in films that were made during moments of great change with respect to established formal and aesthetic conventions: the beginnings of the classical period in Europe and Hollywood, or other 1960s new waves, for example.

The surrealists may not have been able to fully test their intuition that cinema was a powerful tool for transforming the public's attitude towards reality. However, directors involved in defining new conventions of cinematic representation still have great power to influence the way that audiences understand reality on film. My theory of the hybrid object offers a new way of defining a form of surrealism in narrative cinema. Being based on cinema-specific aesthetics rather than just subject matter, this theory overcomes a limitation common to much recent scholarship that has sought to discover surrealist influence in a wider range of films. Hybrid objects in cinema undermine the notion that reality exists as a smooth, unbroken and predictable surface and in this way achieve a considerable part of what the surrealists set out to do.

Note

1   Qtd. in Rémi Fournier-Lanzoni, *French Cinema from its Beginnings to the Present* (New York: Continuum, 2002) 368.

Bibliography

Abel, Richard. *The Ciné Goes to Town: French Cinema 1896–1914*. London: University of California Press, 1994.

———. 'Exploring the Discursive Field of the Surrealist Film Scenario Text'. *Dada and Surrealist Film*. Ed. Rudolf E. Kuenzli. Cambridge, MA: MIT Press, 1996. 58–71.

Adamowicz, Elza, ed. *Surrealism: Crossings/Frontiers*. Bern: Peter Lang, 2006.

Andrew, Dudley. 'Amélie, or Le Fabuleux Destin du Cinéma Français'. *Film Quarterly* 57.3 (2004): 34–46.

———. *Mists of Regret: Culture and Sensibility in Classic French Film*. Princeton: Princeton University Press, 1995.

Aragon, Louis. *Le Paysan de Paris*. Paris: Gallimard, 1926.

Atkinson, Michael. 'À Nous la liberté'. Criterion Collection web site (http://www.criterion.com), 19 August 2002. Viewed 7 November 2007.

Aumont, Jacques et al. *Esthétique du film*. 3rd edn. Paris: Armand Colin, 2004.

Austin, Guy. *Contemporary French Cinema*. Manchester: Manchester University Press, 1996.

Barthes, Roland. *Image-Music-Text*. Trans. Stephen Heath. London: Fontana, 1977.

Baxter, John. *Buñuel*. London: Fourth Estate, 1994.

Billard, Pierre. *L'Âge classique du cinéma français: Du cinéma parlant à la Nouvelle Vague*. Paris: Flammarion, 1995.

———. *Le Mystère René Clair*. Paris: Plon, 1998.

Bordwell, David. *Narration in the Fiction Film*. London: Routledge, 1985.

Bregant, Michal. 'Le cinéma d'avant-garde: entre le rêve et l'utopie'. In *Le Cinéma tchèque et slovaque*. Eds. Eva Zaoralová and Jean-Loup Passek. Paris: Editions du Centre Pompidou, 1996. 75–83.

Breton, André. *L'Amour fou*. In *Breton: Oeuvres complètes*. Ed. Marguerite Bonnet. Vol. 2 of 3 vols. Paris: Gallimard, 1992. 673–785.

———. *Anthologie de l'humour noir*. In *Breton: Oeuvres complètes*. Ed. Marguerite Bonnet. Vol. 2 of 3 vols. Paris: Gallimard, 1992. 863–1176.

———. *La Clé des champs*. Paris: Sagittaire, 1953.

———. 'Comme dans un bois'. In *Les surréalistes et le cinéma*. Eds. Alain and Odette Virmaux. Paris: Éditions Seghers, 1976. 277–82.

———. 'Crise de l'objet'. In *Le Surréalisme et la Peinture (Nouvelle Edition 1928–1965)*. Paris: Gallimard, 1965. 275–81.

———. *Les Manifestes du surréalisme*. Paris: Sagittaire, 1946.

———. *Nadja*. Paris: Gallimard, 1964.

———. *Position politique du surréalisme*. In *Breton: Oeuvres complètes*. Ed. Marguerite Bonnet. Vol. 2 of 3 vols. Paris: Gallimard, 1992. 472–96.

———. *Qu'est-ce que le surréalisme?* In *Breton: Oeuvres complètes*. Ed. Marguerite Bonnet. Vol. 2 of 3 vols. Paris: Gallimard, 1992. 223–62.

———. 'Situation surréaliste de l'objet: Situation de l'objet surréaliste' in *Position politique du surréalisme*. In *Breton: Oeuvres complètes*. Ed. Marguerite Bonnet. Vol. 2 of 3 vols. Paris: Gallimard, 1992. 472–96.

———. *Les Vases communicants*. In *André Breton: Oeuvres complètes*. Ed. Marguerite Bonnet. Vol. 2 of 3 vols. Paris: Gallimard, 1992. 101–215.

Brooke, Michael. 'A Game with Stones'. In notes to BFI DVD release of *Jan Švankmajer: The Complete Short Films*, 2007. 9.

Buchar, Robert. *Czech New Wave Filmmakers in Interviews*. Jefferson, NC: McFarland, 2004.

Cardinal, Roger. 'Thinking Through Things: The Presence of Objects in the Early Films of Jan Švankmajer'. In *The Cinema of Jan Švankmajer: Dark Alchemy*. 2nd edn. Ed. Peter Hames. London: Wallflower, 2008. 67–82.

Carrière, Jean-Claude. *Les années d'utopie 1968–1969: New York-Paris-Prague-New York*. Paris: Plon, 2003.

Ciment, Michel and Noël Herpe, eds. 'Jean-Pierre Jeunet on *Delicatessen*'. In *Projections 9: French Film-makers on Film-making*. London: Faber and Faber, 1999. 144–51.

Clair, René. 'Cinéma et surréalisme'. In *Les surréalistes et le cinéma*. Eds. Alain and Odette Virmaux. Paris: Éditions Seghers, 1976. 318.

Cluzel, Jean. *Propos impertinents sur le cinéma français*. Paris: PUF, 2003.

Crisp, Colin. *The Classic French Cinema: 1930–1960*. Bloomington: Indiana University Press, 1993.

Desnos, Robert. *La liberté ou l'amour!* Paris: Gallimard, 1962.

Drouzy, Maurice. *Luis Buñuel: Architecte du rêve*. Paris: Lherminier, 1978.

Duras, Marguerite. *Le ravissement de Lol V. Stein*. Paris: Gallimard, 1964.

Effenberger, Vratislav. 'Notes sur le cinéma (extraits)'. In *Le cinéma des surréalistes tchèques*. Ed. Petr Král. Cognac: Temps qu'il fait, 2002. 11–14.

Eisenstein, Sergei. *The Film Sense*. London: faber and faber, 1986.

Evans, Peter William. 'An *Amour* Still *Fou*: Late Buñuel'. In *The Unsilvered Screen: Surrealism on Film*. Eds. Graeme Harper and Rob Stone. London: Wallflower, 2007. 38–47.

———. *The Films of Luis Buñuel: Subjectivity and Desire*. Oxford: Clarendon Press, 1995.

———. 'The Indiscreet Charms of the *Bourgeoises* and Other Women'. In *Luis Buñuel: New Readings*. Eds. Peter William Evans and Isabel Santaolalla. London: British Film Institute, 2004. 143–56.

——— and Isabel Santaolalla, eds. *Luis Buñuel: New Readings*. London: British Film Institute, 2004.

Ezra, Elizabeth. 'The Death of an Icon: *Le Fabuleux Destin d'Amélie Poulain*'. *French Cultural Studies* 15.3 (2004): 301–10.

———. *Jean-Pierre Jeunet*. Urbana and Chicago: University of Illinois Press, 2008.

Farassino, Alberto. *Tutto il cinema di Luis Buñuel*. Milan: Baldini & Castoldi, 2000.

Forcer, Stephen. 'Trust Me, I'm a Director: Sex, Sado-Masochism and Institutionalization in Luis Buñuel's *Belle de Jour (1967)*'. *Studies in European Cinema* 1, no. 1 (April 2004): 19–29.

Fotiade, Ramona. 'The slit eye, the scorpion and the sign of the cross: surrealist film theory and practice revisited'. *Screen* 39 (1998): 109–23.

Fournier-Lanzoni, Rémi. *French Cinema from its Beginnings to the Present*. New York: Continuum, 2002.

Freud, Sigmund. *The Interpretation of Dreams*. Trans. Joyce Crick. Oxford: Oxford University Press, 1999.

———. *The 'Wolfman' and Other Cases*. Trans. Louise Adey Huish. London: Penguin, 2002.

Garbarz, Franck. 'Le Fabuleux Destin d'Amélie Poulain: La recolleuse de morceaux'. *Positif*, no. 483, May 2001, 29–30.

Goudal, Jean. 'Surréalisme et cinéma'. In *Les surréalistes et le cinéma*. Eds. Alain and Odette Virmaux. Paris: Éditions Seghers, 1976. 305–16.

Griffiths, Keith, dir. 'The Cabinet of Jan Švankmajer'. Channel Four, 1984. In BFI DVD release of *Jan Švankmajer: The Complete Short Films*, 2007.

Gural-Migdal, Anna. 'Paris comme parc d'attractions à la Disney dans *Le Fabuleux destin d'Amélie Poulain*'. *AUMLA* 108 (2007): 131–48.

Hames, Peter. 'An Appreciation by Peter Hames'. Extra material on Second Run DVD release of *The Party and the Guests*, 2007.

———, ed. *The Cinema of Jan Švankmajer: Dark Alchemy*. 2nd edn. London: Wallflower, 2008.

———. 'The Core of Reality: Puppets in the Feature Films of Jan Švankmajer'. In *The Cinema of Jan Švankmajer: Dark Alchemy*. 2nd edn. Ed. Peter Hames. London: Wallflower, 2008. 83–103.

———. *Czech and Slovak Cinema: Theme and Tradition*. Edinburgh: Edinburgh University Press, 2009.

———. 'Czechoslovakia: After the Spring'. In *Post New Wave Cinema in the Soviet Union and Eastern Europe*. Ed. Daniel J. Goulding. Bloomington: Indiana University Press, 1989. 102–42.

———. *The Czechoslovak New Wave*. 2nd edn. London: Wallflower, 2005.

———. 'The Film Experiment'. In *The Cinema of Jan Švankmajer: Dark Alchemy*. 2nd edn. Ed. Peter Hames. London: Wallflower, 2008. 8–39.

———. 'Interview with Jan Švankmajer'. In *The Cinema of Jan Švankmajer: Dark Alchemy*. 2nd edn. Ed. Peter Hames. London: Wallflower, 2008. 104–39.

Hammond, Paul, ed. and trans. *The Shadow and Its Shadow: Surrealist Writings on the Cinema*. 3rd edn. San Francisco: City Lights Books, 2000.

Harper, Graeme and Rob Stone. Introduction to *The Unsilvered Screen: Surrealism on Film*. Eds. Harper and Stone. London: Wallflower, 2007. 1–8.

———, eds. *The Unsilvered Screen: Surrealism on Film*. London: Wallflower, 2007.

Hašek, Jaroslav. *The Good Soldier Schweik*. Trans. Paul Selver. Harmondsworth, Middlesex: Penguin, 1951.

Hayward, Susan. *Cinema Studies: The Key Concepts*. London and New York: Routledge, 2000.

Hrabal, Bohumil. *Closely Observed Trains*. Trans. Edith Pargeter. London: Abacus, 2005.

Hughes, Alex and James S. Williams, eds. *Gender and French Cinema*. Oxford: Berg, 2001.

Huyssen, Andreas. *After the Great Divide: Modernism, Mass Culture, Postmodernism*. Basingstoke: Macmillan, 1988.

Iampolski, Mikhail. *The Memory of Tiresias: Intertextuality and Film*. Trans. Harsha Ram. Berkeley: University of California Press, 1998.

Jeunet, Jean-Pierre. 'Director's Commentary'. Extra material on Momentum DVD release of *Amélie*, 2002.

———, Guillaume Laurent and Phil Casoar. *Le Fabuleux album d'Amélie Poulain*. Paris: Les Arènes, 2001.

Kessel, Joesph. *Belle de Jour*. Paris: Gallimard, 1928.

Kopaněvová, Galina. 'Un Quart de siècle de métamorphoses'. In *Le Cinéma tchèque et slovaque*. Eds. Eva Zaoralová and Jean-Loup Passek. Paris: Editions du Centre Pompidou, 1996. 95–112.

Kovács, Steven. *From Enchantment to Rage: The Story of Surrealist Cinema*. Cranbury, New Jersey: Associated University Presses, 1980.

Král, Petr, ed. *Le cinéma des surréalistes tchèques*. Cognac: Temps qu'il fait, 2002.

———. 'D'un Imaginaire réaliste'. In *Le cinéma des surréalistes tchèques*. Ed. Petr Král. Cognac: Temps qu'il fait, 2002. 3–10.

———. *Le Surréalisme en Tchécoslovaquie*. Paris: Gallimard, 1983.

Kuenzli, Rudolf E., ed. *Dada and Surrealist Film*. Cambridge, MA: MIT Press, 1996.

———. Introduction to *Dada and Surrealist Film*. Ed. Rudolf E. Kuenzli. Cambridge, MA: MIT Press, 1996. 1–12.

Kundera, Milan. *The Unbearable Lightness of Being*. London: Faber and Faber, 1984.

Kyrou, Adonis. *Le Surréalisme au cinéma*. Paris: Le Terrain Vague, 1963.

Laprévotte, Gilles. 'Les Années d'aujourd'hui (1980–2004)'. In *Une histoire du cinéma français*. Ed. Claude Beylie. Paris: Larousse, 2005. 257–324.

Larcher, Jérôme. 'Le Cabinet de curiosités'. *Cahiers du cinéma*, no. 557, May 2001, 112.

Liebman, Stuart. '*Un Chien andalou*: The Talking Cure'. *Dada and Surrealist Film*. Ed. Rudolf E. Kuenzli. Cambridge, MA: MIT Press, 1996. 143–58.

Malt, Johanna. *Obscure Objects of Desire: Surrealism, Fetishism, and Politics*. Oxford: Oxford University Press, 2008.

Marcus, Laura. 'Cinema and Psychoanalysis'. In *Close Up 1927–1933: Cinema and Modernism*. Eds. James Donald, Anne Friedberg and Laura Marcus. Princeton: Princeton University Press, 1998. 240–46.

Martins, Laura M. 'Luis Buñuel, or Ways of Disturbing Spectatorship'. In *Luis Buñuel: New Readings*. Eds. Peter William Evans and Isabel Santaolalla. London: British Film Institute, 2004. 187–97.

Matthews, J. H. *Surrealism and Film*. Ann Arbor: University of Michigan Press, 1971.

Metz, Christian. *Le signifiant imaginaire*. Paris: Christian Bourgois Éditeur, 2002.

Oms, Marcel. *Don Luis Buñuel*. Paris: Éditions du Cerf, 1985.

O'Pray, Michael. 'In the Capital of Magic: The Black Theatre of Jan Švankmajer'. *Monthly Film Bulletin*, no. 630, July 1986. Reprinted in notes to BFI DVD release of *Jan Švankmajer: The Complete Short Films*, 2007. 1–4.

———. 'Jan Švankmajer: A Mannerist Surrealist'. In *The Cinema of Jan Švankmajer: Dark Alchemy*. 2nd edn. Ed. Peter Hames. London: Wallflower, 2008. 40–66.

Oscherwitz, Dayna and MaryEllen Higgins. *Historical Dictionary of French Cinema*. Lanham, MD: Scarecrow, 2007.

Owen, Jonathan L. *Avant-Garde to New Wave: Czechoslovak Cinema, Surrealism and the Sixties*. Oxford: Berghahn, 2011.

Philippe, Pierre, dir. *René Clair par Bronja Clair*. La Septième Art, 1998. In Criterion DVD release of *À Nous la liberté*, 2002.

Potton, Ed. 'Jean-Pierre Jeunet'. *Times Online*, 9 April 2005.

Přádná, Stanislava. 'Les Personnalités de la Nouvelle Vague'. In *Le Cinéma tchèque et slovaque*. Eds. Eva Zaoralová and Jean-Loup Passek. Paris: Editions du Centre Pompidou, 1996. 127–32.

Richardson, Michael. *Surrealism and Cinema*. Oxford: Berg, 2006.

Sabbadini, Andrea. 'Of Boxes, Peepholes and Other Perverse Objects: A Psychoanalytic Look at Luis Buñuel's *Belle de Jour*'. In *Luis Buñuel: New Readings*. Eds. Peter William Evans and Isabel Santaolalla. London: British Film Institute, 2004. 117–27.

Sadoul, Georges. *Le cinéma français (1890–1962)*. Paris: Flammarion, 1962.

Schmitt, Bertrand and Michel Leclerc, dirs. *Les Chimères des Švankmajer*. 2001. In BFI DVD release of *Jan Švankmajer: The Complete Short Films*, 2007.

Shattuck, Roger. *The Banquet Years: The Arts in France, 1885–1918*. London: Faber and Faber, 1958.

Škapová, Zdena. 'La Cinématographie tchèque: littérature et cinéma, et plus particulièrement dans les années soixante'. In *Le Cinéma tchèque et slovaque*. Eds. Eva Zaoralová and Jean-Loup Passek. Paris: Editions du Centre Pompidou, 1996. 115–25.

Škvorecký, Josef. *All the Bright Young Men and Women: A Personal History of the Czech Cinema*. Trans. Michael Schonberg. Toronto: Peter Martin, 1971.

Šmatlák, Martin. 'La Spécificité du cinéma slovaque'. In *Le Cinéma tchèque et slovaque*. Eds. Eva Zaoralová and Jean-Loup Passek. Paris: Editions du Centre Pompidou, 1996. 145–56.

Šmejkal, František. 'After Devětsil: Surrealism in Czechoslovakia'. In *Devětsil: The Czech Avant-Garde of the 1920s and 30s*. Ed. Rostislav Švácha. Oxford and London: Museum of Modern Art and the Design Museum, 1990. 88–93.

———. 'Devětsil: An Introduction'. In *Devětsil: The Czech Avant-Garde of the 1920s and 30s*. Ed. Rostislav Švácha. Oxford and London: Museum of Modern Art and the Design Museum, 1990. 8–27.

———. 'From Lyrical Metaphors to Symbols of Fate: Czech Surrealism of the 1930s'. In *Czech Modernism: 1900–1945*. Eds. Jaroslav Anděl et al. Houston: The Museum of Fine Arts Houston, 1989. 64–83.

Smith, Alison. '*Nikita* as social fantasy'. In *France on Film: Reflections on Popular French Cinema*. Ed. Lucy Mazdon. London: Wallflower, 2001. 27–39.

Spector, Jack J. *Surrealist Art and Writing 1919/39: The Gold of Time*. Cambridge: Cambridge University Press, 1997.

Stone, Rob. 'Eye to Eye: The Persistence of Surrealism in Spanish Cinema'. In *The Unsilvered Screen: Surrealism on Film*. Eds. Graeme Harper and Rob Stone. London: Wallflower, 2007. 23–37.

Tesson, Charles. *Luis Buñuel*. Paris: Éditions de l'Étoile/Cahiers du cinéma, 1995.

Uhde, Jan. 'Jan Švankmajer: Genius Loci as a Source of Surrealist Inspiration'. In *The Unsilvered Screen: Surrealism on Film*. Eds. Graeme Harper and Rob Stone. London: Wallflower, 2007. 60–71.

Vanderschelden, Isabelle. *Amélie*. Champaign: University of Illinois Press, 2007.

Vincendeau, Ginette. 'Café Society'. *Sight and Sound*, August 2001, 22–25.

Virmaux, Alain and Odette, eds. *Les surréalistes et le cinéma*. Paris: Éditions Seghers, 1976.

Visinet, Arnauld. 'Foutaises: Un film de Jean-Pierre Jeunet'. *Six courts métrages*. Ed. Térésa Faucon. BiFi: Lycéens au cinéma, 2000. 16–19.

Williams, Linda. 'The Critical Grasp: Buñuelian Cinema and its Critics'. *Dada and Surrealist Film*. Ed. Rudolf E. Kuenzli. Cambridge, MA: MIT Press, 1996. 199–206.

———. *Figures of Desire: A Theory and Analysis of Surrealist Film*. Berkeley and Los Angeles: University of California Press, 1981.

Zaoral, Zdenek. 'Histoire, culture et cinéma' In *Le Cinéma tchèque et slovaque*. Eds. Eva Zaoralová and Jean-Loup Passek. Paris: Editions du Centre Pompidou, 1996. 19–59.

Zaoralová, Eva and Jean-Loup Passek, eds. *Le Cinéma tchèque et slovaque*. Paris: Editions du Centre Pompidou, 1996.

Žižek, Slavoj. *The Pervert's Guide to Cinema*. Dir. Sophie Fiennes. 1996.

Index